STUDENT STUDY GUIDE

for

Foundations of

PSYCHOLOGICAL
TESTING

Thomas A. Stetz
Hawaii Pacific University

Leslie A. Miller
LanneM TM, LLC

Robert L. Lovler
Wilson Learning Corporation

STUDENT STUDY GUIDE
for
Foundations of
PSYCHOLOGICAL
TESTING

⑤SAGE

Los Angeles | London | New Delhi
Singapore | Washington DC

Los Angeles | London | New Delhi
Singapore | Washington DC

FOR INFORMATION:

SAGE Publications, Inc.
2455 Teller Road
Thousand Oaks, California 91320
E-mail: order@sagepub.com

SAGE Publications Ltd.
1 Oliver's Yard
55 City Road
London EC1Y 1SP
United Kingdom

SAGE Publications India Pvt. Ltd.
B 1/I 1 Mohan Cooperative Industrial Area
Mathura Road, New Delhi 110 044
India

SAGE Publications Asia-Pacific Pte. Ltd.
3 Church Street
#10-04 Samsung Hub
Singapore 049483

Copyright © 2016 by SAGE Publications, Inc.

Printed in the United States of America

ISBN 978-1-5063-0805-0

This book is printed on acid-free paper.

Acquisitions Editor: Reid Hester
Editorial Assistant: Morgan McCardell
Production Editor: Libby Larson
Copy Editor: Matthew Sullivan
Typesetter: C&M Digitals (P) Ltd.
Proofreader: Alison Syring
Cover Designer: Michael Dubowe
Marketing Manager: Shari Countryman

15 16 17 18 19 10 9 8 7 6 5 4 3 2 1

Contents

Preface

If you are reading the preface of this study guide, you are likely taking a course related to psychological testing and using the fifth edition of Dr. Miller and Dr. Lovler's textbook, *Foundations of Psychological Testing: A Practical Approach*. The current student workbook is designed to help you more actively engage in the learning process. The workbook contains a variety of information and learning activities to help you understand and apply information, and help you make progress toward learning and retaining material related to psychological testing. A thorough understanding of concepts and issues foundational to psychological testing is important for several reasons. First, psychological tests personally affect many individuals, including students such as yourself. Each day, different types of professionals administer psychological tests to many individuals, and the results of these tests are used in ways that significantly affect you and those around you. Second, psychological testing is one of the most common methodological courses required for an undergraduate degree in psychology and for many psychology and counseling master's and PhD degrees. Third, measurement literacy, at both the undergraduate and graduate levels, is lacking. Mastering the material in the textbook will not only help you perform well in the course you are taking, but also help set you apart from other students. We believe that the material in the textbook, combined with the information and learning activities in the workbook, will help you increase your understanding of concepts and issues associated with the psychological tests that affect you and those around you.

The study guide is organized by chapter, corresponding to the chapters in the textbook. Each chapter follows a consistent structure, resulting in straightforward organization and quick access to key pieces of information. Specifically each chapter is organized into 10 sections:

Chapter Overview
Learning Objectives
Chapter Outline
Key Concepts
Key Concepts Crossword Puzzle
Learning Activities by Learning Objective
Exercises
Additional Learning Activities
Practice Test Questions
    Multiple Choice
    Short Answer

Answer Keys
   Crossword
   Exercises
   Multiple Choice
   Short Answer

Every chapter begins with a high-level **overview** using a brief narrative chapter summary, the chapter **learning objectives**, and the **chapter outline** providing quick reference to the main ideas and topics found in the textbook chapters. Next, all of the chapter's **key concepts** are reinforced, by providing an organized list with definitions of the most important concepts from the chapter. The concepts are reinforced with a **crossword puzzle** activity. The crossword puzzle is followed by a set of suggested **learning activities by learning objective**, with study tips and activities directly linked to each of the chapter's learning objectives. In addition, the chapters contain **exercises** directly related to the chapter content. For example, chapters that include statistical concepts contain exercises that require computations and application.

Not only does the study guide content help to reinforce material presented in the textbook, but it also extends the textbook content, introducing new topics related to each chapter. Each chapter next contains a section of **additional learning activities**. Here, new outside material is introduced, and questions and activities are presented to help you develop your critical thinking skills. For instance, Chapter 1 has a section concerning cheating on tests, and you are asked to discuss what prompts cheating, what can be done about it, how it violates the assumptions of tests, and how it impacts decisions based on test information.

The next section of each chapter contains a set of **practice questions**. Both multiple choice and short essay questions are included. You may perhaps find the last section of the study guide the most useful because in this section **answer keys** for the crosswords, exercises, and practice questions are presented. We believe this is a useful feature for students, giving you a variety of low-stakes practice opportunities accompanied with feedback. This will help you progress toward learning and retaining the material.

1

What Are Psychological Tests?

Chapter Overview

In Chapter 1, we discuss what a psychological test is and introduce you to some instruments you might never have considered to be psychological tests. After exploring the history of psychological testing, we discuss the three defining characteristics of psychological tests and the assumptions we must make when using psychological tests. We then discuss how tests are classified and distinguish four commonly confused concepts: assessment, tests, measurement, and surveys. We conclude by sharing print and online resources for locating information about psychological testing and specific tests.

Learning Objectives

After completing your study of this chapter, you should be able to do the following:

- Define what a psychological test is, and understand that psychological tests extend beyond personality and intelligence tests.
- Trace the history of psychological testing from Alfred Binet and intelligence testing to the tests of today.
- Describe the ways in which psychological tests can be similar to and different from one another.
- Describe the three characteristics that are common to all psychological tests, and understand that psychological tests can demonstrate these characteristics to various degrees.
- Describe the assumptions that must be made when using psychological tests.
- Describe the different ways that psychological tests can be classified.
- Describe the differences among four commonly used terms that students often confuse: *psychological assessment*, *psychological tests*, *psychological measurement*, and *surveys*.
- Identify and locate print and online resources that are available for obtaining information about psychological tests.

1

Chapter Outline

Why Should You Care About Psychological Testing?
What Are Psychological Tests?
  Similarities Among Psychological Tests
  Differences Among Psychological Tests
The History of Psychological Testing
  Intelligence Tests
  Personality Tests
  Vocational Tests
  Testing Today
The Defining Characteristics of Psychological Tests
Assumptions of Psychological Tests
Test Classification Methods
  Maximal Performance, Behavior Observation, or Self-Report
  Standardized or Nonstandardized
  Objective or Projective
  Dimension Measured
  Subject Tests
Psychological Assessment, Psychological Tests, Measurements, and Surveys
  Psychological Assessments and Psychological Tests
  Psychological Tests and Measurements
  Psychological Tests and Surveys
Locating Information About Tests
Chapter Summary

Key Concepts

achievement tests:	Tests that are designed to measure a person's previous learning in a specific academic area.
aptitude tests:	Tests that are designed to assess the test taker's potential for learning or the individual's ability to perform in an area in which he or she has not been specifically trained.
behavior:	An observable and measurable action.
behavior observation tests:	Tests that involve observing people's behavior to learn how they typically respond in a particular context.
emotional intelligence:	"type of intelligence defined as the abilities to perceive, appraise, and express emotions accurately and appropriately, to use emotions to facilitate thinking, to understand and analyze emotions, to use emotional knowledge effectively, and to regulate one's emotions to promote both emotional and intellectual growth" (APA, 2015, para. 10).
inference:	Using evidence to reach a conclusion.

intelligence tests:	Tests that assess the test taker's ability to cope with the environment but at a broader level than do aptitude tests.
interest inventories:	Tests that are designed to assess a person's interests in educational programs for job settings and thereby to provide information for making career decisions.
measurement:	The process of assessing the size, the amount, or the degree of an attribute using specific rules for transforming the attribute into numbers.
measurement instrument:	A tool or technique for assessing the size, amount, or degree of an attribute.
nonstandardized tests:	Tests that do not have standardization samples; more common than standardized tests.
norms:	A group of scores that indicate the average performance of a group and the distribution of scores above and below this average.
objective tests:	Tests on which test takers choose a response or provide a response and there are predetermined correct answers, requiring little subjective judgment of the person scoring the test.
personality tests:	Tests that are designed to measure human character or disposition.
projective tests:	Tests that are unstructured and require test takers to respond to ambiguous stimuli.
psychological assessments:	Tools for understanding and predicting behavior that involve multiple methods, such as personal history interviews, behavioral observations, and psychological tests, for gathering information about an individual.
psychological construct:	An underlying, unobservable personal attribute, trait, or characteristic of an individual that is thought to be important in describing or understanding human behavior.
psychological test:	A measurement tool or technique that requires a person to perform one or more behaviors in order to make inferences about human attributes, traits, or characteristics or predict future outcomes.
psychometrics:	The quantitative and technical aspects of psychological measurement.
self-report tests:	Tests that rely on test takers' reports or descriptions of their feelings, beliefs, opinions, and/or mental states.
standardization sample:	People who are tested to obtain data to establish a frame of reference for interpreting individual test scores.
standardized tests:	Tests that have been administered to a large group of individuals who are similar to the group for whom the test has been designed so as to develop norms; also implies a standardized procedure for administration.
surveys:	Instruments used for gathering information from a sample of the individuals of interest.
tests of maximal performance:	Tests that require test takers to perform a particular task on which their performance is measured.
vocational tests:	Tests that help predict how successful a person would be at an occupation before training or entering the occupation.

KEY CONCEPTS CROSSWORD

ACROSS

4. A group of scores that indicate the average performance of a group and the distribution of scores above and below this average.

6. Type of test that does not have standardization samples; more common than standardized tests.

8. An inventory that is designed to assess a person's interests in educational programs for job settings and provide information for making career decisions.

10. People who are tested to obtain data to establish a frame of reference for interpreting individual test scores.

12. Type of intelligence involving the ability to perceive, appraise, and express emotions accurately and appropriately, to use emotions to facilitate thinking, to understand and analyze emotions, to use emotional knowledge effectively, and to regulate one's emotions to promote both emotional and intellectual growth.

15. An observable and measurable action.

16. Type of test that helps predict how successful a person would be at an occupation before training or entering the occupation.

19. The quantitative and technical aspects of psychological measurement.

20. The process of assessing the size, the amount, or the degree of an attribute using specific rules for transforming the attribute into numbers.

22. A measurement tool or technique that requires a person to perform one or more behaviors in order to make inferences about human attributes, traits, or characteristics or predict future outcomes.

23. Type of test designed to measure a person's previous learning in a specific academic area.

24. Type of test administered to a large group of individuals who are similar to the group for whom the test has been designed so as to develop norms; also implies a standardized procedure for administration.

25. An underlying, unobservable personal attribute, trait, or characteristic of an individual that is thought to be important in describing or understanding human behavior.

DOWN

1. Using evidence to reach a conclusion.

2. Type of test designed to assess the test taker's potential for learning or the individual's ability to perform in an area in which he or she has not been specifically trained.

3. Tools for understanding and predicting behavior that involve multiple methods (such as personal history interviews, behavioral observations, and psychological tests) for gathering information about an individual.

5. Instruments used for gathering information from a sample of the individuals of interest.

7. Type of observation test that involves observing people's behavior to learn how they typically respond in a particular context.

9. Type of test that assesses the test taker's ability to cope with the environment, but at a broader level than do aptitude tests.

11. Type of test where the test takers choose a response or provide a response to predetermined correct answers, requiring little subjective judgment of the person scoring the test.

13. A tool or technique for assessing the size, amount, or degree of an attribute.

14. Type of test that requires test takers to perform a particular task on which their performance is measured.

17. Type of test that is designed to measure human character or disposition.

18. Type of test that is unstructured and requires test takers to respond to ambiguous stimuli.

21. Type of test that relies on test takers' reports or descriptions of their feelings, beliefs, opinions, and/or mental states.

LEARNING ACTIVITIES BY LEARNING OBJECTIVE

The following are some study tips and learning activities you can engage in to support the learning objectives for this chapter.

Learning Objectives	*Study Tips and Learning Activities*
After completing your study of this chapter, you should be able to do the following:	The following study tips and learning activities will help you meet these learning objectives:
Define what a psychological test is, and understand that psychological tests extend beyond personality and intelligence tests.	• Write your definition of a psychological test. List examples of psychological tests, from what comes to your mind first to what comes to your mind last. Compare your list of examples with Figure 1.1. • Ask various professionals, inside and outside the psychology field, to explain to you how they would define what a psychological test is. Compare and contrast their definitions. Compare these definitions with the definitions provided in this textbook. Discuss why definitions might vary.
Trace the history of psychological testing from Alfred Binet and intelligence testing to the tests of today.	• Reflect on the history of testing. Create a timeline showing significant events in testing, beginning with testing in ancient China and ending with testing today.
Describe the ways in which psychological tests can be similar to and different from one another.	• Think about two exams you recently took. Make two lists: one of how they were similar and another of how they were different. Compare your lists with Interim Summary 1.1.
Describe the three characteristics that are common to all psychological tests, and understand that psychological tests can demonstrate these characteristics to various degrees.	• Recall the three characteristics common to all psychological tests. Make three columns, and label them "Representative Sample of Behaviors," "Standardized Conditions," and "Rules for Scoring." Select one or two psychological tests that you have taken. Write how the test(s) demonstrates each characteristic. • Construct an eight-question quiz, with one question for each of the eight Chapter 1 learning objectives. Give the quiz to your classmates (your professor will determine the logistics of this). As a class, discuss whether the quiz meets all of the characteristics of a psychological test. What were the strengths of your quiz? How could your quiz have been improved?
Describe the assumptions that must be made when using psychological tests.	• Describe the six assumptions we must make when using psychological tests. Without looking in your book, see how many assumptions you can write. Compare your written assumptions with the assumptions in the book. Explain why we must make these assumptions.

Describe the different ways that psychological tests can be classified.	• Review the test classification methods in your book. Think about the road portion of the driving test, the SAT, a job interview, the NEO Personality Inventory, and a multiple-choice test you took recently. Classify each test using the different test classification methods.
Describe the differences among four commonly used terms that students often get confused: *psychological assessment*, *psychological tests*, *psychological measurement*, and *surveys*.	• Draw a picture or diagram illustrating how these four commonly confused terms overlap.
Identify and locate printed and online resources that are available for locating information about psychological tests.	• Go to your college library and find *Tests in Print* and the *Mental Measurements Yearbook*. Write the names of three tests and what they measure. • Go to each of the websites referenced in your book. Compare and contrast the information found on these websites. • Select a psychological test that is mentioned in Chapter 1 or 2 or that is suggested by your instructor. Using reference books available at your college library and online, collect as much of the information as possible about your test. Keep track of where you found the information.

EXERCISES

1. Match the event in Column A with the time period Column B.

	Column A Event	Column B Time Period
____	1. France begins using civil service examinations.	A. 2200 BCE
____	2. Wechsler-Bellevue Intelligence Scale developed	B. 618–907
____	3. Civil service examinations begin in China assessing knowledge of classics and literary style.	C. 1368–1644
____	4. United States enacts the No Child Left Behind Act causing a great increase in the amount spent on educational testing.	D. 1791
____	5. Hermann Rorschach develops the Rorschach inkblot test.	E. 1883
____	6. First use of tests by Chinese emperor administered examinations to officials every third year to determine if they were suitable to remain in office.	F. 1905
____	7. Binet and Simon publish the first test of mental ability.	G. 1916
____	8. United States enacts a civil service act requiring competitive examinations.	H. 1920
____	9. The U.S. Employment Service develops the General Aptitude Test Battery.	I. 1921
____	10. Civil service examinations become a more formal part of the government application process in China.	J. 1930s
____	11. Stanford-Binet Intelligence Scales published.	K. 1939
____	12. APA commissions Robert Woodworth to develop the Personal Data Sheet.	L. 1947
____	13. Murray and Morgan develop the TAT.	M. 2001

2. For each situation described in Column A, identify if it is best described as a psychological assessment, test, or survey. Place your answers in Column B.

Column A	Column B Type
1. A clinical psychologist interviews a client, administers the MMPI-2, and then devises a treatment plan.	
2. A human resource professional takes a certification examination and then receives feedback that he did not pass.	
3. A student answers a series of verbal questions, which are scored in a standardized manner, and then is admitted to a special education program.	
4. All employees in a department answer a series of questions. Their answers are aggregated and feedback on the group's answers is given to management.	
5. A job applicant is given a personality inventory and is then hired based on the results.	
6. An individual is administered the MacArthur Competence Assessment Tool and the Competence Assessment for Standing Trial for Defendants with Mental Retardation. A forensic psychologist then makes a judgment regarding the individual's competence to stand trial.	

ADDITIONAL LEARNING ACTIVITIES

Activity 1-1 Projective Tests

Background

The American Psychological Association (APA), founded in 1892 and having nearly 130,000 members, is the oldest and largest association involving psychology (APA, 2014). The Association consists of 54 divisions, including experimental psychology, military psychology, and the psychology of women. However, while APA's membership is large and broad, interests tend to lean toward clinical and counseling work. Partly because of this, the Association for Psychological Science (APS) (previously the American Psychological Society) was founded in 1988. The APS now has more than 26,000 members, and one of APS' primary goals is to disseminate scientific psychological research (APS, 2014). The APS is an excellent alternative to APA and has high-quality, high-impact journals that publish rigorous research. One of their journals is called *Psychological Science in the Public Interest* (PSPI), with the lofty goal of providing "definitive assessments of topics where psychological science may have the potential to inform and improve the well-being of society" (APS, 2014, para. 10). Of course, to achieve this goal, people actually have to be able to access and read the assessments and reviews that they publish. As a result, APS makes PSPI articles freely available to the public at this website: http://www.psychologicalscience.org/index .php/publications/journals/pspi/pspi-archive.

A number of years ago, PSPI published an excellent review on a type of test that is briefly discussed in Chapter 1 and Chapter 14 of the textbook—projective tests. Remember that the textbook distinguishes between objective and projective tests, where objectives tests are highly structured and projective tests are highly unstructured. Many students are intrigued by the idea of a wise psychologist sitting back and uncovering deep meaningful unconscious issues that are the key to solving their clients' problems. Therapy does not tend to work in this manner, however. Below is the APA style reference for the PSPI article on projective tests.

Lilienfeld, S. O., Wood, J. M., & Garb, H. N. (2000). The scientific status of projective techniques. *Psychological Science in the Public Interest, 1*(2), 27–66. doi:10.1111/1529-1006.002

The article is quite long and comprehensive, and while it does include discussion of many topics that you may not be familiar with yet, it is definitely worth reading. As the class progresses, however, you will gain a greater understanding of topics such as reliability, validity, norms, generalizability, and so on. Do not let this intimidate you and stop you from trying to read the article. Knowledge, especially knowledge about complex testing topics, builds incrementally, and you have to start somewhere. You may not understand everything right now, but over the course of the semester, you will develop a deeper understanding of these testing topics. In addition, each section of the article has a Summary and Discussion that avoids a lot of technical details. For example, on pages 38 and 39, there is a Summary and Discussion concerning the Rorschach inkblot test.

This exercise, however, only requires that you read how Lilienfeld and his colleagues define projective techniques and their rationale, which can be found on pages 28 and 29. After obtaining the article and reading this section, answer the questions below.

Questions

1. How do the authors define projective tests?

2. Why do the authors believe that objective versus projective is not a hard classification but rather a continuum?

3. What is the underlying rationale for projective tests, and does research support this rationale?

4. Why do the authors use the term *techniques* rather than *tests*? Is the article's use of the words *techniques* and *tests* consistent textbook's characteristics of a test?

Activity 1-2 Cheating on Tests

Background

Based on the material presented in Chapter 1 of the textbook, it is obvious that formalized high-stakes tests have a long history dating back to the Han Dynasty around 200 to 100 BCE. A little-discussed facet of testing is the topic of cheating. It seems that when important decisions will be made based on test results, certain individuals will be motivated to cheat. Interestingly, there is evidence that the early Chinese examiners had to deal with cheating, and test examiners had procedures and instructions about how to search test takers for cheating materials and how to proctor examinations (Elman, 2000). One well-known Chinese garment that some believe may have been used for cheating is housed at the East Asian Library at Princeton University and can be viewed at the link below.

http://eastasianlib.princeton.edu/robe.htm

The garment shown in the images dates back to the late 19th century and contains over 700 well-known essays. However, there is little evidence that such a garment could have been successfully used to cheat. Instead, the garment may have been rented and used for good luck (Cizek, 1999).

Cheating directly affects two of the basic assumptions about psychological tests that were presented in the textbook: *Individuals will report accurately about themselves* and *individuals will report honestly their thoughts and feelings.* Cheating obviously violates these assumptions. The questions below are intended to help you further think about why cheating occurs, what can be done about cheating, and how cheating affects test outcomes.

Find an example of cheating on a high-stakes test (which is a test that is used to make important decisions) in the news and then answer the questions below.

Questions

1. What cheating occurred, who was the cheater, and what might the possible motives have been behind the cheating?

2. How could cheating have been avoided or caught earlier?

3. How does cheating violate assumptions of psychological testing, and how might violating assumptions impact decisions that are made based on test results?

4. On what types of tests (achievement, aptitude, intelligence, personality, and/or interest inventories) are individuals more likely to cheat on and why?

PRACTICE TEST QUESTIONS

The following are some practice questions to assess your understanding of the material presented in this chapter.

Multiple Choice

1. What do all psychological tests require an individual to do?
   a. Answer questions
   b. Fill out a form
   c. Perform a behavior
   d. Sign a consent form

2. According to the textbook, which one of the following is least typical of psychological tests?
   a. Personality tests
   b. Intelligence tests
   c. Structured interviews
   d. Classroom tests

3. Who published the first test of intelligence in 1905?
   a. Lewis Binet
   b. Alfred Simon
   c. Robert Woodworth
   d. Alfred Binet

4. Who published the Stanford–Binet?
   a. Henry Murray
   b. Robert Woodworth
   c. Lewis Terman
   d. Alfred Binet

5. What test did Robert Woodworth develop during World War I to help the U.S. military detect soldiers who would not be able to handle the stress associated with combat?
   a. Thematic Apperception Test
   b. Stanford–Binet
   c. Personal Data Sheet
   d. Rorschach inkblot test

6. What was the first widely used personality inventory?
   a. Woodworth Psychoneurotic Inventory
   b. Personal Data Sheet
   c. Rorschach inkblot test
   d. Thematic Apperception Test

7. A test requiring individuals to demonstrate their driving ability is best classified as what type of test?
   a. Test of maximal performance
   b. Self-report test
   c. Behavior observation test
   d. Projective test

8. A test requiring individuals to respond to test questions about their feelings and beliefs can best be described as what type of test?
   a. Test of maximal performance
   b. Self-report test
   c. Behavior observation test
   d. Projective test

9. Which one of the following types of tests does not have answers that can be scored as correct or incorrect?

   a. Objective test

   b. Projective test

   c. Standardized test

   d. Self-report test

10. What type of test is administered to a large group of individuals who are similar to the group for which the test has been designed?

   a. Nonstandardized test

   b. Standardized test

   c. Projective test

   d. Subjective test

11. What type of test would a classroom teacher most likely administer?

   a. Achievement test

   b. Aptitude test

   c. Intelligence test

   d. Interest inventory

12. If Jose took a test to identify his potential for learning or his ability to perform in an area in which he had not been specifically trained, what type of test would he be taking?

   a. Achievement test

   b. Intelligence test

   c. Aptitude test

   d. Vocational test

13. Joe took three tests. One required him to respond to true/false questions, one to multiple-choice questions, and one to rating scales. What type of tests did Joe take?

   a. Projective tests

   b. Nonstandardized tests

   c. Subjective tests

   d. Objective tests

14. What type of test would a career development counselor most likely administer?

   a. Achievement test

   b. Aptitude test

   c. Intelligence test

   d. Interest inventory

15. If you wanted to locate a professional test review for a published test, which one of the following would be the best source?

   a. *Tests in Print*

   b. *Tests in Microfiche*

   c. *Mental Measurements Yearbook*

   d. *Measures for Psychological Assessment*

Short Answer

1. What is a psychological test? Provide an example of a psychological test and discuss what makes the example a test.

2. Why is it important for test takers, such as yourself, to understand foundations of psychological testing?

3. Identify three different psychological tests. Discuss how they are similar and how they are different.

4. When using a psychological test, what assumptions must be made? Why are these assumptions important?

5. What are the similarities and differences among intelligence tests, aptitude tests, and achievement tests? Provide an example of each.

6. Identify a psychological assessment, psychological test, and measurement. Discuss how they are similar and different?

7. How are psychological tests and surveys similar? How are psychological tests and surveys different?

ANSWER KEYS

Crossword

ACROSS

4. NORMS—A group of scores that indicate the average performance of a group and the distribution of scores above and below this average.

6. NONSTANDARDIZED—Type of test that does not have standardization samples; more common than standardized tests.

8. INTEREST—An inventory that is designed to assess a person's interests in educational programs for job settings and provide information for making career decisions.

10. STANDARDIZATION SAMPLE—People who are tested to obtain data to establish a frame of reference for interpreting individual test scores.

12. EMOTIONAL—Type of intelligence involving the ability to perceive, appraise, and express emotions accurately and appropriately, to use emotions to facilitate thinking, to understand and analyze emotions, to use emotional knowledge effectively, and to regulate one's emotions to promote both emotional and intellectual growth.

15. BEHAVIOR—An observable and measurable action.

16. VOCATIONAL—Type of test that helps predict how successful a person would be at an occupation before training or entering the occupation

19. PSYCHOMETRICS—The quantitative and technical aspects of psychological measurement.

20. MEASUREMENT—The process of assessing the size, the amount, or the degree of

DOWN

1. INFERENCE—Using evidence to reach a conclusion.

2. APTITUDE—Type of test designed to assess the test taker's potential for learning or the individual's ability to perform in an area in which he or she has not been specifically trained.

3. PSYCHOLOGICAL ASSESSMENTS—Tools for understanding and predicting behavior that involve multiple methods (such as personal history interviews, behavioral observations, and psychological tests) for gathering information about an individual.

5. SURVEYS—Instruments used for gathering information from a sample of the individuals of interest.

7. BEHAVIOR OBSERVATION—Type of observation test that involves observing people's behavior to learn how they typically respond in a particular context.

9. INTELLIGENCE—Type of test that assesses the test taker's ability to cope with the environment but at a broader level than do aptitude tests.

11. OBJECTIVE—Type of test where the test takers choose a response or provide a response to predetermined correct answers, requiring little subjective judgment of the person scoring the test.

13. MEASUREMENT INSTRUMENT—A tool or technique for assessing the size, amount, or degree of an attribute.

14. MAXIMAL PERFORMANCE—Type of test that requires test takers to perform a particular task on which their performance is measured.

an attribute using specific rules for transforming the attribute into numbers.

22. PSYCHOLOGICAL TEST—A measurement tool or technique that requires a person to perform one or more behaviors in order to make inferences about human attributes, traits, or characteristics or predict future outcomes.

23. ACHIEVEMENT—Type of test designed to measure a person's previous learning in a specific academic area.

24. STANDARDIZED—Type of test administered to a large group of individuals who are similar to the group for whom the test has been designed so as to develop norms; also implies a standardized procedure for administration.

25. PSYCHOLOGICAL CONSTRUCT—An underlying, unobservable personal attribute, trait, or characteristic of an individual that is thought to be important in describing or understanding human behavior.

17. PERSONALITY—Type of test that is designed to measure human character or disposition.

18. PROJECTIVE—Type of test that is unstructured and requires test takers to respond to ambiguous stimuli.

21. SELF-REPORT—Type of test that relies on test takers' reports or descriptions of their feelings, beliefs, opinions, and/or mental states.

Exercises

1.

	Column A Event	Column B Time Period
D	1. France begins using civil service examinations.	A. 2200 BCE
K	2. Wechsler-Bellevue Intelligence Scale developed.	B. 618–907
B	3. Civil service examinations begin in China assessing knowledge of classics and literary style.	C. 1368–1644
M	4. United States enacts the No Child Left Behind Act causing a great increase in the amount spent on educational testing.	D. 1791
I	5. Hermann Rorschach develops the Rorschach inkblot test.	E. 1883
A	6. First use of tests by Chinese emperor administered examinations to officials every third year to determine if they were suitable to remain in office.	F. 1905
F	7. Binet and Simon publish the first test of mental ability.	G. 1916
E	8. United States enacts a civil service act requiring competitive examinations.	H. 1920

(Continued)

(Continued)

L	9. The U.S. Employment Service develops the General Aptitude Test Battery.	I. 1921
C	10. Civil service examinations become a more formal part of the government application process in China.	J. 1930s
G	11. Stanford-Binet Intelligence Scales published.	K. 1939
H	12. APA commissions Robert Woodworth to develop the Personal Data Sheet.	L. 1947
J	13. Murray and Morgan develop the TAT.	M. 2001

2.

Column A	Column B Type
1. A clinical psychologist interviews a client, administers the MMPI-2, and then devises a treatment plan.	Assessment
2. A human resource professional takes a certification examination and then receives feedback that he did not pass.	Test
3. A student answers a series of verbal questions, which are scored in a standardized manner, and then is admitted to a special education program.	Test
4. All employees in a department answer a series of questions. Their answers are aggregated and feedback on the group's answers is given to management.	Survey
5. A job applicant is given a personality inventory and is then hired based on the results.	Test
6. An individual is administered the MacArthur Competence Assessment Tool and the Competence Assessment for Standing Trial for Defendants with Mental Retardation. A forensic psychologist then makes a judgment regarding the individual's competence to stand trial.	Assessment

Multiple-Choice

1.

Correct: c

Source: Page 6

Explanation: All psychological tests require a person to perform a behavior. Furthermore, a behavior is an observable and measurable action. Some examples of common behaviors associated with testing include solving a math problem or answering an interview question such as, "How would you deal with a difficult customer?" In fact, reading and then circling the best answer option for the question, "What do all psychological tests require that you do?" is an observable and measureable action.

2.

Correct: c

Source: Page 5

Explanation: Most people think of tests in terms of an objective multiple-choice achievement test. However, structured interviews are tests, they just happen to be less typical of the traditional view of a test. Structured interviews require a person to perform a behavior (respond to a question), and the answer is used to infer some attribute, trait, or characteristic. A sample question might be, "Tell me about a time you had to lead a project. What was the situation, what did you do, and what was the result?" For an employment interview, from a person's response to the sample question, we would make an inference that how the person lead the project in the past would be how the person would lead a project in the future.

3.

Correct: d

Source: Page 12

Explanation: Alfred Binet published the first intelligence test in 1905 in France. However, he did have a coauthor: Theodore Simon. The test was based on Binet's work with his own children and French school children, and Parisian school officials used the test to identify kids who could not perform well in school.

4.

Correct: c

Source: Page 12

Explanation: American psychologist Lewis Terman adapted Binet's original intelligence test in 1916 and published it under the name Stanford-Binet Intelligence Scales. Today it is still one of the most used intelligence tests.

5.

Correct: c

Source: Page 13

Explanation: Woodworth developed the Personal Data Sheet during World War I, wanting to identify individuals who might not be able to handle the stress of combat. The test originally consisted of 200 questions, which was reduced to 116 questions answered in a yes/no fashion. The test covered topics such as anxiety, depression, fears, impulse control, sleepwalking, nightmares, and memory problems.

6.

Correct: b

Source: Page 13

Explanation: Woodworth was not able to finish his Personal Data Sheet, and it was not used in World War I. However, after the war, he completed the Woodworth Psychoneurotic Inventory for use with civilians. The Woodworth Psychoneurotic Inventory was the first self-report test, becoming the first widely used personality inventory.

7.

Correct: a

Source: Page 20

Explanation: Tests of maximal performance require test takers to try their best. Many tests, however, fall into more than one category; therefore, the test could also be classified as a behavior observation test because the test taker's driving is observed. The textbook indicates that many times, for behavior observation tests, the test taker does not know he or she is being observed, which is different from a driving ability test.

8.

Correct: b

Source: Page 20

Explanation: Tests made up of questions that ask the test taker about opinions, beliefs, feelings, and so on, are classified as self-report tests. Generally, for these tests, there are no right or wrong answers. An example of such a test is the Hogan Personality Inventory.

9.

Correct: b

Source: Page 21

Explanation: Projective tests are unstructured and require the test taker to respond to vague or ambiguous stimuli. There are no objectively correct or incorrect answers. This is different from the other answer options, which tend to be structured and be as clear as possible.

10.

Correct: b

Source: Page 21

Explanation: Standardized tests are specifically designed to be given to a large group of people who share common characteristics. The goal is to establish a frame of reference for comparing and interpreting scores, and the result are group norms. The SAT is an example of a standardized test because it allows colleges to compare students' scores to one another.

11.

Correct: a

Source: Page 22

Explanation: Achievement tests are designed to measure a person's learning. As a result, these tests are often called *knowledge tests* and are most likely to be used in a classroom learning setting. In contrast, aptitude tests that measure a person's ability to perform in new situations, intelligence tests measure a person's ability to cope with the environment, and interest inventories measure a person's likes and dislikes.

12.

Correct: c

Source: Page 23

Explanation: Aptitude tests assess a test taker's potential for learning or ability to perform in a new job or situation. Aptitude tests measure the product of cumulative life experiences—or what one has acquired over time. Thus, they help determine what "maximum" can be expected from a person.

13.

Correct: d

Source: Page 21

Explanation: Objective tests most often use three types of answering—yes/no, multiple-choice, and rating scales. Objective tests are characterized by structure, clarity, and a correct answer.

14.

Correct: d

Source: Page 23

Explanation: Interest inventories are commonly used for career counseling and making career decisions. They are not used, however, to predict job success; rather, they are used to identify how well a person's characteristics match different careers or jobs.

15.

Correct: c

Source: Page 26-29

Explanation: While both *Tests in Print* and the *Mental Measurements Yearbook* are both very popular sources for test information, the *Mental Measurements Yearbook* tends to contain more information about a test (e.g., validity information, reliability information, test reviews, a list of references to pertinent literature).

Short Answer

1. Perhaps the best way to define a test is to describe the two features common to all psychological tests. First, they all require a person to perform some observable and measurable action (i.e., behavior). Second, the behavior is used to indicate a personal attribute, trait, or characteristic, or to predict an outcome. For example, a multiple-choice job knowledge test requires the test taker

to read and respond to test questions (behavior). The responses are used to indicate a person's level of knowledge.

2. It is important to understand the foundations of psychological testing because testing is widely used in modern society. For example, test results are used to diagnose and treat disorders, to determine who to hire for a job, and to determine whom to admit to college. In each case, test scores are used to make decisions that have significant life impact. As a test taker, it is helpful to understand the foundations of psychological testing so that you can better understand if the tests you are taking are well-designed tests and if the resulting test scores are being properly interpreted and used. As a test user, it is important to ensure that you use tests appropriately leading to the best possible decisions.

3. Although all psychological tests require a behavior to be performed to measure attributes, traits, or characteristics used to predict outcomes, there are many differences across tests. According to your textbook, these differences can be defined in terms of the behavior performed, the attribute measured, the content, the administration and format, the scoring and interpretation, and the psychometric quality. The Stanford-Binet Intelligence Scales, the Wechsler Adult Intelligence Scale, and the Rorschach inkblot test are three commonly used psychological tests. The Stanford-Binet and the Wechsler intelligence scales are very similar on all of areas stated above. However, they are substantially different from the Rorschach. The Rorschach requires test takers to project themselves into the test and interpret content, whereas intelligence scales requires individuals to identify correct answers. Thus, the content, administration, and interpretation are all vastly different. In addition, intelligence scales tend to have excellent psychometric qualities, while the Rorschach has much lower quality psychometric qualities.

4. There are many assumptions that are made when using psychological tests. A test user must assume that

1. the tests measure what they claim to measure,

2. the behavior and scores will remain stable over time,

3. test takers understand and interpret items similarly,

4. test takers will (and can) accurately report about themselves,

5. test takers will honestly report their thoughts and feelings, and

6. the test score represents the test takers true score plus some random error.

These assumptions are important because they affect our confidence in the meaning and interpretation of the scores, and relate to their usefulness. There are many actions that test administrators and test users can take to increase our confidence that each of the assumptions is true.

5. To laypersons, intelligence, achievement, and aptitude tests often get confused because of their similarities. All three can be used to predict similar outcomes, such as success in an education program or job performance. However, there are differences. An achievement test measures learned skill or knowledge in a specific area. This is different from aptitude and intelligence tests, which measure a person's ability. Aptitude tests specifically measure a person's ability to learn

or perform in a new situation, and intelligence tests measure a more general ability to cope with one's environment.

6. Psychological assessments, tests, and measurements have similarities, as they are all commonly used to collect information and make decisions about individuals. However, there are important differences. A psychological assessment is a much broader concept than a test. Psychological assessment involves collecting and assembling information to make a decision. Some of that information may involve test results, but things such as personal histories can also be included. In addition, assessment generally includes some subjective components. In contrast, measurement refers to processes and rules used to assign numbers. Thus, while most psychological tests involve measurement not all psychological tests meet the definition of measurement.

7. Psychological tests and surveys are both used to collect information. However, there are two important distinctions. First, tests focus on individual outcomes, while surveys focus on group outcomes. For example, an organization may give a test to employees to decide whom they want to promote. That same organization may also administer a survey to employees to determine if they are happy with the promotion process as a group. Also, test results are usually reported as a single score, but survey results are often reported at the individual-item level.

References

APA. (2014). *Who we are*. Retrieved from http://www.apa.org/about/apa/index.aspx

APA. (2015). *Glossary of psychological terms*. Retrieved from http://www.apa.org/research/action/glossary.aspx?tab=5

APS. (2014). *History of APS*. Retrieved from http://www.psychologicalscience.org/index.php/about/history-of-aps

Cizek, G. J. (1999). *Cheating on tests: How to do it, detect it, and prevent it*. Mahaway, NJ: Lawrence Erlbaum Associates.

Elman, B. A. (2000). *A cultural history of civil examinations in late Imperial China*. Los Angeles: University of California Press.

2

Why Is Psychological Testing Important?

Chapter Overview

In Chapter 2, we discuss why psychological testing is important, including why individuals and institutions use test results to make both comparative and absolute decisions. We explore who uses psychological tests in educational, clinical, and organizational settings and for what reasons. We also discuss some of the concerns society has about using psychological tests, including controversies about intelligence tests, aptitude tests, and integrity tests. Also covered is one of the most current controversies—the use of high-stakes testing in education.

Learning Objectives

After completing your study of this chapter, you should be able to do the following:

- Describe different types of decisions that are made using the results of psychological tests.
- Explain which professionals use psychological tests, in what settings, and for what reasons.
- Describe some concerns individuals have regarding the use of psychological tests as well as the social and legal implications of psychological testing, especially as they relate to intelligence, achievement, aptitude, and integrity testing.

Chapter Outline

The Importance of Psychological Testing
Individual and Institutional Decisions
Comparative and Absolute Decisions

Key Concepts

absolute decisions:	Decisions that are made by seeing who has the minimum score needed to qualify.
comparative decisions:	Decisions that are made by comparing test scores to see who has the best score.
individual decisions:	Decisions that are made by the person who takes the test using the test results.
institutional decisions:	Decisions that are made by an institution based on the results of a particular test or tests.
integrity tests:	Tests that measure individual attitudes and experiences toward honesty, dependability, trustworthiness, reliability, and prosocial behavior.
nature-versus-nurture controversy:	A debate that focuses on whether intelligence is determined by heredity or develops after birth based on environmental factors.
within-group norming:	The practice of administering the same test to every test taker but scoring the test differently according to the race of the test taker.

KEY CONCEPTS CROSSWORD

ACROSS

4. The norming practice of administering the same test to every test taker, but scoring the test differently according to the test taker's race.
5. Type of decision that is made by an institution by seeing who has the minimum test score needed to qualify.
6. Type of decision an institution makes based on the results of a particular test or tests.
7. Type of decision institutions make by comparing test scores to see who has the best score.

DOWN

1. A controversy that focuses on whether intelligence is determined by heredity or develops after birth based on environmental factors.
2. Type of test that measures individual attitudes and experiences toward honesty, dependability, trustworthiness, reliability, and prosocial behavior.
3. Type of decision that is made by the person who takes the test using the test results.

LEARNING ACTIVITIES BY LEARNING OBJECTIVE

The following are some study tips and learning activities you can engage in to support the learning objectives for this chapter.

Learning Objectives	Study Tips and Learning Activities
After completing your study of this chapter, you should be able to do the following:	The following study tips and learning activities will help you meet these learning objectives:
Describe different types of decisions that are made using the results of psychological tests.	• Make a list of all the psychological tests you have ever taken. Write down any decisions you made about yourself based on the results of each test. Write down any decisions others made about you based on the results of each test. Indicate whether others used a comparative method or an absolute method when evaluating your test score.
Explain which professionals use psychological tests, in what settings, and for what reasons.	• Schedule time to talk with three of the following professionals: a clinical psychologist, a career counselor, a secondary school administrator, a school psychologist, an industrial and organizational practitioner, and a human resources director. Interview these professionals and find out what tests they use on a day-to-day basis, why they use these tests, and how they use the test scores to make decisions. Be prepared to share your findings with your class.
Describe some concerns individuals have regarding the use of psychological tests as well as the social and legal implications of psychological testing, especially as they relate to intelligence, achievement, aptitude, and integrity testing.	• Find two news or journal articles: one discussing controversies in psychological testing prior to 1980 and one discussing legal challenges associated with psychological testing after 1980. Compare and contrast the controversies discussed in each article. Be prepared to share your articles and findings with your class. • On a piece of paper, create three columns: Intelligence and Achievement, Aptitude, and Integrity. Write as many of the social and legal implications as you can remember in each of the categories.

EXERCISES

1. The textbook discusses the role that nature (heredity and genetics) and nurture (environment and learning) play in the determination of intelligence. The debate concerning the amount each factor plays in determining intelligence is often part of discussions concerning group differences in intelligence test scores. For the individuals listed in the table below, identify if they are most likely to say intelligence is determined by nature, nurture, or a combination of the factors. Explain your answers.

Individual	Nature, Nurture, or a Combination
René Descartes	
John Locke	
Arthur Jensen	
Richard Herrnstein and Charles Murray	
Neisser et al. (1996)	
Nisbett et al. (2012)	

2. For each testing scenario described in the first column identify if it is best described as a comparative or absolute decision.

Testing Scenario	Type of Decision
1. A medical school admits 100 students a year, in a top-down fashion, using only scores from the *Medical College Admission Test*.	
2. A radiologist is granted certification based on her score on a test.	
3. A law school evaluates a student's score on the *Law School Admissions Test* to determine if he achieved the minimum score required by the school for admittance.	
4. An attorney passes the bar examination.	
5. A public safety organization has job applicants take a job knowledge test. The highest 30 scoring individuals then partake in a personal interview. Scores on the test and interview are combined, and the 10 highest scoring individuals are offered a job.	
6. A mental health professional administers a test and determines if the patient meets the diagnostic criteria for a disorder.	
7. A government organization decides that it will offer jobs to the highest scoring 25% of the applicants.	

ADDITIONAL LEARNING ACTIVITIES

Activity 2-1 Mainstream Science on Intelligence

Background

While covering the controversy over intelligence tests, the textbook identifies two excellent summary articles written on the state of knowledge concerning intelligence (Neisser et al., 1996; Nisbett et al., 2012). There is another key article on intelligence, however, that has an interesting history. That article is an editorial published in the *Wall Street Journal*, which was endorsed by 54 academic intelligence researchers. The content of the editorial and an account of how it was developed was later published in the scholarly journal *Intelligence*.

During the Bell Curve controversy, Linda Gottfredson, an educational psychologist, approached the *Wall Street Journal* Features Editor, David Brooks, about publishing an essay on misinformation on intelligence. While he was not interested in her essay, he was interested in publishing a short statement signed by knowledgeable experts. Gottfredson was given a two-week timeline to come up with the editorial statement and signatures. Unfortunately for her, this was in 1994, before everyone was constantly tethered to their work e-mail via smart phones, so contacting and communicating with testing experts took much longer than today.

Gottfredson quickly drafted the statement consisting of 25 conclusions regarded as mainstream. She also compiled a list of highly knowledgeable academic intelligence researchers, representing a diverse variety of disciplines ranging from anthropology, genetics, neuropsychology, sociology, and various psychological specialties such as psychometrics, educational psychology, and personnel selection. She then faxed her statement to all of the people she identified (if they had a fax number), requesting that they read the statement and let her know if they endorsed the statement. Because of the tight timeline, the recipients could not modify the statement that she had written. They could only check "yes" or "no" to indicate if they endorsed the statement. If an academic researcher checked "no," they could then select one of three reasons:

1. "I don't agree that the statement represents the mainstream"

2. "I don't know enough to say for sure"

3. "Other reason"

Gottfredson sent a total of 131 invitations and received 100 responses. Of the 100 researchers who replied, 52 checked "yes," indicating that they endorsed the entire statement, and 48 checked "no," indicating that they did not endorse the statement. Of those who declined to endorse and sign the statement, seven thought it did not represent the mainstream, 11 did not feel they knew enough to say if it did or did not, and 30 selected for other reasons. Looking more closely at the 30 who did not sign for other reasons, it is clear that they did not necessarily disagree with the 25 conclusions. For example, six stated that they did not dispute the content, but did disagree with the presentation mode of a *Wall Street Journal* editorial, and stated that they feared that signing it would jeopardize their position. Thus, overall, it seems that only seven of the 100 responding researchers clearly did not agree with Gottfredson's conclusions.

Gottfredson points out that intelligence testing is a complex topic, and entire books have been written about most of the 25 conclusions in the editorial. Thus, there is a lot left out of her editorial and its simplified coverage of the topic. However, this strong collective voice suggests that there is a lot less controversy among intelligence experts than has been portrayed in the popular media.

Locate either the original *Wall Street Journal* article or Gottfredson's (1997) article, and answer the following questions.

Questions

1. How does the Gottfredson editorial define intelligence?

2. What conclusions does Gottfredson make in the editorial about group differences?

3. What position does Gottfredson take on nature-versus-nurture concerning intelligence?

4. What does Gottfredson suggest are the implications for social policy?

5. Research and determine if there is controversy surrounding the Gottfredson article. If you locate criticisms, what are they?

Activity 2-2 How Would You Score?

Background

Testing of military personnel has a long history in the United States dating back to World War I. Perhaps one of the most influential individuals was the American psychologist Robert M. Yerkes. Yerkes earned a PhD in psychology from Harvard and was a president of the American Psychological Association (APA) in 1917. As the founding father of comparative psychology, his name is attached to the famous Yerkes-Dodson Law. He was quite an accomplished person. However, he was also a proponent of eugenics, which promoted the selective breeding of humans so that only the best genes would be passed on, thereby improving the human species. This line of thinking has led to many atrocities, such as forced sterilization of people deemed unfit for reproduction, including those with mental disabilities and low intelligence. As a result, modern thinkers who are against intelligence testing do not necessarily have nice things to say about the man who contributed greatly to its spread and use.

Being the president of APA at the time when the United States entered WWI in 1917, Yerkes established a committee to explore ways that psychology could contribute to the war effort. He surrounded himself on this committee with several well-known testing experts of the time. During his two years of military service during WWI, he "lived military psychology" (Yerkes, 1930, para. 51) and spearheaded the development of the Army Alpha and Army Beta tests. These tests were used to assess over 1.75 million military recruits. The Army Alpha measured verbal ability, numerical ability, ability to follow directions, and knowledge of information, and was administered in a group setting. However, there were a large number of immigrants who could not read English, and as a result, the nonverbal Army Beta was developed.

The textbook provides two examples of questions found on the Army Alpha test. The websites below offer several more examples. Try answering the questions found at both websites, and then answer the questions below.

http://official-asvab.com/armysamples_rec.htm
http://historymatters.gmu.edu/d/5293

Questions

1. How would you have done on the tests?

2. Do you believe it would be appropriate for an important "institutional" decision to be made about you using these tests? Provide a rationale for your answer.

3. Do you believe that the tests would have been suitable for you to make an "individual" decision about your military service? Provide a rationale for your answer.

4. Is it fair to evaluate and judge the Army Alpha and Army Beta tests using today's knowledge of testing and testing standards? Provide a rationale for your answer.

Activity 2-3 Individual and Institutional Decisions

Background

The textbook distinguishes between two different types of decisions we can make using test results. First, there are individual decisions. These are decisions test takers make themselves. Next, there are institutional decisions. These are decisions other people make about those who take tests (test takers).

Chapter 1 of the Study Guide material included a review of projective techniques. The reference again is shown below.

Lilienfeld, S. O., Wood, J. M., & Barb, H. M (2000). The scientific status of projective techniques. *Psychological Science in the Public Interest, 1*(2), 27–66. doi:10.1111/1529-1006.002

Although you may not yet be familiar with the technical language of testing, the article contains several short reviews of various projective tests that, for the most part, can be easily understood. Locate the article above and read the Summary and Discussion section concerning the Rorshach inkblot test found on pages 38 and 39 of the article. Then, answer the questions below.

Questions

1. Would you feel comfortable using the results of a Rorschach to make an individual decision?

2. What two institutional decisions could be made using the results of a Rorschach inkblot test? Explain if you would feel comfortable with others using the results of a Rorschach to make these decisions?

PRACTICE QUESTIONS

The following are some practice questions to assess your understanding of the material presented in this chapter.

Multiple Choice

1. What type of decision is made when a high school administrator uses your test score to determine if you should be in a gifted program?
   a. Absolute
   b. Comparative
   c. Individual
   d. Institutional

2. Hector completed several interest inventories at the career center at his college. He used the results to decide on a college major. What kind of decision did Hector make?
   a. Institutional
   b. Individual
   c. Comparative
   d. Absolute

3. What method is an organizational leader using to make a decision when the leader continues to consider your job application because your score was one of the highest on a pre-employment test?
   a. Absolute
   b. Comparative
   c. Individual
   d. Institutional

4. A manager at XYZ Corporation administers an employment test to help determine which job candidates will be offered a job. The manager first decides what minimum score she will accept and then offers jobs to individuals who scored equal to or more than the minimum score. The manager used the test to make what kind of decision?
   a. Individual
   b. Absolute
   c. Comparative
   d. Normative

5. In educational settings, teachers, administrators, school psychologists, and career counselors use psychological tests for all of the following purposes EXCEPT
   a. measuring student learning.
   b. awarding scholarships.
   c. identifying career interests.
   d. planning treatment programs.

6. In organizational settings, human resources professionals and industrial-organizational psychology practitioners use psychological tests for all of the following purposes EXCEPT
   a. making hiring decisions.
   b. diagnosing disorders.
   c. determining training needs.
   d. evaluating employee performance.

7. Which one of the following beliefs has been a major concern of the general public regarding the use of psychological tests?

    a. Test publishing companies make too much money selling psychological tests.

    b. Psychological tests unfairly discriminate against certain racial groups.

    c. Psychological tests have no evidence of reliability/precision or validity for intended use.

    d. Local and federal government regulation of psychological testing is too prevalent.

8. What debate centers on whether people are born with their intelligence or acquire their intelligence during their lives?

    a. Innate versus learned

    b. Mature versus learned

    c. Innate versus nurture

    d. Nature versus nurture

9. What test is used to determine whether individuals qualify for specific jobs in military branches?

    a. Rorschach inkblot test

    b. General Aptitude Test Battery (GATB)

    c. Armed Service Vocational Aptitude Battery (ASVAB)

    d. Leadership Practices Inventory (LPI)

10. What process was introduced because an examination of GATB scores showed that more Whites were being referred for jobs than African Americans and Hispanics?

    a. Ethnic norming

    b. Situational norming

    c. Within-group norming

    d. Between-group norming

11. What is the term used to describe when test taker's raw scores are compared with those of their own racial or ethnical group?

    a. Ethnic norming

    b. Situational norming

    c. Race norming

    d. Between-group norming

12. What do integrity tests claim to measure?

    a. Ability to perform a job

    b. Personality

    c. Individuals' ethics

    d. Honesty

Short Answer

1. Describe the different types of decisions we make using the results of psychological tests. Provide an example of each.

2. How might individuals use the results of psychological tests? How might organizations use the result of psychological tests?

3. What are the similarities and differences between comparative decisions and absolute decisions? Give examples of each.

4. Who uses the results of psychological tests, and for what reasons do they use the results?

5. What are some of society's concerns about intelligence, aptitude, and integrity testing?

6. How do past controversies over psychological testing compare to current controversies?

7. What concerns exist regarding the use of the following personality tests: Rorschach inkblot test, Minnesota Multiphasic Personality Inventory (MMPI), and Myer-Briggs Type Indicator (MBTI)?

ANSWER KEYS

Crossword

ACROSS

4. WITHIN-GROUP—The norming practice of administering the same test to every test taker, but scoring the test differently according to the test taker's race.
5. ABSOLUTE—Type of decision made by an institution by seeing who has the minimum test score needed to qualify.
6. INSTITUTIONAL—Type of decision an institution makes based on the results of a particular test or tests.
7. COMPARATIVE—Type of decision institutions make by comparing test scores to see who has the best score.

DOWN

1. NATURE-VERSUS-NURTURE—A controversy that focuses on whether intelligence is determined by heredity or develops after birth based on environmental factors.
2. INTEGRITY—Type of test that measures individual attitudes and experiences toward honesty, dependability, trustworthiness, reliability, and prosocial behavior.
3. INDIVIDUAL—Type of decision that is made by the person who takes the test using the test results.

Exercises

1.

Individual	Nature, Nurture, or a Combination
René Descartes	Nature—The 17th-century philosopher Descartes believed that intelligence occurs naturally and is influenced little by the environment.
John Locke	Nurture—The 17th-century philosopher Locke supported the "blank slate" approach and believe that environment shaped intelligence.
Arthur Jensen	Nature—In 1969, Jensen authored an influential *Harvard Educational Review* article where he implied that intelligence was primarily due to genetic factors (80%).
Richard Herrnstein and Charles Murray	Nature and Nurture—Herrnstein and Murray in 1994 authored the *The Bell Curve: Intelligence and Structure in American Life*. They wrote that IQ is somewhere between 40% and 80% inheritable. Thus, it is a combination of both, but nature likely plays a larger role.
Neisser et al. (1996)	Nature and Nurture—Neisser et al. (2012) is an APA task force report titled *Intelligence: Knowns and Unknowns*. The report acknowledges that there are differences in intelligence scores between racial and ethnic groups, but the cause of the difference is unknown.
Nisbett et al. (2012)	Nature and Nurture—Nisbett et al. (2012) published a review of current research findings. They concluded that although we know a great deal about intelligence we do not know much about the roles of both heredity and environment.

2.

Column A	Column B
1. A medical school admits 100 students a year, in a top-down fashion, using only scores from the *Medical College Admission Test.*	Comparative
2. A radiologist is granted certification based on her score on a test.	Absolute
3. A law school evaluates a student's score on the *Law School Admissions Test* to determine if he achieved the minimum score required by the school for admittance.	Absolute
4. An attorney passes the bar examination.	Absolute
5. A public safety organization has job applicants take a job knowledge test. The highest 30 scoring individuals then partake in a personal interview. Scores on the test and interview are combined, and the 10 highest scoring individuals are offered a job.	Comparative
6. A mental health professional administers a test and determines if the patient meets the diagnostic criteria for a disorder.	Absolute
7. A government organization decides that it will offer jobs to the highest scoring 25% of the applicants.	Comparative

Multiple Choice

1.

Correct Answer: d

Source: Page 37–38

Explanation: Institutional decisions are those made based on a test score by someone other than the test taker. For example, a company may decide to hire an individual based on an interview, or a college may decide to admit an applicant based on his or her SAT score.

2.

Correct Answer: b

Source: Page 37–38

Explanation: Based on a test score, a person may make decisions that directly concern him- or herself. These decisions are called individual decisions because they are made by the individual who took the test. Consider a person who takes the Graduate Record Examination—a test many graduate programs use as a part of the admission process. If the individual performs well on the test, he or she may choose to apply to schools that are more selective. However, if he or she does not perform well on the test a less selective schools may be the person's choice.

3.

Correct Answer: b

Source: Page 38

Explanation: The leader is making a comparative decision because the leader is comparing your score to others who have taken the test. With this type of decision, test takers are generally rank ordered based on their test score. Decisions are often made in order, so if the company needed to hire five employees, and the top five performed well, all five might be offered a job. If a person turned the job down, then the sixth person on the list might be offered the job, and so on.

4.

Correct Answer: b

Source: Page 38

Explanation: The manager made an absolute decision. These types of decisions are based on the test taker's score in relation to some defined standard and do not consider the scores of other test takers when decisions are made. For example, the Praxis test is a test that measures teacher candidates' knowledge and skills. States set a minimum score that the candidate must achieve to become licensed in that state.

5.

Correct Answer: d

Source: Page 39–40

Explanation: Planning treatment programs is outside the area of expertise of these individuals, and therefore they should not be using tests for this purpose. The only individuals who should be planning treatment programs are individuals specifically trained in this area—such as clinical psychologists, psychiatrists, social workers, and other health care workers.

6.

Correct Answer: b

Source: Page 39–40

Explanation: Diagnosing disorders is outside the area of expertise of human resource professionals and industrial-organizational psychologists. While industrial-organizational psychologists have "psychologist" in their title, they do not have training in such areas, are not licensed health care providers, and should not provide such services.

7.

Correct Answer: b

Source: Page 43–44

Explanation: While some individuals may have some of the concerns listed in the answer options, a deeply rooted issue is concern over discrimination in psychological testing. In the United States, concerns about discrimination and cultural bias date back to one of the first large-scale testing efforts, the Army Alpha and Beta tests. Such concerns continue today, as evidenced by laws such as the Civil Rights Act and court cases affecting the nature and practices of psychological testing.

8.

Correct Answer: d

Source: Page 45

Explanation: The nature-versus-nurture debate centers the relative importance of genetically inherited factors (nature) versus environmental or learned factors (nurture) and their importance in determining a person's intelligence. What makes this debate important is that certain racial and ethnic groups tend to score lower than other racial and ethnic groups, and explanations as to why this occurs often incorporate and emphasize on side of the nature versus nurture debate. However, there is widespread scientific agreement that both nature and nurture play an important role in the determination of intelligence, but the relative significance of each factor is still an open question.

9.

Correct Answer: c

Source: Page 49–50

Explanation: The military uses the ASVAB to predict personal future academic and occupational success in the military. The ASVAB is administered at over 14,000 locations and to over 1 million people a year.

10.

Correct Answer: c

Source: Page 49

Explanation: Within-group norming is a score adjustment procedure that used to be recommend to deal with group differences between minority and majority groups when making hiring decisions. While the practice was endorsed by a National Research Council study, the practice was controversial and was outlawed by the 1991 Civil Rights Act.

11.

Correct Answer: c

Source: Page 49

Explanation: Race norming is also known as within-group norming. In this practice, raw scores within a racial group are compared and ranked based on their relative standing within the group. The relative ranking for each group is combined into a single overall ranking of candidates. Under this practice, the highest scoring individual in each group would be treated the same regardless of their raw scores. Race norming was a controversial practice and was outlawed by the 1991 Civil Rights Act.

12.

Correct Answer: d

Source: Page 50–52

Explanation: Integrity tests measure a person's attitudes and experiences toward honesty. They also touch on characteristics such as dependability, trustworthiness, reliability, and prosocial behavior. One type of integrity test requires that test takers answer questions about their experiences, based on the notion that past behavior predicts future behavior. A second type requires test takers to share preferences and is similar to a personality measure. There is controversy surrounding the use of integrity tests, but employers regularly use them because of large monetary losses related to counter-productive work behaviors.

Short Answer

1. Decisions based on psychological tests can be classified along two dimensions. The first dimension is individual-versus-institutional decisions. An example of an individual decision is a test taker's decision to apply or not apply to a specific school based on his or her test results. In contrast, an institutional decision involves another entity making a decision concerning the test taker. For example, based on test results, a school may decide to accept or not accept a test taker.

The second dimension is comparative-versus-absolute decisions. A comparative decision involves comparing a test taker's score to other people who have taken the test. For example, an employer may offer jobs to the top five scoring individuals with the understanding that they are the best applicants for the job. On the other hand, an absolute decision involves only looking at an individual's specific score and its relation to some set standard. For example, if a test taker achieves a certain score, he or she may become certified in an area of professional practice. This indicates the test taker has a level of knowledge at or above what has been identified as the minimum required amount for the profession.

2. There are many ways that both individuals and organizations might use test results. For example, a high school student may take a vocational assessment helping him or her decide on career options. Organizations may also give the same vocational assessment when deciding on what type of job to put an employee into.

3. Comparative and absolute decisions are methods institutions commonly use to make decisions using test scores. Comparative decisions involve comparing a person's performance relative to others who have taken the test, while absolute decisions involve comparing a person's performance in relation to some set standard. Although they are different decision-making methods, they can sometimes be used together. For example, an employer may decide to set a minimum test score to establish

basic proficiency. Any applicant who scored higher would be considered employable. This is an absolute decision. Then a comparative decision might be made and jobs offered to the two highest scores (above the minimum cut score). If no one scores above the cut score, then the job is offered to no one.

4. The textbook includes discussion of test uses in three different settings: educational, clinical, and organizational. In *educational settings*, test users can be administrators, teachers, school psychologists, and career counselors. They use test results for a variety of reasons, including to award scholarships, measure learning, identify problems, and identify career interests. In *clinical settings*, test users can be clinical psychologists, psychiatrists, social workers, and counselors. They use test results to diagnose disorders, plan treatment, assess treatment, and counsel others. In *organizational settings*, test users can be human resource professionals and industrial-organizational psychologists. They use test results to make hiring decisions, determine training needs, and evaluate performance.

5. While there are concerns that are specific to each area of testing, one common theme throughout intelligence, aptitude, and integrity testing is cultural bias and discrimination toward minorities. The fear is that test scores will inaccurately represent the knowledge, skills, abilities, or other characteristic of these populations and therefore disadvantage them. Well-developed and appropriately used tests, however, minimize bias and discrimination.

6. Many of the past controversies over testing are quite similar to current controversies and involve bias and discrimination. For example, the first large-scale testing effort during WWI, the Army Alpha test, had language and cultural issues. As a result, a second test, the Army Beta test, was developed, and this kicked off a nature-versus-nurture debate concerning intelligence. This debate has continued with Arthur Jensen's 1969 article, where Jensen stated that 80% of group differences in intelligence are a result of genetic factors. And the concern continued into the 1990s with the publication of the *Bell Curve* where the authors stated that intelligence is between 40% and 80% heritable. An APA task force publication, *Intelligence: Knowns and Unknowns*, did not necessarily disagree with the *Bell Curve*, but stated that there is no support to conclude that the difference is due to genetics.

7. A concern that users of these types of tests and inventories have is that there is not a single identifiably correct answer and thus they are susceptible to faking. It is feared that test takers can intentionally or unintentionally misrepresent themselves to test users. For example, job applicants might give socially desirable answers in hope of landing a job even though they may be poor matches. In an effort to combat this, many tests have test items built into them to attempt to detect faking.

References

Gottfredson, L. S. (1997). Mainstream science on intelligence: An editorial with 52 signatories, history, and bibliography. Intelligence, 24(1), 13–23. Retrieved from http://www.journals.elsevier.com/intelligence/

Neisser, U., Boodoo, G., Bouchard, Jr., T. J., Boykin, A. W., Brody, N., Ceci, S. J., ... & Urbina, S. (1996). Intelligence: Knowns and unknowns. American Psychologist, 51(2), 77. Retrieved from http://www.apa.org/pubs/journals/amp/

Nisbett, R. E., Aronson, J., Blair, C., Dickens, W., Flynn, J., Halpern, D. F., & Turkheimer, E. (2012). Intelligence: New findings and theoretical developments. American psychologist, 67(2), 130. doi:10.1037/a0026699

Yerkes, R. M. (1930). Autobiography of Robert Mearns Yerkes. In C. Murchison (Ed.), A history of psychology in autobiography (Vol., 2, pp. 381–407). Worcester, MA: Clark University Press. Retrieved from http://psychclassics.yorku.ca/Yerkes/murchison.htm

3

Is There a Right or Wrong Way to Use Psychological Tests?

Chapter Overview

In Chapter 3, we introduce you to ethical standards in psychological testing. We discuss the concept of acting ethically and what we mean by *ethics* and *professional standards*. We summarize some of the most commonly referenced and discussed professional practice standards relevant to the field of psychological testing. Following a discussion of the responsibilities of test publishers, test users, and test takers, we discuss issues related to testing special populations.

Learning Objectives

After completing your study of this chapter, you should be able to do the following:

- Define ethics and the importance of acting ethically by following professional practice standards.
- Identify the professional practice standards of associations and societies most relevant to psychological testing.
- Distinguish professional practice standards from certification and licensure.
- Explain the general responsibilities of test publishers, test users, and test takers.
- Explain the issues associated with testing special populations.

Chapter Outline

Acting Ethically
   What Are Ethics?
   Professional Practice Standards
   Certification and Licensure
Appropriate Use of Psychological Tests
   Test Publisher Responsibility
   The Sale of Psychological Tests
   The Marketing of Psychological Tests
   Availability of Comprehensive Test Manuals
   Test User Responsibility
   Test Taker Responsibilities
   Test Taker Rights
Testing Special Populations
   Test Takers With Physical or Mental Challenges
   Test Takers With Learning Disabilities
   Test Takers From Multicultural Backgrounds
Chapter Summary

Key Concepts

anonymity:	The practice of administering tests or obtaining information without obtaining the identity of the participant.
certification:	A professional credential individuals earn by demonstrating that they have met predetermined qualifications (e.g., that they have specific knowledge, skills, and/or experience).
cognitive impairments:	Mental challenges that include intellectual disabilities, learning disabilities, and traumatic brain injuries.
confidentiality:	The assurance that all personal information will be kept private and not be disclosed without explicit permission.
ethical standards:	Statements by professionals (not laws established by governmental bodies) regarding what they believe are appropriate and inappropriate behaviors when practicing their profession.
ethics:	Issues or practices that influence the decision-making process in terms of "doing the right thing."
informed consent:	Individuals' right of self-determination; means that individuals are entitled to full explanations of why they are being tested, how the test data will be used, and what the test results mean.

learning disability:	A hidden handicap that hinders learning and does not have visible signs.
licensure:	A mandatory credential individuals must obtain to practice within their professions.
motor impairments:	Disabilities that hinder physical movement, such as paralysis and missing limbs.
multicultural backgrounds:	Experiences of those who belong to various minority groups based on race, cultural or ethnic origin, sexual orientation, family unit, primary language, and so on.
sensory impairments:	Disabilities that hinder the function of the five senses, such as deafness and blindness.
test security:	Steps taken to ensure that the content of a psychological test does not become public knowledge.
test taker:	The person who responds to test questions or whose behavior is measured.
test user:	A person who participates in purchasing, administering, interpreting, or using the results of a psychological test.
user qualifications:	The background, training, and/or certifications the test purchaser must meet.

KEY CONCEPTS CROSSWORD

ACROSS

2. The assurance that all personal information will be kept private and not be disclosed without explicit permission.
4. Experiences of those who belong to various minority groups based on race, cultural or ethnic origin, sexual orientation, family unit, primary language, and so on.
7. Type of impairment involving mental disorders that include intellectual disabilities, learning disabilities, and traumatic brain injuries.
8. Issues or practices that influence the decision-making process in terms of "doing the right thing."
9. An impairment that hinders the function of the five senses, such as deafness and blindness.
11. The practice of administering tests or obtaining information without obtaining the identity of the participant.
13. A person who participates in purchasing, administering, interpreting, or using the results of a psychological test.
14. Steps taken to ensure that the content of a psychological test does not become public knowledge.
16. A professional credential individuals earn by demonstrating that they have met predetermined qualifications (e.g., that they have specific knowledge, skills, and/or experience).

DOWN

1. Individuals' right of self-determination; means that individuals are entitled to full explanations of why they are being tested, how the test data will be used, and what the test results mean.
3. An impairment that hinders physical movement, such as paralysis and missing limbs.
5. The background, training, and/or certifications the test purchaser must meet.
6. The person who responds to test questions or whose behavior is measured.
10. A mandatory credential individuals must obtain to practice within their professions.
12. Statements by professionals (not laws established by governmental bodies) regarding what they believe are appropriate and inappropriate behaviors when practicing their profession.
15. A hidden disability that hinders learning and does not have visible signs.

LEARNING ACTIVITIES BY LEARNING OBJECTIVE

The following are some study tips and learning activities you can engage in to support the learning objectives for this chapter.

Learrning Objectives	Study Tips and Learning Activities
After completing your study of this chapter, you should be able to do the following:	The following study tips will help you meet these learning objectives:
Define ethics and the importance of acting ethically by following professional practice standards.	• Search the Web for definitions of ethics and professional practice standards. After comparing what you learn with the definitions in the chapter, brainstorm a list of consequences that might result from not acting ethically and/or following professional practice standards.
Identify the professional practice standards of associations and societies most relevant to psychological testing.	• Create a lit of the professional practice standards discussed in the chapter. Search the Web and find 3-4 more professional practice standards that might be relevant to psychological testing. Describe why the standards are relevant to psychological testing. • Review the complete standards for those discussed in the chapter. The chapter includes information on where to find the complete standards. Create a list of best practices based on the commonalities you identify during your review of the standards. • Write a case study in which a psychologist has not complied with one or more ethical points. As part of the study, describe what various parties were able to do about the psychologist's noncompliance.
Distinguish professional practice standards from certification and licensure.	• Search the Web for definitions of professional practice standards, certification, and licensure. Using definitions from the chapter and the Web, create a table that includes the similarities and differences between the three concepts.
Explain the general responsibilities of test publishers, test users, and test takers.	• Think about each of the ethical responsibilities discussed in the chapter. Write a paragraph on why someone might choose or not choose to be responsible for each. • Write one case study in which a test taker's privacy, anonymity, and informed consent rights have been violated. Rewrite the case study to reflect what could be done different so as not to violate the rights. • Review the responsibilities of test publishers, test users, and test takers. Reflect on who has more responsibility? Explain your answer. • Search the test publisher websites referenced in Chapter 1 to learn more about each test publisher's process for selling tests to test users. Identify the similarities and differences in test publisher processes.
Explain the issues associated with testing special populations.	• Define each of the three types of impairments, and describe what kind of testing accommodations you think a person with that impairment might need. • Interview a friend who has been diagnosed as having a learning disability, and ask what accommodations that person needs when testing.

EXERCISES

College students, particularly those majoring in psychology, take psychological tests often. Not only are college students tested on academic knowledge, but they also may be asked to participate in class exercises or research studies that involve psychological tests. The following situations, adapted from a casebook on ethical teaching (Keith-Spiegel, Wittig, Perkins, Balogh, & Whitley, 1994), are examples of situations where students might take one or more psychological tests. After reading each situation, search your chapter and the web to find answers to the following questions for each situation:

1. Are there any ethical issues given the information provided?

2. If yes, what are the ethical issues?

3. If yes, how could the ethical issue(s) be avoided?

   a. **Situation 1: Marketing Research Participation.** A professor teaching an introductory psychology course informs his students at the beginning of the semester that they will be required to either participate in a research study or complete another assignment that takes about the same amount of time and effort. The study is one that he is conducting on intelligence and requires students to take a number of psychological tests, including IQ tests. The professor describes to the students the department's rules on test administration that follow American Psychological Association guidelines regarding confidentiality, informed consent, debriefing, and coercion. He then tells the students that he definitely prefers that they serve as research participants.

   b. **Situation 2: Class Demonstrations of Secure Tests.** In an upper division undergraduate course on psychological testing, the professor demonstrates two tests designated as "secure": the Rorschach inkblot test and the Minnesota Multiphasic Personality Inventory (MMPI). Although the professor does not teach students how to score or interpret the tests, she does show actual Rorschach cards to the students and reads actual items from the MMPI.

   c. **Situation 3: Student Disclosures in Class.** A professor in a social psychology class likes to administer tests that measure attitudes and personality as class demonstrations and exercises. The tests measure constructs such as attitudes toward women and the "Just World" theory, as well as locus of control and self-efficacy. He uses only instruments that are published in professional journals for public access. The professor asks the students to complete one or more tests and then gives them the scoring key for the test(s). After the students have determined their scores, he asks them to form groups and discuss their results. Often he also requires students to include their test results in their journals, which the professor reads at the end of the semester.

ADDITIONAL LEARNING ACTIVITIES

Activity 3-1 Classroom Tests and Security

Publishers often make test banks available to instructors who have adopted their textbooks. A test bank is a ready-made resource where instructors can choose from previously written test items. However, there is wide variation in the quality of the test items in the test banks. Some test items are very well written. Other items are not well written. Some test banks are expansive, consisting of hundreds of questions per textbook chapter. Other test banks are quite limited, containing only a few questions. Some publishers require the instructor to accept a licensing agreement with statements about proper use and handling of the test questions. Other publishers have no restrictions. Furthermore, some tests banks are widely known to be compromised and available to students. An example of this occurred at the University of Central Florida, where the publisher's test bank was shared with all 200 students in a large strategic management class (Postal, 2010). This incident raised questions in regards to academic integrity for the students who viewed the material. However, the incident also raised some concerns over responsible test use by the instructor. In addition, questions were raised about third parties who might illegally obtain and sell such test material.

Within in the context above, answer the following questions concerning the ethical use of test banks for classroom tests.

Questions

1. What are the ethical responsibilities of the test takers? Are they required not to share knowledge of test items with other students?

2. Are professors who use test banks being unethical? Why or why not?

3. Do textbook publishers' have ethical responsibilities when they provide test banks for instructors to use in the classroom?

4. Locate your university's academic integrity or honesty statement. Often these are found in the student handbook. Would obtaining a test bank to use as a study guide be a violation of the policy?

Activity 3-2 Ethical Case Study

Scenario

Because of managed care, a clinical psychologist's income has drastically declined over the last few years. As a result, she is looking to increase her income. After talking to an industrial and organizational (I-O) psychology practitioner at a conference, she does a little investigating. She finds a salary survey for I-O psychology practitioners and decides to move into advising top leadership on making executive hires. She quickly gets her first job.

In her new job, she decides to use the same clinical tests and assessments that she used in her clinical practice (including assessments such as clinical interviews and the Rorschach inkblot test). She makes broad judgments about job candidates' mental health and makes hiring recommendations. The top leadership who hired her believed that she contributed valuable information to the hiring process and hire her to help with executive hires on several more occasions.

Questions

1. What is right and what is wrong with this incident?

2. What modifications could have been made to the testing process to best serve the applicants and the organization that hired the psychologist?

PRACTICE QUESTIONS

The following are some practice questions to assess your understanding of the material presented in this chapter.

Multiple Choice

1. Which one of the following statements about ethical standards is FALSE?

   a. Members of professional organizations can be expelled for violating ethical standards.

   b. Ethical standards are laws federal or local government agencies pass.

   c. Ethical standards are statements by professional regarding appropriate behavior.

   d. No one can be tried or sued in a court of law for violating an ethical standard.

2. Which one of the following statements about misuse of psychological tests is TRUE?

   a. Misuse is not a problem in today's society.

   b. Misuse is sometimes a problem, but rarely with serious consequences.

   c. Misuse is a chronic and disturbing problem that can result in serious harm.

   d. Misuse is only a concern to researchers who are likely to be most affected.

3. Which one of the following is a right of test takers?

   a. Keep a copy of any test they take

   b. Receive a copy of the test manual

   c. Review the test before administration

   d. Have their test score kept private

4. A group of teachers at Alfred E. Newman High School decided that it would be helpful to administer intelligence tests to first-year students to be used for placing students in appropriate classes. They also decided that it would be best not to tell the students what they were being tested for and not to tell them their scores on the intelligence tests. When teachers discussed their plan with the school psychologist, he strongly opposed it because he said it violated students' right to

   a. assemble.

   b. withdraw.

   c. know their IQ.

   d. informed consent.

5. Belinda conducted a research project in which she interviewed workers about their work standards and integrity on the job. She assured her study participants that all personal information they disclosed would be kept private and would not be disclosed without their permission. Which one of the following was she guaranteeing her participants?

   a. Anonymity

   b. Reliability

   c. Confidentiality

   d. Obscurity

6. Phillip is a supervisor at the LMNOP Corporation. He is very concerned about helping his workers and meeting their needs. Therefore, he sent a request to the human resources department asking for the scores on pre-employment tests that his workers had taken. The human resources department replied they could not give him the scores because the test takers had been assured of what?

    a. Their right to informed consent
    b. Their right to confidentiality
    c. Protection from invasion of privacy
    d. Protection from stigma

7. Coding test materials in such a way that test takers can be identified without their knowledge or consent would be a violation of test user's promise of what?

    a. Anonymity
    b. Protection from invasion of privacy
    c. Protection from stigma
    d. Confidentiality

8. For whom are ethical standards written?

    a. Test publishers and test users
    b. Members of a professional organization
    c. Test takers with disabilities
    d. Everyone involved in the testing process

9. Test publishers ensure every psychological test has

    a. adequate marketing.
    b. an unlimited number of test users.
    c. a complete test manual.
    d. a record of satisfied test users.

10. When test questions are published or given to persons other than test takers, there may be a problem with test

    a. test scoring.
    b. test security.
    c. evidence of validity.
    d. evidence of reliability.

11. Which one of the following is listed in your textbook as a responsibility of the test publisher?

    a. Ensuring that only qualified persons purchase it psychological tests
    b. Marketing the psychological tests it publishes
    c. Giving a copy of the test to each potential purchaser
    d. Giving a copy of the test manual to each potential purchaser

12. Intellectual disabilities, learning disabilities, and traumatic brain injuries are examples of what type of impairment?

    a. Cognitive
    b. Motor
    c. Sensory
    d. Personality

13. What do testing guidelines that protect people with physical and mental challenges require?

    a. Modifying the testing process to prevent impairments from affecting test outcomes
    b. Giving all tests individually (instead of in groups) and orally (instead of in written form)
    c. Relieving the challenged test taker from the ethical standard of informed consent
    d. Not administering tests to people with challenges in a specific way

14. A structured interview might need to be substituted for paper-and-pencil tests for individuals with what type of impairment?

    a. Visual
    b. Motor
    c. Hearing
    d. Cognitive

15. Which one of the following is TRUE about learning disabilities?

    a. They are much like physical and mental disabilities.

    b. They do not have visible signs.

    c. They do not require special testing administration.

    d. They do not affect test scores.

16. What is one of the best ways instructors can help students with learning disabilities?

    a. Tape-record their lectures

    b. Encourage learning-disabled students to self-disclose

    c. Request reasonable accommodations for the student

    d. Determine how each student learns best

17. Which one of the following is TRUE?

    a. Most psychological tests are appropriate for test takers from various cultures and backgrounds.

    b. The Rorschach inkblot test is appropriate for Blacks and Hispanics as well as Whites.

    c. Test appropriate for people with learning disabilities are also appropriate for normal Blacks and Hispanics.

    d. The revision of the original MMPI provides a model for revising older tests that were not developed with minorities in mind.

18. Which one of the following organizations published the fourth edition of the *Principles for the Validation and Use of Personnel Selection Procedures* in 2003 to reflect the current research on selecting, developing, and using testing instruments to make employment-related decisions?

    a. American Psychological Association

    b. Association for Psychological Science

    c. Society for Human Resource Management

    d. Society for Industrial-Organizational Psychology

19. Who has the responsibility to request a test accommodation for a physical condition, illness, or language issue that may interfere with test performance?

    a. Test developer

    b. Test administrator

    c. Test user

    d. Test taker

Short Answer

1. Discuss three ethical issues of concern to testing professionals and consumers.

2. What documents about ethics are published by the APA? Why is it important for test users to be familiar with these documents? What would be the consequence of test users not being familiar with these documents?

3. Describe how organizations can and cannot enforce compliance with their ethical standards.

4. Compare and contrast ethical standards and ethical guidelines.

5. What rights do test takers have regarding privacy, anonymity, and informed consent?

6. What actions or activities would you see a test publisher performing if the publisher were fulfilling its ethical responsibilities?

7. Explain what test user qualifications are and why they are important.

8. Explain what the *Standards* (AERA, APA, & NCME, 2014) say about testing special populations.

9. If you thought you had a learning disability, what steps would you take to be eligible for test modifications?

10. Describe the issues associated with test takers from multicultural backgrounds.

ANSWER KEYS

Crossword

ACROSS

2. CONFIDENTIALITY—The assurance that all personal information will be kept private and not be disclosed without explicit permission.
4. MULTICULTURAL BACKGROUNDS—Experiences of those who belong to various minority groups based on race, cultural or ethnic origin, sexual orientation, family unit, primary language, and so on.
7. COGNITIVE—Type of impairment involving mental disorders that include intellectual disabilities, learning disabilities, and traumatic brain injuries.
8. ETHICS—Issues or practices that influence the decision-making process in terms of "doing the right thing."
9. SENSORY—An impairment that hinders the function of the five senses, such as deafness and blindness.
11. ANONYMITY—The practice of administering tests or obtaining information without obtaining the identity of the participant.
13. TEST USER—A person who participates in purchasing, administering, interpreting, or using the results of a psychological test.
14. TEST SECURITY—Steps taken to ensure that the content of a psychological test does not become public knowledge.
16. CERTIFICATION—A professional credential individuals earn by demonstrating that they have met predetermined qualifications (e.g., that they have specific knowledge, skills, and/or experience).

DOWN

1. INFORMED CONSENT—Individuals' right of self-determination; means that individuals are entitled to full explanations of why they are being tested, how the test data will be used, and what the test results mean.
3. MOTOR—An impairment that hinders physical movement, such as paralysis and missing limbs.
5. USER QUALIFICATIONS—The background, training, and/or certifications the test purchaser must meet.
6. TEST TAKER—The person who responds to test questions or whose behavior is measured.
10. LICENSURE—A mandatory credential individuals must obtain to practice within their professions.
12. ETHICAL STANDARDS—Statements by professionals (not laws established by governmental bodies) regarding what they believe are appropriate and inappropriate behaviors when practicing their profession.
15. LEARNING—A hidden disability that hinders learning and does not have visible signs.

Exercises

a. Marketing Research Participation. Although the professor has assured his students that the research study will conform to the APA's guidelines for ethical research, Keith-Spiegel and colleagues (1994) point out that when professors make their preferences known, students may interpret the situation as less than voluntary or even coercive. Insisting that there is no penalty for not complying with the professor's preference might not be enough to relieve the pressure that some students feel to conform to the instructor's preferences.

b. Class Demonstrations of Secure Tests. Making secure test items available to anyone who is not authorized to use them—outside of the standard testing situation described in the test manual—is inappropriate. Assessment demonstrations should be limited to those in the textbook because the professor can assume that items were released by the test publisher (as is the case in this textbook). Using secure materials in graduate courses for training purposes is an exception to this limitation (Keith-Spiegel et al., 1994).

c. Student Disclosures in Class. Requiring students to disclose personal information in class or to their instructor is a violation of their right to privacy. Such disclosures also have the potential for embarrassment and harm. Asking students to complete attitude scales in class without divulging the results is acceptable when the professor is careful to provide adequate debriefing regarding how the results can be interpreted. However, no student should be required to participate against his or her will. Scales for which there is no reliability or validity information should be clearly designated by the instructor as learning activities, not psychological tests.

Multiple Choice

1.

Correct Answer: b

Source: Page 59

Explanation: Ethical standards are established by professional organizations stating what they believe to be acceptable and unacceptable professional behavior. Because they are not established by governmental agencies, no one can be tried or sued in a court of law for violating an ethical standard. However, the professional organization can take action such as expulsion from the organization.

2.

Correct Answer: c

Source: Page 58

Explanation: Unfortunately, test misuse is a continuing and chronic problem. Most times, misuse is unintentional and a result of poor technical knowledge. However, this does not lessen the serious consequences of misuse. For example, incorrect decisions can prevent an individual from being hired into a job or result in an individual receiving unneeded treatment. These poor decisions based on misuse of testing information can have emotional and financial impact harming both the individual and society.

3.

Correct Answer: d

Source: Page 77

Explanation: The right to privacy and confidentiality is a core standard of the *APA Ethical Principles and Code of Conduct*. The standard assures test takers that all personal information they disclose will not be divulged without their explicit permission, except as mandated by law. However, a court order can overrule this the principle.

4.

Correct Answer: d

Source: Page 78

Explanation: All test takers have a right to determine their involvement. This is called informed consent. In addition, they are entitled to an explanation of why they are being tested, how the test date will be used, and what their test scores mean. Because this scenario involves high school students (minors), informed consent from both the parent and the student should have been obtained.

5.

Correct Answer: c

Source: Page 77

Explanation: In this case, the researcher assured the participant confidentiality. Anonymity, a closely related concept, is achieved when personal identifying information is not collected and therefore the responses of any individual cannot be known. In this scenario, that is not the case because she interviewed the workers and collected personal information.

6.

Correct Answer: c

Source: Page 77–78

Explanation: Although the manager has good intentions, test takers have a right to privacy.

This means the human resources department acted in accordance with the APA ethical principles by safeguarding the private information that the employees had disclosed. Human resources could release the information if the employees approved it, but they would need to ensure that the employees were doing so without any undue pressure or fear of reprisals from the manager.

7.

Correct Answer: a

Source: Page 77

Explanation: Anonymity means that no data is collected that can tie an individual to his or her test results. Thus, if the test user promises anonymity, but collects and codes data in ways that allow results to be tied to a specific individual, then this has violated the person's promised anonymity.

8.

Correct Answer: b

Source: Page 59

Explanation: Ethical standards are specifically written for the members of a professional organization. However, these same organizations can state what they believe the rights of test takers are, but rights are not ethical standards that the test takers need to live up to. In addition, test organizations are not required by law to follow the ethical standards, but they do voluntarily attempt to be consistent with them such as ensuring user qualifications.

9.

Correct Answer: c

Source: Page 72

Explanation: Test publishers should ensure that all tests have a comprehensive test manual that includes information about the psychometrics of the test, detailed administration information, proper use of the test, and norms. The textbook does discuss test marketing, but it does so in terms of ensuring that the publisher truthfully markets the test, not with extent of marketing.

10.

Correct Answer: b

Source: Page 72 & 76

Explanation: Test security concerns the safe keeping of test information ensuring the fair and equitable opportunity for all who take the test. If information is released giving access to some test takers but not others, then the test security has been compromised, and some individuals may have an unfair advantage.

11.

Correct Answer: a

Source: Page 71–72

Explanation: Test publishers voluntarily follow testing ethical standards, which state that they should only sell tests to qualified users. The publishers often create guidelines and standards stating the minimum training, education, and experience a user must have to purchase and administer a test.

12.

Correct Answer: a

Source: Page 79

Explanation: Cognitive impairments is a broad term used to describe deficiencies or characteristics that affect intellectual performance. The textbook lists intellectual disabilities, learning disabilities, and traumatic brain injuries as examples of cognitive impairments. By contrast, motor impairments include paralysis and missing limbs, and sensory impairments include deafness and blindness.

13.

Correct Answer: a

Source: Page 79–81

Explanation: According to professional testing standards, test results and outcomes should indicate the intended skills or attributes accurately and not be affected by a disability. In other words, an unrelated disability should not affect the outcome of a test. As a result, test users often alter testing procedures and score interpretation to accurate reflect the skills or attributes being measured.

14.

Correct Answer: a

Source: Page 79–81

Explanation: Depending on the extent of the visual impairment, these individuals will most likely be unable to read the paper-and-pencil test. Therefore, a structured interview, which is conducted orally, is a reasonable accommodation. Other accommodations might include large print and braille test materials.

15.

Correct Answer: b

Source: Page 81

Explanation: Learning disabilities, like physical and mental disabilities, may require special testing accommodations. Unlike other disabilities, however, they do not have visible signs. A learning disability is a disability that affects any aspect of learning. This can include language abilities, mathematical abilities, and focus and attention. Some examples include dyslexia, dyscalculia, and dysgraphia.

16.

Correct Answer: b

Source: Page 84

Explanation: Instructors can indeed make adjustments that allow the students to learn in the manner appropriate for their disability and test more effectively. However, before instructors can do this, the student must self-declare to school administrators who will ensure that the diagnosis was made by an appropriately qualified professional.

17.

Correct Answer: d

Source: Page 85

Explanation: The MMPI was originally developed in the 1930s using a sample of White residents of Minnesota, which was mostly rural at the time. This sample with little diversity lead psychologists to question if the test provided accurate information for individuals with a different background. As a result, the test was revised using a more diverse sample.

18.

Correct Answer: d

Source: Page 62

Explanation: In 2003, the Society for Industrial and Organizational Psychology (SIOP) published the fourth edition of the *Principles for the Validation and Use of Personnel Selection Procedures* to reflect current research and to be consistent with the *Standards for Educational and Psychological Testing*. The

Principles reflect the official statement from SIOP regarding professionally accepted practices for selecting, developing, and using testing instruments to make employment-related decisions. The *Principles* include four main sections:

- Overview of the Validation Process
- Sources of Validity Evidence
- Generalizing Validity Evidence
- Operational Considerations in Personnel Selection

19.

Correct Answer: d

Source: Page 76

Explanation: The 2014 *Standards* has an extensive discussion concerning the responsibilities of test takers. One of the explicitly stated responsibilities of test takers is to request an accommodation if he or she believes there is a physical condition, illness, or language issue that might affect his or her test performance.

Short Answer

1. Ethical issues and concerns abound in testing, and they are practically limitless in number. For example, many scenarios could be conceived that relate to the four issues of primary concern: the right to privacy, the right to informed consent, the right to know and understand test results, and the right to protection from stigma. The right to privacy means that test information will not be released to others unless expressly authorized by the test taker. The right to informed consent means that individuals have the right of self-determination of participation (i.e., the right to freely choose whether to continue with testing). The right to know and understand the results means that test takers should be provided a nontechnical explanation of their scores. Finally the right to protection from stigma means that they should not be labeled with derogatory terms. Instead, testing should facilitate growth and development.

2. The APA has published several documents concerning general ethics for psychologists and others specifically for testing. For example, the APA has published *Ethical Principles of Psychologists and Code of Conduct*, which includes five general principles, and specific ethical standards to guide psychologists. They have also published the *Standards for Educational and Psychological Testing* jointly with AERA and NCME, *Test User Qualifications: A Data-Based Approach to Promoting Good Test Use*, and *Report of the Task Force on Test User Qualifications*. While these documents are not laws, it is important to be familiar with (and follow) them because

the APA can sanction or expel member psychologists who do not adhere to the published standards and guidelines.

3. Ethics and law are different things. Law is created and enforced by governments to control or mediate the behavior of individuals, while ethical standards concern what people believe is right and wrong. The APA's ethical standards are what the professional organizational believes is the appropriate behavior of a psychologist. No one can be sued or tried in a court of law for violating the APA's ethical standards. However, the APA can sanction or even expel member psychologists who do not adhere to their ethical standards.

4. Ethical standards and ethical guidelines both state expected appropriate behaviors and inappropriate behaviors. Where they differ is that standards developed by an organization such as the APA explicitly apply only to their members. As a result, these same organizations may publish broader reaching guidance or guidelines to others outside their membership to help shape and influence their behaviors.

5. The APA's *Ethical Principles of Psychologists and Code of Conduct* addresses each of these issues. Test takers have privacy rights, meaning that their personal and test information will not be disclosed unless they expressly approve the disclosure (or as required by law). Taking steps to ensure anonymity can help to guarantee the test taker's right to privacy. To ensure anonymity, no information is collected that could be used to identify the test taker; therefore, he or she cannot be identified. Finally, informed consent means that test takers have the right to know why they are being tested, how the data are being used, and what their test scores mean. The information should be communicated in plain nontechnical language. Often, the test taker will provide written consent indicating that he or she has been informed about and understands the information shared.

6. Test publishers should follow the ethical guidelines. Test publishers should ensure they have defined minimum test user qualifications for each test they publish, stating the required training, education, and experience that a test user must have to purchase the test. Test publishers should also ensure that all of their marketing practices are accurate and truthful. They should ensure the security of the test. Finally, test publishers should also make available to test users a comprehensive test manual that includes the psychometric properties of the test, detailed administration instructions and scoring information, proper norms, and proper scoring interpretation practices.

7. Test publishers establish test user qualifications that state the minimum training, education, and experience that is needed to purchase tests. Test user qualifications are important because misuse of tests is a chronic and disturbing problem that harms individuals and society as a whole. Most test misuse is unintentional and results from a lack of knowledge. One way to combat the problem of test misuse is by ensuring test purchasers meet minimum test users qualifications. This helps to ensure that only knowledgeable individuals use the tests, decreasing the likelihood of misuse.

8. The *Standards* state that test users should make sure test outcomes accurately represent the intended skills or attributes. Those outcomes should not be inadvertently altered because of an individual's disability. Because of this standard, test users often use information in addition to test scores for diagnostic and intervention decisions. Test users may also modify a test's administration or score interpretation to ensure that the interpretation and use is accurate and consistent with the test's purpose.

9. Before you could be considered for a test modification, you would need to self-disclose to the appropriate individuals using official diagnoses information. Once a learning disability has been established and confirmed, there are many possible modifications, and their use depends on the specific diagnosis. Some common modifications include more testing time, allowing verbal rather than written responses, allowing breaks, and arranging for individual testing rooms with fewer distractions.

10. As diversity of the United States has increased, so has attention to cultural issues and their effect on testing. One obvious concern is language, as different demographic groups have different levels of English proficiency. There has also been an increase in the numbers of individuals for whom English is their second language. Another important issue concerns the sample of people used to develop the test. For example, the Exner scoring system for Rorschach inkblot test appears to be inappropriate for several groups because of large cultural differences within the norming group. The MMPI is another example. This test was developed using a rural White population. The test has been updated using a diverse sample more representative of the population of the United States.

References

American Educational Research Association, American Psychological Association, & National Council on Measurement in Education. (2014). *Standards for educational and psychological testing*. Washington, DC: American Educational Research Association.

Keith-Spiegel, P., Witting, A. R., Perkins, D. V., Balogh, D. W., & Whitley, B. E., Jr. (1994). *The ethics of teaching: A casebook*. Muncie, IN: Ball State University Press.

Postal, L. (2010, November 21). Test banks are at the center of UCF's cheating scandal. *Orlando Sentinel*. Retrieved from http://articles.orlandosentinel.com/2010-11-21/news/os-ucf-cheating-online-20101121_1_studies-cheating-large-lecture-classes-test-banks

4

How Does Computerized Testing Work?

Chapter Overview

In Chapter 4, we look at issues and concepts that have transformed psychological testing. First, we discuss computer-based testing—how computers are used in the psychological testing process. Second, we look at computerized adaptive testing, which can decrease the number of test questions required to provide accurate measurements. Third, we consider the advantages and disadvantages of psychological testing using the Internet. Finally, we discuss the implications of web-based testing for the testing and survey industry in the future.

Learning Objectives

After completing your study of this chapter, you should be able to do the following:

- Describe how computers have enhanced the development, administration, and scoring of psychological tests.
- Discuss the advantages and disadvantages of computerized testing.
- Explain the differences between adaptive testing and traditional testing.
- Discuss the advantages and disadvantages of administering tests using the web.
- Discuss the implications of web-based technology for testing in the future.

Chapter Outline

Computerized Testing
  Test Development
  Test Administration

Key Concepts

adaptive testing:	Using tests developed from a large test bank in which the test questions are chosen to match the skill and ability level of the test taker.
computerized adaptive rating scales (CARS):	Testing in which the computer software, as in computerized adaptive testing, selects behavioral statements for rating based on the rater's previous responses.
computerized adaptive testing (CAT):	Testing in which the computer software chooses and presents the test taker with harder or easier questions as the test progresses, depending on how well the test taker answered previous questions.
e-learning:	Any learning that occurs on a computer, providing individuals the opportunity to learn at any location and at any time.
employee assistance programs (EAP):	Programs provided as an employee benefit to help employees with problems not related to the workplace.
enterprise services:	Online standardized tests offered by companies for large numbers of test takers at multiple sites.
hosted services:	Server space, web design, and maintenance provided by companies for the purpose of instruction and assessment.
nonhosted services:	Instructional and assessment services that run on local area networks or private websites.
proctor:	A person who supervises a testing location; similar to a test administrator.
survey research firms:	Companies that specialize in the construction and administration of surveys and analysis of survey data for purposes such as marketing, political opinion assessment, and employee organizational satisfaction.
test bank:	A large number of multiple-choice, true/false, and short-answer questions that assess knowledge of a subject or group of subjects.
virtual time:	The time that a computer records elapsing during a test, which might not be equal to the actual time that passes during test administration.

KEY CONCEPTS CROSSWORD

ACROSS

1. A type of firm that specializes in constructing and administering surveys and analyzing survey data for purposes such as marketing, political opinion assessment, and employee organizational satisfaction.

7. A person who supervises a testing location; similar to a test administrator.

9. The time that a computer records elapsing during a test, which might not be equal to the actual time that passes during test administration.

10. Computerized adaptive _____ occurs when computer software chooses and presents the test taker with harder or easier questions as the test progresses, depending on how well the test taker answered previous questions.

11. Any learning that occurs on a computer, providing individuals the opportunity to learn at any location and at any time.

12. _____ programs provided as an employee benefit to help employees with problems not related to the workplace.

DOWN

2. Online standardized tests offered by companies for large numbers of test takers at multiple sites.

3. A large number of multiple-choice, true/false, and short-answer questions that assess knowledge of a subject or group of subjects.

4. Using tests developed from a large test bank in which the test questions are chosen to match the skill and ability level of the test taker.

5. Instructional and assessment services that run on local area networks or private websites.

6. Server space, web design, and maintenance provided by companies for the purpose of instruction and assessment.

8. Computerized adaptive _____ is when computer software selects behavioral statements for rating based on the rater's previous responses.

LEARNING ACTIVITIES BY LEARNING OBJECTIVE

The following are some study tips and learning activities you can engage in to support the learning objectives for this chapter.

Learning Objectives	Study Tips and Learning Activities
After completing your study of this chapter, you should be able to do the following:	The following study tips and learning activities will help you meet these learning objectives:
Describe how computers have enhanced the development, administration, and scoring of psychological tests.	• Contact your college's career services office. Inquire about what assessments or tests they have available that students can take on a computer. Ask questions to understand how computerized tests (vs. paper-and-pencil tests) have helped career services staff members and benefited students. Think about the benefits in terms of development, administration, scoring, and interpretation.
Discuss the advantages and disadvantages of computerized testing.	• Choose a partner. Together, think about a paper-and-pencil test you have both taken on a computer. Discuss and list the benefits of the computerized testing, using your own experience and what you learned in the chapter as a guide.
Explain the differences between adaptive testing and traditional testing.	• Make a list of various test characteristics, including method of administration, length of time to complete the test, selection of questions, and method of scoring. Explain each characteristic for traditional testing and adaptive testing.
Discuss the advantages and disadvantages of administering tests using the web.	• Go to the web, and search for a test you can take online. As you take the test, make notes about what you like and dislike about web-based testing.
Discuss the implications of web-based technology for testing in the future.	• Make a list of technologies that are currently possible, but impractical. How does the technology of computerized tests, CAT, and web-based assessment compare with the other technologies on your list?

EXERCISES

1. As described in the textbook, computer adaptive testing (CAT) software selects test questions based on the test takers previous answers. In this exercise, you will select test questions in a manner similar to CAT software. Suppose a test developer has assigned each question a difficulty level from 1 to 10, with Level 1 being the easiest and Level 10 being the most difficult level. For each situation described below, circle the level that would most likely be administered next.

    a. A test taker correctly answers a Level 5 question.

    Level 4   Level 6

    b. A test taker incorrectly answers a Level 8 question.

    Level 7   Level 9

    c. A test taker correctly answers a Level 1 question, then a Level 2, and then incorrectly answers a Level 3 question.

    Level 2   Level 4

    d. A test taker correctly answers a Level 6 question, then incorrectly answers a Level 7 question, then correctly answers a Level 6 question, and incorrectly answers a Level 7 question.

    Level 6   Stop, best estimate of the test taker's score is 6

2. For each of the following statements concerning CAT indicate if the statement is *True* or *False*.

a. CAT begins by asking very difficult questions.	True	False
b. CAT allows a fuller profile of the test taker's ability in less time than traditional paper-and-pencil tests.	True	False
c. CAT for standardized tests was feasible and prevalent before the widespread use of modern computers.	True	False
d. All test takers receive the same number of questions.	True	False
e. CAT requires a large bank of test questions.	True	False
f. CAT uses a statistical technique called Item Response Theory.	True	False
g. A good test-taking strategy to use when taking a CAT is to incorrectly answer the first few questions so easier test questions will be administered.	True	False
h. Test takers can skip questions on a CAT.	True	False

ADDITIONAL LEARNING ACTIVITIES

Activity 4-1 Neuropsychological Testing on Computers and Mobile Devices

Computers and the Internet have offered and continue to offer tremendous opportunities for the advancement and availability of psychological tests. One area that has progressed greatly is neuropsychological testing because important cognitive measures, such as reaction time and object tracking, can only be precisely measured using computers. However, with great opportunities also come great challenges and risks. Consider the example of the Automated Neuropsychological Assessment Metrics, or ANAM. The ANAM is a computer-based set of cognitive assessments consisting of 22 different tests measuring constructs like attention, concentration, reaction time, memory, processing speed, and decision making. Some specific tests include pursuit tracking, the Stroop test, finger tapping, and spatial processing. Most of these types of tests are simply not possible to administer using paper and pencil. Furthermore, the U.S. Department of Defense, in response to a congressional mandate requiring them to better address traumatic brain injury of military personnel in war zones, began testing all personnel deployed to Iraq or Afghanistan before deployment to establish a baseline. Later, on return, the personnel were to be tested again. The Department of Defense selected the ANAM for this required testing. Although the ANAM has been in development since the 1980s and has been used in hundreds research studies (Reeves, Winter, Bleiberg, & Kane, 2007), it is not without its problems. Critics argue that there are newer, cheaper tests with better psychometric properties, and they also argue that the ANAM has been misused and the project mismanaged (Zwerdling, Sapien, & Miller, 2011).

One suggested alternative assessment for concussions and traumatic brain injury is the ImPACT, which is used in the National Hockey League and the National Football League. This test has three main components: a demographic component, current concussion symptoms and conditions component, and a neurocognitive component. Specific tests include

- **word discrimination**, which evaluates verbal recognition;
- **design memory**, which evaluates attention;
- **X's and O's**, which evaluates working memory and visual process speed;
- **symbol matching**, which evaluates visual processing speed, learning, and memory;
- **color matching**, which evaluates reaction time and impulse control; and
- **three-letter memory**, which evaluates memory and visual-motor response speed (ImPACT, 2014).

One interesting application of the ImPACT is that it is available on mobile devices such as smartphones and can easily be used on the playing field or sidelines immediately after a potential injury. While the company markets the product in part to parents of student athletes, trained individuals, such as school nurses and certified athletic trainers, are to administer the assessment.

Questions

1. What may be some of the advantages, disadvantages, and difficulties of performing neuro-psychological tests using mobile devices?

2. In addition to concussion testing, what are some other types of psychological tests that may be appropriate to administer via a mobile device?

3. The ImPACT is specifically marketed to parents. Locate the ImPACT website and evaluate the site in terms of how ethically the publisher markets the product.

Activity 4-2 Teaching Machines

Background

Computer assessment and testing has a wide array of applications as described in the textbook. One area of application discussed is that of e-learning, which has long and deep roots. However, using the "e" terminology is relatively recent. Previously, computer assessment was referred to as *programmed instruction* and *teaching machines*. Although there are various definitions of a teaching machine, one well-known definition proposed by Benjamin (1988) is that a teaching machine is an automatic or self-controlling device that (a) presents a unit of information, (b) provides some means for the learner to respond, and (c) provides feedback about the correctness of the learner's responses.

While many attribute the first teaching machine to B. F. Skinner in the 1950s, the machines have a much longer history. The U.S. Patent Office in 1866 issued a patent to Halcyon Skinner (no relation to B. F.) for a teaching machine that "taught" spelling (Benjamin, 1988). However, Halcyon's machine did not provide feedback, so it seems to be more of a testing machine rather than a teaching machine. Later, in 1928, psychologist Sidney Pressey received a patent for a "Machine for Intelligence Tests." As described by Benjamin (1988), this machine presented material printed on a scroll that was loaded onto a drum. The learner would use a crank to expose the written material through a small window. The material consisted of multiple-choice questions with four answer options. The machine had four keys that corresponded to the answers and the learner would press the appropriate key to make a response. In addition, there were two modes. The first was called *test*. In this mode, the machine would record the response and advance to the next question. In the *teaching* mode, the machine would not advance until the correct answer option was selected. Finally, the machine had a dispenser that could be used to provide a piece of candy after a predetermined number of questions were answered correctly.

Pressey continued his work on teaching machines into the 1950s and 1960s when Skinner was actively involved with teaching machines. B. F. Skinner began work on teaching machines in 1953 after observing his daughter's fourth-grade class. He noted that all students had to proceed at the same pace and that students had to wait an extended time period for feedback from the teacher (Skinner, 1983). Skinner and Pressey even met and discussed the use of teaching machines. During this time, Pressey had cautioned that Skinner's approach could do away with textbooks (Pressey, 1962). Interestingly similar concerns have recently been expressed about interactive ebooks (as a teaching machine).

Skinner's work resulted not just in a teaching tool but an entirely new educational technology that promoted a new approach to teaching (Benjamin, 1988), and there was boom in the development and production of machines. In fact, there were even door-to-door "salesmen" who sold teaching machines. There was an extensive interest in the concept, and in 1962 even the U.S. Central Intelligence Agency (CIA) explored the possible applications for programmed instructions in the covert operations to include the following:

- Training in observation and description
- Lip reading
- Shorthand
- Recording spoken language without knowing the language
- Learning a foreign language
- Reading and interpreting gauges
- Learning of an agent's cover story
- Orienting material such as geography, customs and monetary practices of a country, and sounds of engines or airplanes. (Fulcher, 1962)

However, teaching machines may have been too much of a good thing, and there was soon pushback and criticism. Critics claimed that it was a dehumanizing approach and that kids were being taught by robots and being treated like pigeons (as Skinner was well-known for his experimental work with pigeons) (Benjamin, 1988). Overall, interest in teaching machines has fluctuated over the years. There was extreme interest in the early 1960s, but by the late 1960s, the interest had died out. Then, in the 1980s, when personal computers were introduced into classrooms, interest began to rise only to fade once again. Due to the widespread availability of high-speed Internet access and mobile computing, the basic ideas of individualized instruction and testing has once again become popular. One could refer to these approaches teaching machines, programmed learning, e-learning, interactive textbooks, or self-paced instruction.

Questions

1. Skinner believed that the world was not ready for teaching machines, and that was partially the reason Pressey's first machine was not widely accepted by the public (Benjamin, 1988). Is the world now ready for computerized teaching machines? Why or why not?

2. An article in the CIA journal *Studies in Intelligence* (Fulcher, 1962) discussed the need to have programmed instruction and teaching machines at a specialized location, but envisioned a time when it could be accomplished "at the agent's home." With the advent of new mobile computing technologies, what are the potential benefits and difficulties of e-learning and testing on mobile devices such as smartphones?

3. Find an example of computerized programmed instruction and describe it.

4. How would you feel about not having an instructor for this class and instead taking it as preprogrammed e-learning computerized instruction?

PRACTICE QUESTIONS

The following are some practice questions to assess your understanding of the material presented in this chapter.

Multiple Choice

1. Ursula took a test on a computer. She was told the computer would choose questions from a large test bank matched to her skill level. What kind of test did she take?

   a. Adaptive test

   b. Achievement test

   c. Skills test

   d. Performance test

2. Which one of the following is TRUE about computerized adaptive tests?

   a. They are not as psychometrically sound as paper-and-pencil tests.

   b. They provide a fuller profile in less amount of time than traditional tests.

   c. They provide the same questions in the same order for each test taker.

   d. They may present too many questions that are either too difficult or too easy.

3. Which one of the following is TRUE about computerized tests?

   a. The test taker must understand computer programming to take them.

   b. They are time-consuming for the test taker.

   c. They make standardized administration easier.

   d. They can increase the chance of scoring errors.

4. Which one of the following is TRUE about computerized tests?

   a. Men have an advantage over women because they are more experienced with computers.

   b. Computer-based test administration often compromises the psychometric quality of tests.

   c. Test takers may not be able to use similar strategies when responding to paper-and-pencil tests.

   d. Computer-based tests are not as fair as traditional tests.

5. What is a database containing a large number of multiple-choice, true/false, and short-answer questions on topics in a textbook called?

   a. An adaptive test

   b. A test bank

   c. A computerized test

   d. A classroom test

6. What did research studies comparing test scores on two types of test administration—computerized and paper-and-pencil—reveal?

   a. The resulting test scores were similar.

   b. The administration times were the same.

   c. Students preferred paper-and-pencil tests.

   d. Instructors preferred paper-and-pencil tests.

7. Which one of the following tests was NOT practical until computerized testing became possible?

   a. Standardized tests

   b. Pre-employment tests

   c. Surveys

   d. Adaptive tests

8. Whether administering or scoring tests, computers can save test users from

    a. administering an inappropriate test.

    b. using tests inappropriately.

    c. the cost of shipping answer sheets.

    d. the problems of using a database.

9. Which one of the following is a possible issue unique to web-based testing?

    a. Perpetual cheating

    b. Timing of the test questions

    c. Discrimination against some groups

    d. Difficulty selecting test questions

10. Adaptive testing would be impractical without

    a. standardized tests.

    b. paper-and-pencil administration.

    c. psychometric theory.

    d. powerful computers.

11. Traditionally, why was standardized testing a lengthy process?

    a. The need to rely heavily on the postal service

    b. The need for more scorer training than for non standardized tests

    c. The need for different tests at each testing location

    d. More concern with cheating than other types of tests

12. What does e-learning refer to?

    a. Any learning that occurs using a computer

    b. Web-based assessment of students

    c. One source of software for web-based assessment

    d. Programs that teach educators how to use web-based assessment

13. According to your textbook, what was the "old-fashioned" method of assessment?

    a. Replicating paper-and-pencil tests on the computer

    b. Administering exams quarterly or at the end of a semester

    c. Giving schools scores or grades and compare them

    d. Asking children to respond to essay questions

14. The tests we take as students reflect what?

    a. How educated our parents are

    b. How much effort we put into studying

    c. The environment of our classrooms

    d. The performance of our teachers, schools, and colleges

15. What do employee-assistance programs provide?

    a. Services to their clients using a secure website

    b. A website that employees can use for assessment

    c. Health and life insurance for employees

    d. Assistance to employees who need training in job skills

16. What is one solution to the problem of administering web-based assessment without a proctor?

    a. Require test takers to sign an informed consent form

    b. Adjust test taker scores to account for possible cheating

    c. Ask test takers to provide photocopies of drivers' licenses

    d. Require a second round of testing in a proctored environment

Short Answer

1. Describe how computers have enhanced the development, administration, and scoring of psychological tests.

2. How do the advantages of computerized testing compare to the disadvantages of computerized testing?

3. Explain the difference between adaptive testing and traditional testing.

4. How might test users and test takers benefit from a test administered online? What might be some disadvantages?

5. Explain how the technology of web-based testing is likely to influence the fields of education, mental health, and industry.

ANSWER KEYS

Crossword

ACROSS

1. SURVEY RESEARCH—A type of firm that specializes in constructing and administering surveys and analyzing survey data for purposes such as marketing, political opinion assessment, and employee organizational satisfaction.
7. PROCTOR—A person who supervises a testing location; similar to a test administrator.
9. VIRTUAL TIME—The time that a computer records elapsing during a test, which might not be equal to the actual time that passes during test administration.
10. TESTING—Computerized adaptive _____ occurs when computer software chooses and presents the test taker with harder or easier questions as the test progresses, depending on how well the test taker answered previous questions.
11. E-LEARNING—Any learning that occurs on a computer, providing individuals the opportunity to learn at any location and at any time.
12. EMPLOYEE ASSISTANCE—_____ programs provided as an employee benefit to help employees with problems not related to the workplace.

DOWN

2. ENTERPRISE SERVICES—Online standardized tests offered by companies for large numbers of test takers at multiple sites.
3. TEST BANK—A large number of multiple-choice, true/false, and short-answer questions that assess knowledge of a subject or group of subjects.
4. ADAPTIVE TESTING—Using tests developed from a large test bank in which the test questions are chosen to match the skill and ability level of the test taker.
5. NONHOSTED SERVICES—Instructional and assessment services that run on local area networks or private websites.
6. HOSTED SERVICES—Server space, web design, and maintenance provided by companies for the purpose of instruction and assessment.
8. RATING SCALES—Computerized adaptive _____ is when computer software selects behavioral statements for rating based on the rater's previous responses.

Exercises

1a. Level 6
1b. Level 7
1c. Level 2

1d. Stop, best estimate of the test taker's score is 6

2a. False
2b. True
2c. False

2d. False

2e. True

2f. True

2g. False

2h. False

Multiple Choice

1.

Correct Answer: a

Source: Page 94

Explanation: Adaptive tests select test questions from a large test bank based on the test taker's performance on previous items. For example, if a test taker is presented a moderately difficult item and gets it correct, the adaptive software will select a slightly harder question. If the test taker gets that question correct, then a slightly harder question will be administered, and so on. Likewise, if the test taker gets a question wrong, then a slightly easier question will then be administered. This process continues until the software determines the test taker's skill level with a predetermined level of precision.

2.

Correct Answer: b

Source: Page 94

Explanation: Research shows that adaptive tests result in a fuller profile in less time than traditional testing procedures. This is because the software selects questions based on the test taker's previous correct answers and avoids items that are either too easy or too hard. This saves time and results in more accurate measurements.

3.

Correct Answer: c

Sources: Page 91

Explanation: Because the computer is programmed and executes the exact same procedures

for each test taker, computers increase standardization in the administration process. When human test administrators are used, they can make a variety of mistakes, such as not allowing the proper time for testing or not properly communicating the instructions to the test takers. Different administrators may make different mistakes in administration, which will increase the amount of error in the test scores.

4.

Correct Answer: c

Source: Page 93

Explanation: Because of the manner that computerized tests are administered, test-taking strategies for paper-and-pencil tests often do not work. For example, questions cannot be skipped, as a response is required before moving to the next question. Also, test takers often cannot go back to review answers or change answers.

5.

Correct Answer: b

Source: Page 90

Explanation: A test bank is a large group of test items that assess a particular knowledge or skill. The items can be can be categorized by topic, difficulty, type, and so on. During the testing process items can be randomly selected.

6.

Correct Answer: a

Source: Page 100

Explanation: Most of the research to date has shown that test administration mode has little effect on test scores. Thus, computerized and paper-and-pencils scores can be easily compared and considered equivalent.

7.

Correct Answer: d

Source: Page 94

Explanation: While the concept of adaptive testing dates back to the beginning of the 20th century, it was not feasible until computing power sufficiently increased. Adaptive testing requires powerful software, sophisticated algorithms, and a large bank of test items to work effectively.

8.

Correct Answer: c

Source: Page 91

Explanation: Computerized tests are simply more efficient than traditional paper-and-pencil tests. They save time and money for both test taker and test user. For example, test users and test takers often receive the results immediately after the test is completed. The reason for this immediate feedback is the fact that answers sheets no longer need to be mailed, saving time and money.

9.

Correct Answer: b

Source: Page 99

Explanation: One minor difficulty with web-based testing is that transitions between questions or screens can take a variable amount of time to load on the test taker's computer. The exact amount depends on a many factors. Sometimes, this time can be tracked, and the page loading time can be added to the test so all test takers have the same amount of time with the questions displayed.

10.

Correct Answer: d

Source: Page 94

Explanation: Computer adaptive testing (CAT) is impractical (or impossible) without powerful computers. This is because CAT requires the adaptive selection of test items from a large test bank. The determination of what question to administer is based on the test takers answers to previous questions and known characteristics of items in the test bank. CAT uses an algorithm to select the optimal question to

determine the test taker's standing on the construct the test is measuring.

11.

Correct Answer: a

Source: Page 90

Explanation: With traditional standardized testing, booklets and other administration materials have to be mailed to the testing locations. After the test administration, all testing materials have to be mailed back to a central location to be scored. Finally, test results have to be mailed out. Computerized and web-based testing has made this extensive use of the postal service obsolete and drastically decreased the total time of administration, scoring, and feedback.

12.

Correct Answer: a

Source: Page 101

Explanation: E-learning often goes by other names such as *online learning*, *distance education*, and *web-based training*. The defining feature of e-learning is that it occurs on a computer and provides the learner the opportunity to learn at any location at any time. Other advantages include increased ease and opportunities for assessment and feedback, faster feedback, and greater possibility for individualized instruction.

13.

Correct Answer: b

Source: Page 101

Explanation: Because testing (e.g., administration, scoring, and feedback) took so long under the traditional testing paradigm, assessments tended to be given much less frequently than is now possible with e-learning and computer-based testing. As a result, the old method of assessment only involved occasional quizzes and then larger tests at the midterm and the end of the semester.

14.

Correct Answer: d

Source: Page 101–102

Explanation: Although testing is generally examined at the individual outcome level, the results for individuals sometimes can be aggregated, providing a great deal of information concerning the performance of specific groups. For example, test results of students can be grouped based on teacher, school, school district, college, state, and so on. These results can then be used to evaluate the performance of the group.

15.

Correct Answer: a

Source: Page 102

Explanation: Employee assistance programs are provided by employers to offer help to their employees with problems that may not be related to the workplaces, such as substance abuse or stress. Because of encryption software and secure connections, the providers can ensure a degree of confidentiality.

16.

Correct Answer: d

Source: Page 97

Explanation: The textbook makes the recommendation of requiring a second round of testing for verification purposes in a proctored environment for dealing with the issues of identification and cheating on web-based assessments. Unfortunately, a second round of testing may not be practical for organizations. Interestingly, there has been some research suggesting that the differences in test taker performance in a proctored versus unproctored setting may not be as great as one would imagine. However, the question is still an open one.

Short Answer

1. Computerized and web-based testing have transformed the testing industry. Test development has been changed by computers by enabling convenient storage of large test banks of test items. In addition, testing software allows easier creation of tests from these test banks. Test administration has been affected, which has created the opportunity to use many more types of questions and made innovations such as adaptive testing possible. Scoring and score reporting has changed as well. No longer do scoring sheets need to be mailed to a central location, scored, and then results mailed back to the test taker. With computerized testing, test takers can often sign up, pay, take the test, and receive feedback in a single day. Overall, computers have increased the speed of test development, registration, payment, administration, scoring, and feedback, which has transformed the testing industry.

2. The textbook lists three main disadvantages of computerized testing: computer anxiety, interpretation of test scores, and testing strategies. However, computer anxiety is the main disadvantage unique to computer testing. Some people still have little experience with computers and feel anxiety, but there are protocols and software to lessen the effect of anxiety. The advantages far outweigh the disadvantages. Computerized tests are efficient, are easy to schedule, can be administered individually in comfortable settings, increase standardization, allow for novel question types such as 3-D graphics and sound, decrease scoring errors, and allow many types of test accommodations to be easily made.

3. In traditional testing, the same questions are asked to all test takers. In contrast, computer adaptive testing the tests start with a set of moderately difficult test questions. Then, based on test taker performance, a computer program selects test questions that are easier or harder. This continues until the software has established the test taker's standing on the attribute the test is designed to measure within a predetermined level of accuracy. Because there is targeted selection of test questions based on the test takers' ability, fewer questions are needed and testing time is reduced.

4. Web-based tests have the same basic advantages as computerized testing in general. They are efficient, are easy to schedule, can be administered individually in comfortable settings, increase standardization, allow for novel and rich question types that can include 3-D graphics and sound, decrease scoring errors, and allow many test accommodations to be easily made. In addition, they have the added benefit of being able to be administered nearly anywhere in the world. They also have the same disadvantages and a few new ones. For example, when delivering tests on the web, loading pages does take time. Depending on the circumstances, this time can add up, significantly affecting the total testing time. It is also more difficult to monitor test takers on the web. In the past, there were concerns that paper-and-pencil tests and web-based tests may not be equivalent; however, research has shown that this is not the case.

5. Web-based testing technology makes testing more convenient and assessable in the fields of education, mental health, and industry. For example, in education there are many new online testing tools that can be incorporated into classroom instruction. In mental health fields, web testing has allowed clinicians quick access to specialized tools and allows clinicians to quickly and privately communicate with clients. In industry, web-based certification tests provide increased opportunities for employers to ensure that their employees have the required skills and abilities to properly and safely perform a job. With the increased use of tests, it will be even more important that test users have the knowledge to develop, administer, and interpret test scores. For example, the Society of Human Resource Management and the HR Certification Institute develop and administer certification tests to a large number of individuals. These organizations have a great deal of expertise in all areas of testing. Not all organizations are as capable, however.

References

Benjamin, L. T. (1988). A history of teaching machines. *American Psychologist, 43*, 703–712. Retrieved from http://aubreydaniels.com/institute/sites/aubreydaniels.com.institute/files/History%20of%20teaching%20machines.pdf

Fulcher, J. (1962, Winter). Comes the teaching machine. *Studies in Intelligence, 6*(1), A5–A20. Retrieved from https://www.cia.gov/library/center-for-the-study-of-intelligence/kent-csi/vol6no1/html/v06i1a08p_0001.htm

ImPACT (2014). *The ImPACT test*. Retrieved from https://www.impacttest.com/products/?The-ImPACT-Test-2

Reeves, D. L., Winter, K. P., Bleiberg, J., & Kane, R. L. (2007). ANAM® Genogram: Historical perspectives, description, and current endeavors. *Archives of Clinical Neuropsychology*, 22, 15–37. doi:10.1016/j.acn.2006.10.013

Pressey, S. L. (1962). Basic unresolved teaching-machine problems. *Theory into Practice, 1*, 30–37. Retrieved from http://www.tandfonline.com/loi/htip20

Skinner, B. F. (1983). *A matter of consequences*. New York: Knopf.

Zwerdling, D., Sapien, J., & Miller, T. C. (2011). Military's brain-testing program a debacle. *NPR*. Retrieved from http://www.npr.org/2011/11/28/142662840/militarys-brain-testing-program-a-debacle

5

How Do Test Users Interpret Test Scores?

Chapter Overview

In Chapter 5, we focus on increasing your understanding of the procedures used to interpret test scores. Because these procedures depend on the type of data that a test produces, we begin with a discussion of the four levels of measurement of psychological test data. We then discuss frequency distributions, measures of central tendency, measures of variability, and measures of relationship. After discussing how to convert raw scores into more meaningful units (e.g., z scores, T scores), we discuss the role of norms in interpreting test scores.

Learning Objectives

After completing your study of this chapter, you should be able to do the following:

- Describe and identify the different levels of measurement.
- Summarize test scores using class intervals and frequency distributions.
- Describe the characteristics of the normal curve as well as skewed, peaked, and bimodal distributions.
- Describe the purpose and calculate measures of central tendency, measures of variability, and measures of relationship.
- Convert raw test scores into more meaningful units.
- Describe norm-based interpretation and the different types of norms.

Chapter Outline

Levels of Measurement
   Nominal Scales
   Ordinal Scales
   Interval Scales
   Ratio Scales
Procedures for Interpreting Test Scores
   Frequency Distributions
   The Normal Curve
   Descriptive Statistics
Standard Scores
   Linear Transformations
   Area Transformations
The Role of Norms
   Types of Norms
Chapter Summary

Key Concepts

age norms:	Norms that allow test users to compare an individual's test score with scores of people in the same age group.
area transformations:	A method for changing scores for interpretation purposes that changes the unit of measurement and the unit of reference, such as percentile ranks.
categorical data:	Data grouped according to a common property.
class intervals:	A way of grouping adjacent scores to display them in a table or graph.
correlation coefficient:	A statistic that provides an index of the strength and relationship between two sets of scores; a statistic that describes the relationship between two distributions of scores.
descriptive statistics:	Numbers calculated from a distribution that describe or summarize the properties of the distribution of test scores, such as the mean, median, mode, and standard deviation.
frequency distribution:	An orderly arrangement of a group of numbers (or test scores) showing the number of times each score occurred in a distribution.
grade norms:	Norms that allow test users to compare a student's test score with scores of other students in the same grade.
histogram:	A bar graph used to represent frequency data in statistics.

interval scales: | Level of measurement in which numbers are assigned with the assumption that each number represents a point that is an equal distance from the points adjacent to it.

level of measurement: | The relationship among the numbers we have assigned to the information—nominal, ordinal, equal interval, or ratio.

linear transformations: | A method for changing raw scores for interpretation purposes that does not change the characteristics of the raw data in any way, such as z scores and T scores.

mean: | The arithmetic average of a group of test scores in a distribution.

measure of central tendency: | A value that helps us understand the middle of a distribution or set of scores.

measures of relationship: | Statistics that describe the relationship between two sets of scores, such as the correlation coefficient.

measures of variability: | Numbers that represent the spread of the scores in the distribution, such as range, variance, and standard deviation.

median: | The middle score in a distribution.

mode: | The most frequently occurring score in a distribution.

nominal scale: | The most basic level of measurement, in which numbers are assigned to groups or categories of information.

normal curve: | A symmetrical distribution of scores that, when graphed, is bell shaped.

normal probability distribution: | A theoretical distribution that exists in our imagination as a perfect and symmetrical distribution; also referred to as the normal curve.

norm-based interpretation: | The process of comparing an individual's score with the scores of another group of people who took the same test.

norm group: | A previously tested group of individuals whose scores are used for comparison purposes.

norms: | A group of scores that indicate the average performance of a group and the distribution of scores above and below this average.

ordinal scales: | The second level of measurement, in which numbers are assigned to order or rank individuals or objects from greatest to least (or vice versa) on the attribute being measured.

outliers: | Scores that are exceptionally higher or lower than other scores in a distribution.

Pearson product–moment correlation coefficient: | Represented by r, a correlation coefficient that measures the linear association between two variables, or sets of test scores, that have been measured on interval or ratio scales.

percentage: | A linear transformation of raw scores obtained by dividing the number of correctly answered items by the total number of items.

percentile: An area transformation that indicates the percentage of people who scored at or below a particular raw score.

percentile rank: The percentage of scores that fall at or below a given score.

range: A measure of variability calculated by subtracting the lowest number in a distribution from the highest number in the distribution.

ratio scales: The level of measurement in which numbers are assigned to points with the assumption that each point is an equal distance from the numbers adjacent to it and there is a point that represents an absolute absence of the property being measured, called zero (0).

raw score: The basic score calculated when an individual completes a psychological test.

standard deviation: A measure of variability that represents the degree to which scores vary from the mean.

standard deviation unit: A number that represents how many standard deviations an individual score is located away from the mean.

standard scores: Universally understood units in testing, such as z scores and T scores, that allow the test user to evaluate a person's performance in comparison with other persons who took the same test or a similar test.

stanine: A standard score scale with nine points that allows us to describe a distribution in words instead of numbers (from 1 = *very poor* to 9 = *very superior*).

T scores: Standard scores, which have a mean of 50 and a standard deviation of 10, that are used to compare test scores from two tests that have different characteristics.

variance: A measure of variability that indicates whether individual scores in a distribution tend to be similar to or substantially different from the mean of the distribution.

z scores: Standard scores, which have a mean of zero (0) and a standard deviation of 1, that are used to compare test scores from two tests that have different characteristics.

KEY CONCEPTS CROSSWORD

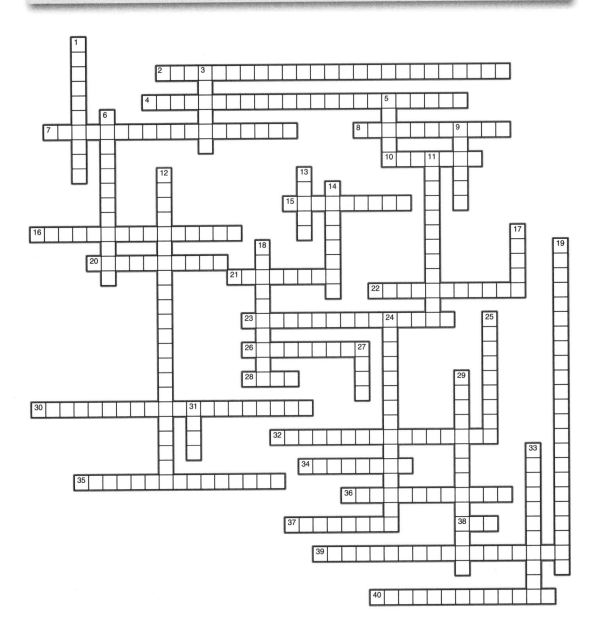

ACROSS

2. The process of comparing an individual's score with the scores of another group of people who took the same test.

4. A number that represents how many standard deviations an individual score is located away from the mean.

7. Type of theoretical distribution that exists in our imagination as a perfect and symmetrical distribution; also referred to as the normal curve.

8. Measures that represent the spread of the scores in the distribution, such as range, variance, and standard deviation.

10. A standard score scale with nine points that allows us to describe a distribution in words instead of numbers (from 1 = *very poor* to 9 = *very superior*).

15. The basic score calculated when an individual completes a psychological test.

16. Universally understood units in testing, such as *z* scores and *T* scores, that allow the test user to evaluate a person's performance in comparison with other persons who took the same test or a similar test.

20. A linear transformation of raw scores obtained by dividing the number of correctly answered items by the total number of items.

21. A measure of variability that indicates whether individual scores in a distribution tend to be similar to or substantially different from the mean of the distribution.

22. Statistics calculated from a distribution that describe or summarize the properties of the distribution of test scores, such as the mean, median, mode, and standard deviation.

23. Level of measurement in which numbers are assigned with the assumption that each number represents a point that is an equal distance from the points adjacent to it.

26. A bar graph used to represent frequency data in statistics.

DOWN

1. A previously tested group of individuals whose scores are used for comparison purposes.

3. The middle score in a distribution.

5. A group of scores that indicate the average performance of a group and the distribution of scores above and below this average.

6. The level of measurement in which numbers are assigned to points with the assumption that each point is an equal distance from the numbers adjacent to it and there is a point that represents an absolute absence of the property being measured, called zero (0).

9. Type of transformation that does not change the characteristics of the raw data, such as *z* scores and *T* scores.

11. A symmetrical distribution of scores that, when graphed, is bell shaped.

12. Type of correlation coefficient that is represented by *r*, that measures the linear association between two variables, or sets of test scores, that have been measured on interval or ratio scales.

13. A type of norm that allows us to compare a student's test score with scores of other students in the same grade.

14. Standard scores, which have a mean of 50 and a standard deviation of 10, that are used to compare test scores from two tests that have different characteristics.

17. A measure of variability calculated by subtracting the lowest number in a distribution from the highest number in the distribution.

18. An area transformation that indicates the percentage of people who scored at or below a particular raw score.

19. A statistic that provides an index of the strength and relationship between two sets of scores; a statistic that describes the relationship between two distributions of scores.

28. The arithmetic average of a group of test scores in a distribution.

30. The relationship among the numbers we have assigned to the information—nominal, ordinal, equal interval, or ratio.

32. Measures that help us understand the middle of a distribution or set of scores.

34. Scores that are exceptionally higher or lower than other scores in a distribution.

35. The percentage of scores that fall at or below a given score.

36. Measures that describe the relationship between two sets of scores, such as the correlation coefficient.

37. Standard scores, which have a mean of zero (0) and a standard deviation of 1, that are used to compare test scores from two tests that have different characteristics.

38. A type of norm that allows us to compare an individual's test score with scores of people in the same age group.

39. A measure of variability that represents the degree to which scores vary from the mean.

40. The most basic level of measurement, in which numbers are assigned to groups or categories of information.

24. A way of grouping adjacent scores to display them in a table or graph.

25. Type of distribution that presents an orderly arrangement of a group of numbers (or test scores) showing the number of times each score occurred in a distribution.

27. The most frequently occurring score in a distribution.

29. The second level of measurement, in which numbers are assigned to order or rank individuals or objects from greatest to least (or vice versa) on the attribute being measured.

31. Type of transformation that changes the unit of measurement and reference, such as percentile ranks.

33. Data grouped according to a common property.

LEARNING ACTIVITIES BY LEARNING OBJECTIVE

The following are some study tips and learning activities you can engage in to support the learning objectives for this chapter.

Learning Objectives	*Study Tips and Learning Activities*
After completing your study of this chapter, you should be able to do the following:	The following study tips and learning activities will help you meet these learning objectives:
Describe and identify the different levels of measurement.	• List the levels of measurement. For each level, identify a real-life example that is not described in your textbook. Describe the types of statistics that could be calculated for each of your examples.
Summarize test scores using class intervals and frequency distributions.	• Gather the shoe size and height of all students in your class. In groups or individually, summarize these two distributions of scores in a frequency table and histogram. Compare answers as a class.
Describe the characteristics of the normal curve as well as skewed, peaked, and bimodal distributions.	• Draw a variety of histograms. Indicate whether each resembles a normal curve, a positively or negatively skewed distribution, a peaked distribution, or a bimodal distribution.

Describe the purpose and calculate measures of central tendency, measures of variability, and measures of relationship.	• Write your answers to the following questions (be prepared to read them in class):
	  o Why do we use measures of central tendency? What are the different measures of central tendency?
	  o Why do we use measures of variability? What are the different measures of variability? What is the formula for each?
	  o Why do we use measures of relationship? How do we measure relationships, and what is one formula discussed in your textbook?

Convert raw test scores into more meaningful units.	• List the different linear and area transformations we use to convert raw scores into more meaningful units. What is the formula for each?

Describe norm-based interpretation and the different types of norms.	• Review norm data for several psychological tests. (You may find them online, or your instructor may provide them.) Document the following information:
	  o What norms are provided?
	  o Can you explain these norms based on the information in this chapter?
	  o How were these norms developed?
	  o How are these norms displayed?
	  o Be prepared to share your findings with the rest of the class.

EXERCISES

1. Read each of the following situations. Then determine whether the level of measurement in each situation is nominal, ordinal, equal interval, or ratio.

   a. A professor scores a multiple-choice test by counting the number of correct answers.

   b. Eggs in the supermarket are graded as 1 = *small*, 2 = *medium*, 3 = *large*, and 4 = *jumbo*.

   c. A teacher measures the height of her first-grade students in inches.

   d. A trucking company has 10 vehicles numbered 1 through 10.

   e. An intelligence test is normed so that the average score is 100.

   f. Employees are assigned random identification numbers.

   g. A local hockey team is ranked the best in the conference because it won the most games.

2. Suppose that you have magically changed places with the professor teaching this course. You have just administered the final exam. The final exam, like the midterm exam, consisted of 100 multiple-choice items (where 1 point is awarded for each correct answer). The scores your students earned on the midterm and final exams are shown below. Calculate measures of central tendency and measures of variability for each distribution of test scores. Calculate a measure of relationship between the two distributions. Be prepared to share with your classmates how students performed on each test and the relationship between the two tests.

Name	Midterm Exam	Final Exam
John	78	75
David	67	63
Kate	69	55
Zachary	63	60
Taylor	85	100
Peter	72	0
Kia	92	91
Jackie	67	75
Roger	94	90
Bill	62	65
Monique	61	60
Iara	44	55
Tonya	66	66
Amanda	87	88
Cindy	76	79
Terry	83	88

Name	Midterm Exam	Final Exam
Robert	42	50
Linda	82	80
Ruth	84	82
Tara	51	50
Kristen	69	60
Nancy	61	60
Bo	96	100
William	73	77
Sally	79	89

3. Assume that you designed a 10-item standardized test to measure college students' knowledge of psychological testing. You administer your new test to a representative group of college students who have taken a psychological testing course. You obtain the following raw scores. Create a table showing the percentage, z score, and T score for each raw score. Compare answers as a class.

Raw Score	Number of Students Who Obtained the Score
1	1
2	2
3	2
4	3
5	5
6	6
7	5
8	4
9	3
10	1

4. Imagine that you are a clinical psychologist. While conducting a comprehensive assessment of your client, Hulbert, you decide to administer various psychological tests to him. One of these tests is the Wallibee Test of Anxiety (this is not a real test). The Wallibee Test consists of 50 questions, and Hulbert answers 32 correctly. Given that the appropriate norm group has a mean of 28 and that the standard deviation of the norm group is 6, provide the following information:

    a. Assuming that the scores from the norm group are normally distributed, plot the scores (using the standard deviation) of the norm group.

    b. Calculate Hulbert's percentage, z score, and T score.

ADDITIONAL LEARNING ACTIVITIES

Activity 5-1 Mean, Median, Mode, and Bill Gates

Background

The question always arises when to use each type of measure of central tendency. Statistics are not necessarily good or bad. There are, however, appropriate and inappropriate uses of statistics. Vickers (2010) created a little scenario that illustrates this point.

Consider this example. The owner of a restaurant wants to determine the average annual salary of his customers to help decide if he can increase his prices. At a random point in time, he walks out and surveys all of the customers. They are quite friendly and actually tell him their annual salary, which is shown in below.

$40,000

$45,000

$55,000

$65,000

$70,000

Which measure of central tendency should you use to understand the typical value in this distribution? The mode is pretty useless as there are five most frequently occurring values (every value occurs once). Rarely do you want to use frequencies when describing the data or making decisions, which is what the mode is based on. For example, what if the next two people who walked in had incomes of $35,000? The mode is $35,000, which clearly does not describe the typical value or center of the data.

In the set of scores above, the mean is $55,000. It happens that the median is also $55,000. Either one of these would work equally well. However, what would happen if Bill Gates walked into the restaurant to get a quick bite? Let's assume that he makes $1,000,000,000 a year!

With Bill Gates added the mean now becomes $166,712,500 and our median becomes $60,000. Which is most descriptive of the typical salary now? The median still falls in what seems to be the center of the data. However, the mean is far to the right of what appears to be the center.

Most people would say that Bill Gates is rich. Statisticians call him an outlier. An outlier is an extreme score and this example illustrates that the mean is highly affected by outliers or extreme scores. The median, on the other hand, is not. As a result, when there are extreme scores the median is *generally* best. If the restaurateur used the mean with Bill Gates in the sample he might decide $1,500 for a hamburger is an appropriate price. However, if he used the median, $7.50 would be a more reasonable conclusion and probably a better decision.

Vickers' (2010) next example takes place in a hospital. Here a hospital administrator is writing next year's budget. He is trying to determine the typical expenses the hospital incurs for an operation. He takes eight cases and finds the following total costs:

$85,000

$50,000

$45,000

$35,000

$30,000

$30,000

$250,000

The mean of these values is just over $70,000 and the median is $42,500. It is obvious that the outlier of $250,000 is causing an increase in the value of the mean substantially above the median. Which is better to use—the mean or the median? In this case, probably the mean is the better choice because if he used the median there is a real chance that he would underestimate the hospital's expenses for next year.

Questions

1. A company gives a test to 10 applicants. The scores are 35, 35, 35, 45, 45, 50, 50, 50, 50, and 100. The company CEO states that she will only hire individuals who scored above average. What are the mean, median, and mode for the test score data? Which measure(s) of central tendency would you use to represent "average," and what would you tell the CEO about measures of central tendency and how they can affect the hiring decisions in this instance?

2. While researching a test, you come across two published studies. The first study reported that the mean test score for men and women in Australia was 45.0 and 45.7, respectively. The second study reported that the median test score for men and women in the United States was 44.8 and 46.0, respectively. Explain why we can or cannot compare these measures of central tendency to make comparisons between men and women and across countries.

Activity 5-2 Graduate School and the GRE

Background

If you are planning on applying to graduate school, it is likely that you will need to take the GRE. This test allows programs to compare applying students using a consistent standard or metric. There are several GRE tests. There is a general test and seven subject tests. Different graduate programs have different requirements, so it is import to check to see what tests are required for schools that you are interested in attending.

The general test consists of three sections: a verbal reasoning measure, a quantitative reasoning measure, and an analytical writing measure. The verbal reasoning section assesses mainly reading and reasoning, while the quantitative section assesses mathematical knowledge and reasoning. The analytical writing section measures "the ability to articulate and support complex ideas, support ideas with relevant reasons and examples, and examine claims and accompanying evidence" (ETS, 2014, p. 4). The section consists of two written essays. The essay topics range from the fine arts and humanities to the social and physical sciences, and do not measure specific content knowledge.

Scoring of the written section is somewhat unique. First, each essay is scored holistically assigning a single score for the essay using a 0 to 6 scale with each point having descriptive scoring anchors. Next, the essay receives a score from ETS's computerized scoring system called e-rater. If the human score and computer score agree, then that is the final score the essay receives. If the scores differ by a certain amount, then a second human scores the essay and the final essay score is the average of the two human scores. However, if the two human scores disagree by a certain amount, then the final score is determined by a third human scorer. The test taker's overall final written essay score is the average of the scores obtained on the two essays rounded to the nearest half-point on the 0–6 score scale.

In 2014, ETS reported there were 1,467,387 test takers between August 1, 2011 and April 30, 2014. The mean analytic writing score was 3.56, with a standard deviation of 0.86. When ETS reports the test takers scores they present a raw score as well as a percentile rank. The raw scores and percentile ranks for the essays are in the table below.

Score	Percentile Rank
6.0	99
5.5	98
5.0	93
4.5	80
4.0	56
3.5	38
3.0	15
2.5	7
2.0	2
1.5	1
1.0	
0.5	
0.0	

Using the information above and the textbook material answer the following questions.

Questions

1. What is the likely shape of the distribution of scores for the written essay section of the GRE?

2. What would a score of 5.0 mean on the written essay section of the GRE?

3. What type of score transformation is the percentile rank?

4. The table above shows that the highest score of 6.0 corresponds to the 99th percentile. Why does a 6.0 not correspond to the 100th percentile?

PRACTICE QUESTIONS

The following are some practice questions to assess your understanding of the material presented in this chapter.

Multiple Choice

1. If 10 students arrange themselves from shortest to tallest and we assign the shortest a score of 1 and the tallest a score of 10, what level of measurement would we be using?
   a. Interval scale
   b. Nominal scale
   c. Ordinal scale
   d. Ratio scale

2. Most psychological tests produce which level of measurement?
   a. Nominal and ratio
   b. Ordinal and ratio
   c. Ordinal and interval
   d. Nominal and ordinal

3. Which one of the following provides us with a visual representation of a distribution of scores?
   a. Measures of variation
   b. Measures of central tendency
   c. Descriptive statistics
   d. Frequency distributions

4. What would you calculate to find out more about the middle of a distribution of scores?
   a. Levels of measurement
   b. Frequency distributions
   c. Measures of variability
   d. Measures of central tendency

5. What would you calculate if you wanted to find out whether individuals who took a test performed similarly to or differently from one another?
   a. Measures of variation
   b. Measures of central tendency
   c. Descriptive statistics
   d. Frequency distributions

6. What would be the most accurate index or indices when a distribution of scores has outliers?
   a. Mode and median
   b. Mean and mode
   c. Mean and median
   d. Mean only

7. The correlation between two distributions of scores can range from
   a. −10.0 to +10.0.
   b. −1.0 to +1.0.
   c. 0 to 1.0.
   d. −0.5 to +0.5.

8. Which one of the following correlation coefficients would you most likely see if students' performance on a midterm exam was inversely related to their performance on a final exam?
   a. −10.0
   b. −0.6
   c. +0.2
   d. +6.0

9. What type of distribution is skewed to the left, has one high point, and has many high scores?

    a. Negatively skewed distribution

    b. Positively skewed distribution

    c. Evenly distributed distribution

    d. Peaked distribution

10. In a normal distribution, approximately what percentage of test scores will fall between 2 and 3 standard deviations above the mean?

    a. 68%

    b. 34.1%

    c. 13.6%

    d. 2.1%

11. In a normal distribution, approximately what percentage of test scores will fall between one standard deviation below the mean and one standard deviation above the mean?

    a. 95%

    b. 68%

    c. 34.1%

    d. 13.6%

12. Which one of the following standard scores always has a mean of 50 and a standard deviation of 10?

    a. *T* scores

    b. *z* scores

    c. Percentiles

    d. Standard deviation units

13. If your score on a test is calculated to be equivalent to a percentile rank of 80, which one of the following is TRUE?

    a. You scored better than 79% of the norm group.

    b. You scored equal to or better than 80% of the norm group.

    c. You scored equal to or less than 80% of the norm group.

    d. 80% of the norm group scored higher than you.

14. If the mean of a distribution of test scores is 70 and the standard deviation is 5, what would John's *z* score be if he scored an 80?

    a. 0

    b. 1

    c. 2

    d. 3

15. Which one of the following standard scores changes the unit of measurement?

    a. Percentage

    b. Percentile

    c. *z* score

    d. *T* score

16. Which one of the following is FALSE about the use of norms?

    a. There is one right population that is regarded as the normative group.

    b. Test publishers often develop and publish the results of various norm groups.

    c. Test users should always be careful to use up-to-date norms.

    d. The smaller the norm group, the more likely the norm group is not representative.

Short Answer

1. What are the potential consequences of not understanding the level of measurement of data?

2. Compare and contrast the levels of measurement. What mathematical operations can you perform for each level of measurement?

3. How does the normal probability distribution help us understand a distribution of test scores? Describe the characteristics of the normal probability distribution.

4. What procedures do we use to interpret test scores? What is the value of calculating measures of central tendency, measures of variability, and measures of relationships? Give an example of each.

5. Can we calculate all descriptive statistics for all levels of measurement? Why or why not?

6. What is the purpose of transforming raw scores into standard scores? What are three commonly used standard scores, and how do you calculate each one?

7. How do norms help us understand test scores? How might norms be used incorrectly?

ANSWER KEYS

Crossword

ACROSS

2. NORM-BASED INTERPRETATION— The process of comparing an individual's score with the scores of another group of people who took the same test.

4. STANDARD DEVIATION UNIT—A number that represents how many standard deviations an individual score is located away from the mean.

7. NORMAL PROBABILITY—Type of theoretical distribution that exists in our imagination as a perfect and symmetrical distribution; also referred to as the normal curve.

8. VARIABILITY—Measures that represent the spread of the scores in the distribution, such as range, variance, and standard deviation.

10. STANINE—A standard score scale with nine points that allows us to describe a distribution in words instead of numbers (from 1 = *very poor* to 9 = *very superior*).

15. RAW SCORE—The basic score calculated when an individual completes a psychological test.

16. STANDARD SCORES—Universally understood units in testing, such as *z* scores and *T* scores, that allow the test user to evaluate a person's performance in comparison with other persons who took the same test or a similar test.

20. PERCENTAGE—A linear transformation of raw scores obtained by dividing the number of correctly answered items by the total number of items.

21. VARIANCE—A measure of variability that indicates whether individual scores in a distribution tend to be similar to or substantially different from the mean of the distribution.

DOWN

1. NORM GROUP—A previously tested group of individuals whose scores are used for comparison purposes.

3. MEDIAN—The middle score in a distribution.

5. NORMS—A group of scores that indicate the average performance of a group and the distribution of scores above and below this average.

6. RATIO SCALES—The level of measurement in which numbers are assigned to points with the assumption that each point is an equal distance from the numbers adjacent to it and there is a point that represents an absolute absence of the property being measured, called zero (0).

9. LINEAR—Type of transformation that does not change the characteristics of the raw data, such as *z* scores and *T* scores.

11. NORMAL CURVE—A symmetrical distribution of scores that, when graphed, is bell shaped.

12. PEARSON PRODUCT–MOMENT— Type of correlation coefficient that is represented by *r*, that measures the linear association between two variables, or sets of test scores, that have been measured on interval or ratio scales.

13. GRADE—A type of norm that allows us to compare a student's test score with scores of other students in the same grade.

14. *T* SCORES—Standard scores, which have a mean of 50 and a standard deviation of 10, that are used to compare test scores from two tests that have different characteristics.

22. DESCRIPTIVE—Statistics calculated from a distribution that describe or summarize the properties of the distribution of test scores, such as the mean, median, mode, and standard deviation.

23. INTERVAL SCALES—Level of measurement in which numbers are assigned with the assumption that each number represents a point that is an equal distance from the points adjacent to it.

26. HISTOGRAM—A bar graph used to represent frequency data in statistics.

28. MEAN—The arithmetic average of a group of test scores in a distribution.

30. LEVEL OF MEASUREMENT—The relationship among the numbers we have assigned to the information—nominal, ordinal, equal interval, or ratio.

32. CENTRAL TENDENCY—Measures that help us understand the middle of a distribution or set of scores.

34. OUTLIERS—Scores that are exceptionally higher or lower than other scores in a distribution.

35. PERCENTILE RANK—The percentage of scores that fall at or below a given score.

36. RELATIONSHIP—Measures that describe the relationship between two sets of scores, such as the correlation coefficient.

37. Z SCORES—Standard scores, which have a mean of zero (0) and a standard deviation of 1, that are used to compare test scores from two tests that have different characteristics.

38. AGE—A type of norm that allows us to compare an individual's test score with scores of people in the same age group.

39. STANDARD DEVIATION—A measure of variability that represents the degree to which scores vary from the mean.

40. NOMINAL SCALE—The most basic level of measurement, in which numbers are assigned to groups or categories of information.

17. RANGE—A measure of variability calculated by subtracting the lowest number in a distribution from the highest number in the distribution.

18. PERCENTILE—An area transformation that indicates the percentage of people who scored at or below a particular raw score.

19. CORRELATION COEFFICIENT—A statistic that provides an index of the strength and relationship between two sets of scores; a statistic that describes the relationship between two distributions of scores.

24. CLASS INTERVALS—A way of grouping adjacent scores to display them in a table or graph.

25. FREQUENCY—Type of distribution that presents an orderly arrangement of a group of numbers (or test scores) showing the number of times each score occurred in a distribution.

27. MODE—The most frequently occurring score in a distribution.

29. ORDINAL SCALES—The second level of measurement, in which numbers are assigned to order or rank individuals or objects from greatest to least (or vice versa) on the attribute being measured.

31. AREA—Type of transformation that changes the unit of measurement and reference, such as percentile ranks.

33. CATEGORICAL—Data grouped according to a common property.

Exercises

1.

   a. Ratio
   b. Ordinal
   c. Ratio
   d. Nominal
   e. Interval
   f. Nominal
   g. Ordinal

2.

Midterm Exam:
Mean = 72.12
Mode = 61, 67, 69
Median = 72
Standard deviation = 14.10
Final Exam:
Mean = 70.32
Mode = 60
Median = 75
Standard deviation = 20.70
Correlation = .66

3.

Standard Scores			
Raw Score	Percentage	z Score	T Score
1	10	−2.18	28.21
2	20	−1.73	32.68
3	30	−1.29	37.14
4	40	−0.84	41.61
5	50	−0.39	46.07
6	60	0.05	50.54
7	70	0.50	55.00
8	80	0.95	59.46
9	90	1.39	63.93
10	100	1.84	68.39

4.

   a.

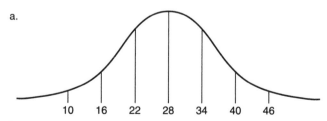

   b.

Percentage = 64%
z score = 0.66
T score = 56.66

Multiple Choice

1.

Correct Answer: c

Source: Page 112–114

Explanation: Ordinal scales are rank order-ings. This type of scale indicates an individual's or object's value based on its relationship to others in the group. The rank only has mean-ing in relationship to the group being com-pared. For example, if you were one of the tallest in the group it would matter greatly if the group was composed of third graders or professional basketball players. In addition, the magnitude of difference between individu-als is not known. Continuing with a height example, if you were the second tallest you could be one inch shorter or two feet shorter, and it does not matter because it is your posi-tion in the rank that has meaning.

2.

Correct Answer: c

Source: Page 112–116

Explanation: Very few psychological tests have a true zero point indicating a complete absence of an attribute. For example, a person cannot have a complete absence of a personal-ity. In addition, nominal scales group individu-als into categories. While this is sometimes used in psychological testing, ordinal and interval scales are most characteristic of psy-chological tests.

3.

Correct Answer: d

Source: Page 118–120

Explanation: A frequency distribution is a visual summary of scores. It is often presented in a table or a histogram. The data are sum-marized showing the count of occurrences at a specific value or range of values.

4.

Correct Answer: d

Source: Page 123

Explanation: Measures of central tendency are descriptive statistics we use to describe the central, middle, or most characteristic score in a distribution. There are three commonly used measures of central tendency: mean, median, and mode. Each has its use, so there is not one best measure of central tendency, instead selec-tion and use depends on the situation and the test user's needs.

5.

Correct Answer: a

Source: Page 127

Explanation: Variability refers to the spread of scores in a distribution, and therefore mea-sures of variation can be used to determine if test scores are close together or far apart. There are three commonly used measures of variation: range, variance, and standard devia-tion. Each has their strengths and weaknesses, but the most commonly used measure is the standard deviation.

6.

Correct Answer: a

Source: Page 127–128

Explanation: In a skewed distribution or a distribution with outliers, the mean is more affected than the mode or median. This is because the mean gets "pulled" toward the extreme values. In contrast, the mode and median are much less affected and as a result can be considered better descriptions the cen-ter of the distribution.

7.

Correct Answer: b

Source: Page 134

Explanation: The correlation coefficient is a measure describing the relationship between two variables. The correlation can range from −1.00 to +1.00. A correlation of −1.00 indicates a perfect negative correlation showing that as one variable increases, there is an exact matching decrease in the other variable. A correlation of +1.00 indicates a perfect positive correlation showing that as one variable increases, the other variable increases an equal amount. Perfect correlations rarely, if ever, occur.

8.

Correct Answer: b

Source: Page 134

Explanation: A correlation coefficient can range from −1.00 to +1.00. Therefore, the correct answer cannot be −10.0 or +6.0. A positive correlation indicates that as one variable increases the other also increases. A negative correlation indicates that as one variable increases the other variable decreases, which is another way of describing an inverse relationship. Thus, the correct answer is −0.6.

9.

Correct Answer: a

Source: Page 124–125

Explanation: A negatively skewed distribution is one that has a single high point to the right and a long tail to the left. One way to remember the difference between positive and negative skew is that a negatively skewed distribution has a long tail in the negative direction and a positively skewed distribution has a long tail in the positive direction.

10.

Correct Answer: d

Source: Page 122

Explanation: A normal distribution is a theoretical distribution that is useful for interpreting test scores. Figure 5.3 in your textbook shows the percentage of scores

falling between various standard deviations. Approximately 34.1% of the scores will fall between the mean and one standard deviation above the mean. Approximately 13.6% of the scores will fall between one standard deviation and two standard deviations above the mean. Finally, about 2.1% of the scores will fall between two and three standard deviations above the mean. Because the normal distribution is symmetric these percentages hold for standard deviations below the mean as well. These percentages are very important in testing and statistics in general and it is worthwhile to memorize these percentages.

11.

Correct Answer: b

Source: Page 122

Explanation: This question can easily be answered by referring to Figure 5.3 in your textbook, which shows the normal probability distribution. Looking at the figure, we can see that approximately 34.1% of the scores will fall between the mean and one standard deviation above the mean. Because we know that the normal distribution is symmetrical we then also know that approximately 34.1% of the scores will fall between the mean and one standard deviation below the mean. Thus adding these values together, approximately 68% of the scores will fall between one standard deviation below the mean and one standard deviation above the mean.

12.

Correct Answer: a

Source: Page 137

Explanation: Raw scores are often difficult to interpret. Therefore, they are often transformed into a different score allowing for easier interpretation and comparison with other test scores. The *T* score is a common linear transformation that is based on the standard deviation. The *T* score has a mean of 50 and standard deviation of 10.

13.

Correct Answer: b

Source: Page 137–138

Explanation: A percentile is a common area score transformation. A score's percentile indicates the percentage of scores that fall at or below that score. Thus, if the percentile is 80 then 80% of the scores were at or below the score. Put another away, the score is equal to or better than 80% of the scores.

14.

Correct Answer: c

Source: Page 137

Explanation: A *z* score is a linear transformation that converts the raw score into standard deviation units. Using the *z* score formula, $\frac{x-\mu}{\sigma}$ we subtract the mean from the obtained score and then divide by the standard deviation. Thus, $z = (80 - 70) / 5 = 2$.

15.

Correct Answer: b

Source: Page 136–138

Explanation: There are two types of transformations, linear and area. Linear transformations do not change the unit of measurement, but area transformations do change the unit of measurement. A percentage, *z* score, and *T* score are linear transformation, while the percentile is an area transformation.

16.

Correct Answer: a

Source: Page 143–145

Explanation: Because psychological tests produce scores that are at the ordinal or interval levels of measurement, scores generally only have meaning in relation to other scores. Norms provide us with the ability to compare scores and are used as the comparison group. There is NOT one norm group. Instead the norm group should be selected based on the individual(s) to whom the test is to be administered. For example, we would not use norms based on third graders if we are testing college students.

Short Answer

1. Levels of measurement are an important consideration in determining which statistical procedures are appropriate to perform and how to interpret test results. For example, nominal variables may have numbers assigned to different categories, but the numbers are just a label or name. They have no mathematical meaning, so mathematical operations on nominal variables are inappropriate. Or consider ordinal data for level of education, which has the groups 1 = *elementary school*, 2 = *high school*, 3 = *college*, 4 = *graduate school*. An individual with a 4 does not have twice as much education as a person with a 2. This type of interpretation would require ratio level data.

2. The levels of measurement can be thought of as a hierarchy with each successive level possessing the characteristics of the lower levels plus additional characteristics. The nominal level is the lowest level on the hierarchy. This level of data is for classification into categories and math operations are inappropriate. The next level is ordinal, which has the property of rank order. At this level, math operations, such as addition, subtraction, multiplication, and division, are inappropriate. However, you can determine rank ordering in terms of magnitude of the characteristic or attribute measured.

Interval level is the next level of measurement. Interval level has all the characteristics of the lower levels plus the intervals between numbers are equidistant. You can use mathematical operations at this level, allowing for the calculation of means and standard deviations. The highest level of measurement is the ratio level of measurement. In addition to the properties already mentioned, this level of measurement also has a zero point that indicates a total absence of what is being measured. Thus, ratios can be computed allowing you to say things like Mary has twice as much of XYZ than John.

3.   The normal distribution is important because many human traits conform to this theoretical distribution. For example, if we created a graph showing heights of adults from the general population, the graph would look like a normal distribution. Most heights would be in the middle, and numbers would gradually taper off symmetrically as we move away from the center peak. We would find that about 34.1% of the individuals would fall between the mean and one standard deviation, about 13.6% would fall between one standard deviation and two standard deviations away from the mean, and about 2.1% would fall between two and tree standard deviations from the mean. These characteristics have important statistical implications.

4.   Descriptive statistics such as central tendency and variability describe test scores, allowing us to understand key features of the distribution and interpret test scores. Measures of relationship, such as the correlation, allow us to easily understand how two variables are associated or vary together. Examples of measures of central tendency include the mean, median, and mode. Examples of measures of variability include the range, variance, and standard deviation. Finally, an example of a measure of relationship is the correlation.

5.   No, we cannot calculate descriptive statistics for all levels of measurement. Each level of measurement has certain characteristics that lend themselves to specific mathematical operations. For example, with nominal and ordinal level data you cannot meaningfully perform addition, subtraction, multiplication, and division. At the interval and ratio levels, however, these operations are appropriate.

6.   Raw scores are transformed into standard scores to aid in the interpretation of test results and scores. With a transformed score, it is often easier to compare individual scores on the same test or similar tests. Three common transformations are percentages, z scores, and percentiles. To calculate a percentage, divide the raw score by the total possible score. To calculate a z score, subtract the mean from the raw score and then divide this amount by the standard deviation. Finally, to calculate the percentile rank, find the number of scores below the given score, add 0.5 for each score that is exactly the same as the given score, and then divide this total by the number of people who took the test.

7.   Norms help us understand test scores because they provide a comparison group. Very few psychological tests produce scores at the ratio level of measurement. Therefore, scores must be compared to understand what the scores mean. Norms provide us with a relative measure to make interpretations of test scores. However, selection of an appropriate norm group is an important consideration. For example, if you are testing fifth graders on math concepts, you would want to use a norm based on the general population of fifth graders and not a norm based on third graders or high school students.

References

ETS. (2014). GRE: *Guide to the use of scores*. Retrieved from https://www.ets.org/s/gre/pdf/gre_guide.pdf
Vickers, A. (2010). *What is a p-value anyway? 34 stories to help you actually understand statistics*. Boston: Addison-Wesley.

6

What Is Test Reliability/Precision?

Chapter Overview

In Chapter 6, we describe three methods of estimating a test's reliability/precision test–retest or stability over time, internal consistency or homogeneity of the test questions, and scorer reliability or agreement. We provide an introduction to classical test theory and describe the relationship between reliability/precision and random measurement error. We discuss how to calculate an index of reliability called the *reliability coefficient*, an index of error called the *standard error of measurement*, and an index of agreement called *Cohen's kappa*. Finally, we discuss factors that increase and decrease reliability of test scores.

Learning Objectives

After completing your study of this chapter, you should be able to do the following:

- Define reliability/precision, and describe three methods for estimating the reliability/precision of a psychological test and its scores.
- Describe how an observed test score is made up of the true score and random error, and describe the difference between random error and systematic error.
- Calculate and interpret a reliability coefficient, including adjusting a reliability coefficient obtained using the split-half method.
- Differentiate between the KR-20 and coefficient alpha formulas, and understand how they are used to estimate internal consistency.
- Calculate the standard error of measurement, and use it to construct a confidence interval around an observed score.
- Identify four sources of test error and six factors related to these sources of error that are particularly important to consider.
- Explain the premises of generalizability theory, and describe its contribution to estimating reliability.

Chapter Outline

Key Concepts

alternate forms:	Two forms of a test that are alike in every way except for the questions; used to overcome problems such as practice effects; also referred to as *parallel forms*.
Cohen's kappa:	An index of agreement for two sets of scores or ratings.
confidence interval:	A range of scores that the test user can feel confident includes the true score.
correlation:	A statistical procedure that provides an index of the strength and direction of the linear relationship between two variables.

generalizability theory: A method for systematically analyzing the many causes of inconsistency or random error in test scores, seeking to find systematic error that can then be eliminated.

heterogeneous test: A test that measures more than one trait or characteristic.

homogeneous test: A test that measures only one trait or characteristic.

internal consistency: The internal reliability of a measurement instrument; the extent to which each test question has the same value of the attribute that the test measures.

interrater agreement: The consistency with which scorers rate or make yes/no decisions.

interscorer agreement: The consistency with which scorers rate or make decisions.

intrarater agreement: How well a scorer makes consistent judgments across all tests.

intrascorer reliability: Whether each scorer was consistent in the way he or she assigned scores from test to test.

measurement error: Variations or inconsistencies in the measurements yielded by a test or survey.

order effects: Changes in test scores resulting from the order in which tests or questions on tests were administered.

parallel forms: Two forms of a test that are alike in every way except questions; used to overcome problems such as practice effects; also referred to as *alternate forms*.

practice effects: When test takers benefit from taking a test the first time (practice) because they are able to solve problems more quickly and correctly the second time they take the same test.

random error: The unexplained difference between a test taker's true score and the obtained score; error that is nonsystematic and unpredictable, resulting from an unknown cause.

reliability/precision: The consistency with which an instrument yields measurements.

reliable test: A test that consistently yields the same measurements for the same phenomena.

scorer reliability: The degree of agreement between or among persons scoring a test or rating an individual; also known as *interrater reliability*.

split-half method: A method for estimating the internal consistency or reliability of a test by giving the test once to one group of people, making a comparison of scores, dividing the test into halves, and correlating the set of scores on the first half with the set of scores on the second half.

standard error of measurement (SEM):   An index of the amount of inconsistency or error expected in an individual's test score.

systematic error: When a single source of error can be identified as constant across all measurements.

test–retest method: A method for estimating test reliability in which a test developer gives the same test to the same group of test takers on two different occasions and correlates the scores from the first and second administrations.

KEY CONCEPTS CROSSWORD

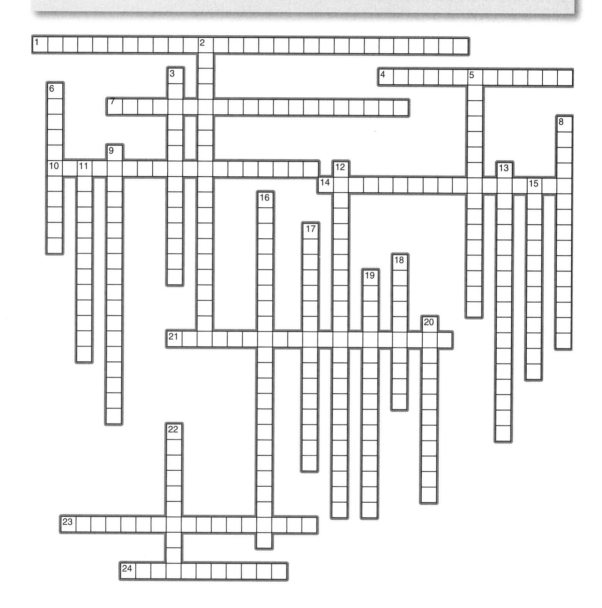

ACROSS

1. An index of the amount of inconsistency or error expected in an individual's test score.

4. An index of agreement for two sets of scores or ratings.

7. The internal reliability of a measurement instrument; the extent to which each test question has the same value of the attribute that the test measures.

10. The degree of agreement between or among persons scoring a test or rating an individual; also known as *interrater reliability*.

14. Variations or inconsistencies in the measurements yielded by a test or survey.

21. A range of scores that the test user can feel confident includes the true score.

23. A method for estimating the internal consistency or reliability of a test by giving the test once to one group of people, making a comparison of scores, dividing the test into halves, and correlating the set of scores on the first half with the set of scores on the second half.

24. A statistical procedure that provides an index of the strength and direction of the linear relationship between two variables.

DOWN

2. The consistency with which an instrument yields measurements.

3. Two forms of a test that are alike in every way except questions; used to overcome problems such as practice effects; also referred to as *alternate forms*.

5. When a single source of error can be identified as constant across all measurements.

6. Type of agreement/consistency with which scorers rate or make decisions.

8. Two forms of a test that are alike in every way except for the questions; used to overcome problems such as practice effects; also referred to as *parallel forms*.

9. A method for estimating test reliability in which a test developer gives the same test to the same group of test takers on two different occasions and correlates the scores from the first and second administrations.

11. Changes in test scores resulting from the order in which tests or questions on tests were administered.

12. A method for systematically analyzing the many causes of inconsistency or random error in test scores, seeking to find systematic error that can then be eliminated.

13. A test that measures more than one trait or characteristic.

15. A test that consistently yields the same measurements for the same phenomena.

16. Whether each scorer was consistent in the way he or she assigned scores from test to test.

17. A test that measures only one trait or characteristic.

18. Type of agreement/consistency concerning how well a scorer makes consistent judgments across all tests.

19. When test takers benefit from taking a test the first time because they are able to solve problems more quickly and correctly the second time they take the same test.

20. The unexplained difference between a test taker's true score and the obtained score; error that is nonsystematic and unpredictable, resulting from an unknown cause.

22. Type of agreement/consistency with which scorers rate or make yes/no decisions.

LEARNING ACTIVITIES BY LEARNING OBJECTIVE

The following are some study tips and learning activities you can engage in to support the learning objectives for this chapter.

Learning Objectives	*Study Tips and Learning Activities*
After completing your study of this chapter, you should be able to do the following:	The following study tips and learning activities will help you meet these learning objectives:
Define reliability/precision, and describe three methods for estimating the reliability/precision of a psychological test and its scores.	• Distinguish among the three methods by writing down who, what, and when for each method.
Describe how an observed test score is made up of the true score and random error, and describe the difference between random error and systematic error.	• Weigh yourself several times on your bathroom scale. Do you get the same weight each time? If not, your scale may have random error. Now try another scale. Compare your weights on the first and second scales. Does your first scale weigh too heavy or too light? If so, your scale may have systematic error.
Calculate and interpret a reliability coefficient, including adjusting a reliability coefficient obtained using the split-half method.	• The learning activities that follow are designed to help you understand how to calculate and interpret reliability coefficients. Complete the activities. If you have questions, be sure to ask your instructor.
Differentiate between the KR-20 and coefficient alpha formulas, and understand how they are used to estimate internal consistency.	• Write a short answer in complete sentences that answers these questions: ○ What kinds of questions require the KR-20 formula? ○ What kinds of questions require the coefficient alpha formula?
Calculate the standard error of measurement, and use it to construct a confidence interval around an observed score.	• Weigh yourself again three times in a row. Do not adjust the scale if your weight appears to vary. Calculate the standard error of measurement of the three weights, and construct a confidence interval around your mean weight. Interpret your weight in terms of the confidence interval.
Identify the four sources of test error and six factors related to these sources of error that are particularly important to consider.	• Try to come up with your own examples for each of these. Check with a classmate and/or your instructor to see whether he or she agrees with your examples.
Explain the premises of generalizability theory, and describe its contribution to estimating reliability.	• Review the example study proposed in the section on generalizability theory. Then propose your own study for detecting systematic error in test results. Share your proposed study with your classmates or your instructor.

EXERCISES

1. The following matrix shows data on a test that was administered on two occasions three weeks apart. Do the following:

   a. Calculate test–retest reliability and the standard error of measurement.

   b. Construct a 95% confidence interval around the score of Test Taker 1 on the first administration.

   c. Interpret the reliability coefficient you have calculated. Do the test scores show sufficient test–retest reliability? Do the confidence intervals of some scores overlap?

Test Taker	First Occasion	Second Occasion
1	80	82
2	70	75
3	50	45
4	60	60
5	80	78
6	65	70
7	50	50
8	55	60
9	78	80
10	78	76

2. Below are the data for a test that was administered on one occasion to the same people to estimate reliability of the test scores. Answer the following questions regarding these data:

   a. What type of reliability/precision can be estimated from these data?

   b. What is the reliability coefficient for the test when corrected using the Spearman–Brown formula?

   c. What is the standard error of measurement?

d. What is the confidence interval that we can be 95% confident contains Tony's true score?

e. Would you say that Tony definitely scored higher than Tina did?

Test Taker	Scores	
	First Half	Second Half
Tony	6	6
Meg	5	4
Chris	8	7
Sam	4	2
Tina	5	5
Ted	2	1
Abe	9	10
Ricardo	3	3

3. Following are descriptions of situations in which the researcher needs to identify one or more ways to estimate reliability/precision. In each instance, choose one or more methods for estimating reliability/precision, tell why you chose the method(s), and describe the steps necessary for gathering the data needed to calculate your reliability coefficient:

a. An instructor has designed a comprehensive math exam for students entering community college. The exam contains multiple-choice questions that measure a student's ability to read formulas, carry out math calculations, and solve word problems. Because students may score higher on the second administration purely because they have taken the test one time already, when gathering evidence of reliability/precision, the instructor can give the exam only once. However, the instructor needs to know how reliable the test scores are. What method should the instructor use for gathering evidence of reliability/precision?

b. An HR professional wants to assess employee attitudes about quality of work life. She wants to be sure that her self-designed instrument is reliable. Her instrument contains 20 statements that employees will rate from 1 to 5. The HR professional has designed the instrument to be homogeneous. What method(s) should she use to estimate reliability/precision?

c. An I-O psychology practitioner designed two-parallel promotion tests for firefighters. Both tests required two fire chiefs to observe firefighters completing job-related activities (e.g., use and maintenance of safety equipment). Each firefighter was required to take two parallel tests rated by the same fire chiefs. How can the ratings be checked for reliability?

d. A test developer is constructing a measure of critical thinking. The instrument consists of a number of anagrams and riddles—problems for which answers are not readily apparent until solved. The test score depends on the percentage of questions the test taker solved correctly. How should the test developer estimate reliability/precision?

Scenario	Possible Method(s) for Estimating Reliability/ precision	Why Each Method Chosen	Steps Necessary for Gathering Data Needed to Calculate Reliability Coefficient
A	1.		
	2.		
	3.		
B	1.		
	2.		
	3.		
C	1.		
	2.		
	3.		
D	1.		
	2.		
	3.		

4. Explaining Various Reports of Reliability/Precision. Julian Rotter (1966) published a monograph describing a personality construct he called *locus of control*—the extent to which a person believes that the reinforcements received in life are due to his or her own effort and ability. The monograph also contains a personality test to measure the extent of this belief in individuals.

The following table contains the reliability/precision information that Rotter published for his test. Identify the types of reliability/precision measured and explain why the reliability coefficients differ.

Internal Consistency				
Sample	Type	N	Sex	r
Ohio State University elementary psychology students	Split-half, Spearman Brown	50	M	.65
		50	F	.79
		100	Combined	.73
	Kuder-Richardson	50	M	.70
		50	F	.76
		100	Combined	.73
Ohio State University elementary psychology students	Kuder–Richardson	200	M	.70
		200	F	.70
		400	Combined	.70
National stratified students sample Purdue Opinion Poll 10th, 11th and 12th grades	Kuder–Richardson	1,000	Combined M & F approximately equal N	.69

Test–Retest Reliability				
Sample	Type	N	Sex	r
Ohio State University elementary psychology students	1 month Group administration	30 30 60	M F Combined	.60 .80 .72
Prisoners Colorado Reformatory	1 month	28	M	.78
Ohio State University elementary psychology students	2 months	63 54 117	M F Combined	.49 .61 .55

What types of reliability/precision were measured?

Why do the reliability coefficients differ?

ADDITIONAL LEARNING ACTIVITIES

Activity 6-1 Reliability/Precision and Target Practice

Background

The textbook presents reliability/precision as the consistency in measurement of a group of test scores. The concept of reliability/precision is often illustrated using a bull's-eye and target practice and this is shown in Figure 6.1. Imagine that your instructor takes two students to a shooting range and asks each one to take 10 shots at a target 50 yards away. The resulting targets are shown below.

Neither student is particularly accurate because each target has four shots in the outer most ring, four in the middle ring, and two in the bull's-eye. Notice, however, that on the target on the left the shots are quite spread out. In contrast, on the target on the right the shots are much more clustered together and are all to the upper left of the bull's-eye. As a result, we would say the student who shot at the right target was more consistent or reliable in his or her shooting.

Next, the textbook presents three methods of looking at or measuring reliability/precision. The methods are test–retest, alternate forms, and internal consistency. We can continue with the target analogy to further understand each method. A day after the initial trip to the shooting range, the instructor takes both students back to the range and has them shoot 10 more shots. Comparing how closely the results of Day 1 were to the results of Day 2 would be an analogous to test–retest reliability.

Now suppose that immediately after the students fire the first 10 shots, the instructor places another target 50 yards away, but this target is a different color. The students take 10 shots at

Figure 6.1   Reliability/Precision of Target Shooting

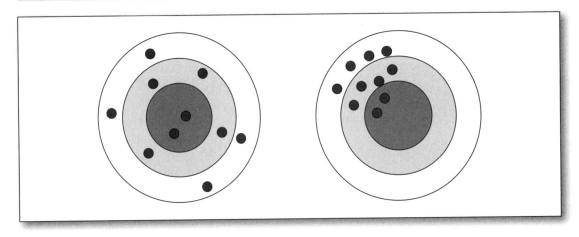

the new target, and then the instructor examines how similar the results of the first 10 shots were to the second 10 shots. While the two targets were very similar to each other, they were not exactly the same. This is an example of alternate-forms reliability.

Finally, we come to internal consistency. Using this method, the students could compare their odd numbered shots to their even numbered shots to see if the results were consistent. For example, the triangles in Figure 6.2 represent odd numbered shots and the circles even numbered shots. This would be analogous to the split-half method of assessing reliability/precision.

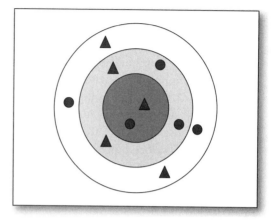

Figure 6.2 Split-Half Reliability/ Precision of Target Shooting

Questions

1. Create a target with shots that represents high internal consistency reliability and high accuracy.

2. Create a target with shots that represents high internal consistency reliability and low accuracy.

3. Create a target with 10 shots that illustrates order effects. Represent the first five shots using a circle and the second five shots using a triangle.

Lee Cronbach: 50 Years After Cronbach's Alpha

Background

Lee Cronbach was an educational psychologist who is best known for his work on reliability. In 1951, Cronbach published his seminal work on reliability where he proposed "alpha." As he later described, alpha was not anything revolutionary or particularly new. In fact, he drew heavily on the works of others. Cronbach was just one of many investigators who were applying similar ideas at the time. Fifty years later, he reflected that "to make so much use of an easily calculated translation of a well-established formula scarcely justifies the fame it has brought me. It is an embarrassment to me that the formula became conventionally known as 'Cronbach's α'" (Cronbach & Shavelson, 2004, p. 397). The article with this statement was published posthumously in the journal of *Educational and Psychological Measurement* three years after Cronbach's death in 2001. However, the work was supported by a grant by the U.S. Department of Education, and therefore there is an open source version available to the public at the web site for the Nation Center of Research on Evaluation, Standards, and Student Testing shown below.

https://www.cse.ucla.edu/products/reports/r643.pdf

In this version, there is an editor's preface in which Richard Shavelson pays tribute to and reflects on his final time with Cronbach, which is quite touching. The open source article is suggested reading for anyone who wants to know more about the people behind the articles found in scientific journals.

For the most part, the article is quite readable for those with an introductory understanding of statistics and psychometrics. However, those with deeper understanding of the concepts will obviously get more out of the article. In the paper, Cronbach reflects on the development of reliability from its beginnings in the early 20th century. He discusses the reliability approaches found in textbooks, such as Spearman's split-half approach and Kuder and Richardson's K-R Formula 20. He then discusses more modern approaches such as generalizability theory. Interestingly, 50 years after he developed the formula, he is not much of a fan of the use of Cronbach's alpha, which brought him so much fame.

Questions

1. Knowing the history behind testing and psychometric ideas can add greatly to your understanding and appreciation for the ideas. Research biographical information for one historical person who has been discussed in the textbook and write a short summary.

2. Write your own testing biography, describing you as a student of testing. Recount your testing experiences before this class, during this class, and project out what your future testing experience may look like.

PRACTICE QUESTIONS

The following are some practice questions to assess your understanding of the material presented in this chapter.

Multiple Choice

1. When we talk about how each inch on a yardstick is the same length, we are talking about the yardstick's
   a. reliability/precision.
   b. internal consistency.
   c. order effects.
   d. score reliability.

2. Which one of the following methods do we use to examine the performance of a test over time and provide an estimate of a test's stability?
   a. Test–retest reliability
   b. Split-half reliability
   c. Score reliability
   d. Alternative forms reliability

3. Marsha, a student teacher, wanted to check the reliability of a math test that she developed for her fourth graders. She gave the test to students on Monday morning and then again on Tuesday morning. On the first administration of her test, there was a wide variety of scores, but on the second administration, nearly all of the children made A's on the test. Marsha wondered, "Why did all the students make A's on Tuesday, but not on Monday?" Which one of the following would most likely account for this outcome?
   a. Order effects
   b. Practice effects
   c. Measurement error
   d. Scorer error

4. Researchers administered the Personality Assessment Inventory (PAI) to two samples of individuals. First, they administered the PAI twice to 75 adults, with the second administration following the first by an average of 24 days. They also administered the PAI to 80 college students who took the test twice, with an interval of 28 days. In each case, the researchers were conducting studies to measure the PAI's
   a. internal consistency.
   b. score reliability.
   c. split-half reliability.
   d. test–retest reliability.

5. Jon developed a math test for fourth graders, but he was not able to administer the test twice. What method can Jon use to estimate the reliability/precision of the math test?
   a. Criterion related
   b. Construct
   c. Internal consistency
   d. Test–retest

6. When using the split-half method, an adjustment must be made to compensate for splitting the test into halves. Which one of the following would we use to make this adjustment?
   a. Coefficient alpha
   b. Pearson product–moment correlation
   c. Spearman–Brown formula
   d. KR-20

7. Which one of the following is the appropriate method for estimating reliability for tests with homogeneous questions that have more than two possible responses?
   a. Coefficient alpha
   b. Pearson product–moment correlation
   c. Spearman–Brown formula
   d. KR-20

8. While _____ describes the degree to which questions on a test or subscale are interrelated, _____ refers to whether the questions measure the same trait or dimension.

   a. homogeneity; coefficient alpha

   b. coefficient alpha; homogeneity

   c. heterogeneity; coefficient alpha

   d. homogeneity; test–retest reliability

9. Researchers conducted two studies on the reliability of the Wisconsin Card Sorting Test (WCST) using adult psychiatric inpatients. In these studies, more than one person scored the WCST independently. What kind of reliability/precision were the researchers interested in establishing?

   a. Test–retest reliability

   b. Scorer reliability

   c. Split-half reliability

   d. Internal consistency

10. Katie and Kathy are roommates who share the same bathroom scale. Neither Katie nor Kathy is on a special diet to lose or gain weight. Each morning, they both weigh themselves. From day to day, it seems that each gains or loses two to three pounds. Some days Katie gains three pounds and Kathy loses two pounds. Other days Katie loses two pounds and Kathy gains three pounds. Every day their weights are different from their weights the previous day, and they cannot distinguish a pattern. Katie and Kathy decide to start weighing themselves on a scale at the wellness center. To their surprise, they neither gain nor lose weight from time to time when using the scale at the wellness center. Which one of the following best explains this situation?

   a. Their home scale has systematic error, and the wellness center scale is more accurate.

   b. Their home scale has random error, and the wellness center scale is more accurate.

   c. The scale at the wellness center has systematic error, and their home scale is accurate.

   d. The scale at the wellness center has random error, and their home scale is accurate.

11. Which one of the following formulas do test developers who wish to increase the reliability of a test use to estimate how many homogeneous test questions should be added to a test to raise its reliability to the desired level?

   a. Coefficient alpha

   b. KR-20

   c. Spearman–Brown

   d. Pearson product–moment correlation

12. Which one of the following is important for both interpreting individual test scores and calculating confidence intervals?

   a. Standard error of measurement

   b. Pearson product–moment correlation

   c. Test Variance

   d. Spearman–Brown formula

13. When test reliability is high, the standard error of measurement is _____. As test reliability decreases, the standard error of measurement _____.

   a. high; decreases

   b. low; decreases

   c. high; increases

   d. low; increases

14. As a rule, adding more questions that measure the same trait or attribute can _____ a test's reliability.

   a. increase

   b. decrease

   c. overestimate

   d. underestimate

15. What makes generalizability theory different from classical test theory?
    a. Generalizability theory focuses on identifying systematic error.
    b. Generalizability theory focuses on identifying random error.
    c. Generalizability theory focuses on identifying systematic and random error.
    d. Generalizability theory focuses on identifying systematic and random true scores.

16. Which one of the following is associated with generalizability theory?
    a. Pearson product–moment correlation
    b. Interrater reliability
    c. Analysis of variance (ANOVA)
    d. Cohen's kappa

17. Who is the most likely to apply generalizability theory?
    a. Test taker
    b. Test user
    c. Test administrator
    d. Test developer

Short Answer

1. Identify three methods of estimating test reliability/precision. What are the similarities and differences among the methods?

2. Explain the difference between test–retest reliability and internal consistency. Provide an example of each.

3. Explain the concepts of interscorer agreement and intrascore agreement. On what types of tests are these concepts most important?

4. What is the difference between random error and systematic error?

5. What is the purpose of the Spearman–Brown formula?

6. Describe the purpose of the KR-20 formula and the coefficient alpha formula. When should each be used?

7. What is a confidence interval? How does the confidence interval help testing professionals interpret an individual's test score?

8. Name six factors that affect a test's reliability. Explain each in terms of how the factor increases or decreases reliability.

9. How is systematic error associated with generalizability theory?

ANSWER KEYS

Crossword

ACROSS

1. STANDARD ERROR OF MEASURE-MENT—An index of the amount of inconsistency or error expected in an individual's test score.

4. COHEN'S KAPPA—An index of agreement for two sets of scores or ratings.

7. INTERNAL CONSISTENCY—The internal reliability of a measurement instrument; the extent to which each test question has the same value of the attribute that the test measures.

10. SCORER RELIABILITY—The degree of agreement between or among persons scoring a test or rating an individual; also known as *interrater reliability*.

14. MEASUREMENT ERROR—Variations or inconsistencies in the measurements yielded by a test or survey.

21. CONFIDENCE INTERVAL—A range of scores that the test user can feel confident includes the true score.

23. SPLIT-HALF METHOD—A method for estimating the internal consistency or reliability of a test by giving the test once to one group of people, making a comparison of scores, dividing the test into halves, and correlating the set of scores on the first half with the set of scores on the second half.

24. CORRELATION—A statistical procedure that provides an index of the strength and direction of the linear relationship between two variables.

DOWN

2. RELIABILITY/PRECISION—The consistency with which an instrument yields measurements.

3. PARALLEL FORMS—Two forms of a test that are alike in every way except questions; used to overcome problems such as practice effects; also referred to as *alternate forms*.

5. SYSTEMATIC ERROR—When a single source of error can be identified as constant across all measurements.

6. INTERSCORER—Type of agreement/consistency with which scorers rate or make decisions.

8. ALTERNATE FORMS—Two forms of a test that are alike in every way except for the questions; used to overcome problems such as practice effects; also referred to as *parallel forms*.

9. TEST–RETEST METHOD—A method for estimating test reliability in which a test developer gives the same test to the same group of test takers on two different occasions and correlates the scores from the first and second administrations.

11. ORDER EFFECTS—Changes in test scores resulting from the order in which tests or questions on tests were administered.

12. GENERALIZABILITY THEORY—A method for systematically analyzing the many causes of inconsistency or random error in test scores, seeking to find systematic error that can then be eliminated.

13. HETEROGENEOUS TEST—A test that measures more than one trait or characteristic.

15. RELIABLE TEST—A test that consistently yields the same measurements for the same phenomena.

16. INTRASCORER RELIABILITY—Whether each scorer was consistent in the way he or she assigned scores from test to test.

17. HOMOGENEOUS TEST—A test that measures only one trait or characteristic.

18. INTRARATER—Type of agreement/consistency concerning how well a scorer makes consistent judgments across all tests.

19. PRACTICE EFFECTS—When test takers benefit from taking a test the first time because they are able to solve problems more quickly and correctly the second time they take the same test.

20. RANDOM ERROR—The unexplained difference between a test taker's true score and the obtained score; error that is non-systematic and unpredictable, resulting from an unknown cause.

22. INTERRATER—Type of agreement/consistency with which scorers rate or make yes/no decisions.

Exercises

1. Calculations and answers are shown below. Evidence of test–retest reliability for this test is very good. Confidence intervals for some scores may overlap (for example, 78 and 80). This overlap should be taken into account when making decisions based on individual test scores. Your results may vary a somewhat depending on when you rounded the results of the correlation and standard deviation before calculating the SEM and confidence intervals. Results below were calculated using Excel without rounding.

Test Taker	X_1	X_2	D_1	D_1^2	D_2	D_2^2	$D_1 \times D_2$	X_1^2
1	80	82	13.4	179.56	14.4	207.36	192.96	6,400
2	70	75	3.4	11.56	7.4	54.76	25.16	4,900
3	50	45	−16.6	275.56	−22.6	510.76	375.16	2,500
4	60	60	−6.6	43.56	−7.6	57.76	50.16	3,600
5	80	78	13.4	179.56	10.4	108.16	139.36	6,400
6	65	70	−1.6	2.56	2.4	5.76	−3.84	4,225
7	50	50	−16.6	275.56	−17.6	309.76	292.16	2,500
8	55	60	−11.6	134.56	−7.6	57.76	88.16	3,025
9	78	80	11.4	129.96	12.4	153.76	141.36	6,084
10	78	76	11.4	129.96	8.4	70.56	95.76	6,084

(Continued)

(Continued)

Test Taker	X_1	X_2	D_1	D_1^2	D_2	D_2^2	$D_1 \times D_2$	X_1^2
Sum	666	676	1,362.4	1,536.4	1,396.4	45,718		
Mean	66.6	67.6						
Standard deviation of X_1	11.67							
r_{xx}	0.97							
SEM	2.18							
95% confidence Interval	$80 + 4.27 = 84.27$ and $80 - 4.27 = 75.73$							

2. Estimating Reliability/Precision

   a. Split-half

   b. $r_{xx} = .79$ when corrected with Spearman–Brown formula (.96 if uncorrected)

   c. SEM ± 0.71

   d. 95% CI = X = 1.96(SEM) = X = 1.4, so Tony's 95% CI is 12 ± 1.4 = 10.6 to 13.4. Tina's is 10 ± 1.4 = 8.6 to 11.4 (You must add the scores from the first and second halves of the test together to get the total test score for each person.)

   e. No. Tony's confidence interval and Tina's confidence interval overlap.

3. Estimating Reliability/Precision Appropriately

   a. Because the test covers several dimensions, it is heterogeneous. The instructor needs to estimate internal consistency because he can administer the test only once. The best he can do is to calculate the internal consistency of the questions that measure each concept. He can use split-half reliability, correlating the scores on two halves selected randomly and adjusting for test length using the Spearman–Brown formula, or he can use the KR-20 or coefficient alpha formula to estimate the internal consistency of all possible split halves. He will end up with three reliability coefficients—one for each section of the test.

   b. The researcher may estimate reliability/precision using the test–retest method provided that there are no intervening developments, such as a change in company benefits that will change employee attitudes between administrations. The researcher cannot use alternate forms unless she develops another parallel form—a lengthy and difficult task. She can use either form of internal consistency—split-half or coefficient alpha. (Coefficient alpha is used when there are more than two possible responses.)

   c. This is a case for interrater reliability. The ratings given by each expert can be correlated to determine how well they agreed. Intrarater agreement can also be calculated to determine how consistently each expert assigned the ratings.

d. Because test takers are likely to remember the answers to the problems, the test–retest method will not work. The developer can calculate internal consistency.

4. Type of reliability test appears at the top of each table with details listed in the second column. Coefficients differ due to sample size, sex differences, and type of reliability tested.

Multiple Choice

1.

Correct Answer: b

Source: Page 151

Explanation: In a measurement context, reliability refers to consistency, and internal consistency is a specific type of reliability. In this example, an inch is always a same length regardless if it is the first inch or the tenth inch on the yardstick. Thus, every inch is uniform in its measurement, and the yardstick is internally consistent.

2.

Correct Answer: a

Source: Page 151–152

Explanation: Test–retest reliability requires that a test be given at two points in time. Then the scores from the first and second administration are compared using correlation. For a test to be reliable, the scores should be relatively stable over time; therefore, there should be a high correlation between the two sets of scores.

3.

Correct Answer: b

Source: Page 152

Explanation: Practice effects are a common problem when using the test–retest method to establish reliability. Practice effects occur when test takers benefit from taking the test a second time. Because they are familiar with the test, test takers can answer the questions faster the second time

and can potentially remember the questions and answers from the first administration.

4.

Correct Answer: d

Source: Page 151–152

Explanation: When a test is administered to the same individuals more than once the researchers are investigating test–retest reliability. Under this method, it is important to administer the test under similar conditions. In addition, the time spacing between administrations should be long enough to minimize the effect of remembering questions and answers, but not so long as to allow growth and learning.

5.

Correct Answer: c

Source: Pages 153

Explanation: Criterion-related and construct are types of validity evidence and therefore cannot be used to determine reliability. Because the test cannot be administered twice, Jon cannot use test–retest to establish the reliability of the test. Therefore, the answer must be internal consistency which is a measure of reliability that helps us examine how related the items within the test are to each other.

6.

Correct Answer: c

Source: Page 154

Explanation: There is a relationship between test length and reliability, such that the longer the test the higher the reliability. This becomes an issue when using the split-half method because the test is divided into two halves, which results in a lower reliability estimate. To compensate for this, the Spearman–Brown formula is used to adjust the reliability coefficient to estimate what it would be for the full-length test.

7.

Correct Answer: a

Source: Page 154

Explanation: KR-20 and coefficient alpha are two methods for estimating the internal consistency of a test. However, the KR-20 can only be used when test items are scored in a dichotomous fashion such as right or wrong. In contrast, coefficient alpha can be used for scales as well as right or wrong questions. When coefficient alpha is used on dichotomous items it will yield the same result as the KR-20.

8.

Correct Answer: b

Source: Pages 154–155

Explanation: Coefficient alpha is a specific method that measures the internal consistency of a test, which is just another way of saying that the items are interrelated. In contrast, homogeneity is a broader term that means all test items measure the same trait or attribute. Heterogeneity, on the other hand, means that the test items measure more than one trait or attribute. A test can have a high coefficient alpha and still be heterogeneous.

9.

Correct Answer: b

Source: Page 155–158

Explanation: When multiple scorers or judges are required to score an exam, their scores or ratings will often differ. Scorer reliability assesses the amount of consistency or agreement among the scorers. When there are only two raters or judges, the correlation coefficient between the ratings can be used to assess scorer reliability. When there are more than two judges, the intraclass correlation coefficient, a special type of correlation, is the statistical procedure generally used to assess scorer reliability.

10.

Correct Answer: b

Source: Page 158–159

Explanation: Random error is just that— random. Neither Katie nor Kathy can distinguish a pattern in the fluctuations of the weight when they use their scale at home. This suggests that there is random error in the measurement. In contrast to their home scale, the wellness center scale does not have these fluctuations and is consistent in its measurement, which would suggest (but not guarantee) a higher degree of accuracy.

11.

Correct Answer: c

Source: Page 163–164

Explanation: The Spearman–Brown formula represents the relationship between the length of a test and the test's reliability/precision. The formula is often used to adjust the reliability estimate when using the split-half method. However, it can also be used to estimate what the reliability of a test would be if the test were made shorter or longer or to determine the number of items that need to be added to a test to obtain a specific level of reliability.

12.

Correct Answer: a

Source: Page 167 & 170–174

Explanation: The standard error of measurement is an index of the amount of inconsistency or error that can be expected in a single test score. It indicates how much an individual's test score is likely to deviate from his or her true score and as a result, it is used when constructing confidence intervals.

13.

Correct Answer: d

Source: Page 173–174

Explanation: When a test's reliability/precision is high, an individual's observed test score will be a better estimate of his or her true score, so the standard error of measurement will be low. In contrast, as reliability/precision decreases, an individual's observed score is a poorer estimate of his or her true score, and therefore the standard error of measurement will be larger.

14.

Correct Answer: a

Source: Page 175

Explanation: Adding more questions that measure the same construct will increase the reliability of a test. Conversely, as a general rule, if you removed items from a test, the reliability would most likely decrease. Reliability would most likely decrease because there is a positive relationship between the length of the test and the reliability of the test. Longer tests designed to measure a single construct provide more precise measurement because random measurement error, which is always present, is more likely to cancel itself out.

15.

Correct Answer: c

Source: Pages 176–178

Explanation: Classical test theory only identifies random error. However, generalizability theory allows the researcher not only to identify random error, but also to identify sources of systematic error as well. Using a statistical procedure called *analysis of variance*, or ANOVA for short, the researcher call examine factors such as the administration as a source of systematic error.

16.

Correct Answer: c

Source: Page 177

Explanation: Analysis of variance or ANOVA is the statistical method that is used in generalizability theory. This procedure allows the researcher to identify different sources that may systematically be introducing error into the test scores. This is different from classical test theory that only looks at random error and does not include systematic error.

17.

Correct Answer: d

Source: Page 176–178

Explanation: Test developers are the individuals who are responsible for establishing the reliability of a test and therefore are the ones who are most likely to use generalizability theory.

Short Answer

1. There are three main methods used to estimate reliability: test–retest, internal consistency, and scorer reliability or agreement. While each method is similar because they all assess the consistency of scores, each method has a unique approach and provides different types of evidence. First, test–retest assesses the consistency of scores across one or more administrations of the test. The second type, internal consistency, assesses how the items within the test are consistent with each other. The third and final approach, scorer reliability, is used when there are multiple raters or judges who score the test. The scorer reliability approach examines how consistent raters or

judges scored the test takers. If the raters or judges have scored each test taker more than once, the degree to which each rater is consistent in his or her ratings can also be evaluated.

2. Test–retest assesses reliability by comparing test scores from two different testing occasions. In contrast, internal consistency looks at the items within a single administration of a test to confirm that the items share something in common (measure the same construct). An example of internal consistency is coefficient alpha, which is an index of how related the individual test items are. Thus, internal consistency and test–retest are different in that the test–retest method uses the total test score on two different testing occasions to estimate the reliability of the test, while the internal consistency method uses the correlation of the individual items from a single testing session. One test–retest method is called *parallel forms*. Rather than giving the same test twice, two very similar tests are given on different occasions in an attempt to avoid practice effects.

3. Interscorer and intrascorer reliability are important for tests that require judges in the scoring process. Interscorer reliability is the amount of agreement across different judges. For example, a test may require that each essay answer be assessed by two independent graders. Interscorer reliability would look at the agreement between the graders. In contrast, intrascorer reliability is the amount of agreement or consistency within a single judge. For example, a single grader may score the same essay more than once to determine his or her consistency.

4. Random errors have meaning within classical measurement theory. According to classical measurement theory, a person's observed score is equal to his or her true score plus random error. Random means that the measurement errors are unpredictable and cannot be attributed to any known cause. While random measurement error may cause individual measurements to be higher or lower than a person's true score, over repeated measurements, the errors will cancel out. On the other hand, systematic error affects tests scores in a consistent way and can be attributed to some cause. For example, practice effects will consistently increase scores on the second administration of a test. Unlike random error, systematic error will not cancel itself out.

5. The Spearman–Brown formula was independently developed by two different researchers: Charles Spearman and William Brown. The formula provides an estimate of a test's reliability if test items measuring the same trait or attribute are added or subtracted from a test. This is possible because there is a relationship between test length and reliability, with longer tests being more reliable. For example, a test developer may have a test with 100 questions, but may wish to cut down on testing time and only use 80 questions. The Spearman–Brown formula would allow the researcher to estimate what the reliability of the shortened test will be.

6. The KR-20 is the Kuder-Richardson formula. This formula measures the internal consistency of a test using items that are dichotomously scored as either right or wrong. This dichotomous nature of the formula distinguishes it from coefficient alpha, which can be used on items with multiple possible responses or levels. However, when coefficient alpha is used on dichotomous items, the results are the same as with the KR-20.

7. Any single test sore is called a *point estimate*. According to classical test theory, measurement error can cause this estimate to be too high or too low. A confidence interval provides a range of scores within which the true score is likely to fall. Generally this interval is statistically determined using the 95% confidence level. Thus, a researcher could say that he is 95% confident that a person's true score is within the range specified by the confidence interval.

8. The textbook describes six factors that can affect a test's reliability: test length, test homogeneity, test–retest interval, test administration, scoring, and cooperation of the test takers.

(1) Test length—Generally, adding items that measure the same trait or attribute will increase the test's reliability.

(2) Homogeneity—Generally, if items measuring the same attribute or trait are added, reliability will increase; however, if heterogeneous items are added, test reliability is more likely to decrease.

(3) Test–retest interval—As a general rule, the longer the interval between administrations of a test, the lower the reliability coefficient will be.

(4) Test administration—Standardization and consistency between administrations is expected to increase reliability because extraneous factors will be limited or at least controlled.

(5) Scoring—As a general rule, the more qualitative judgments that graders must make, the lower the reliability will be.

(6) Cooperation of the test taker—Test takers who are not motivated to cooperate with the test instructions are likely to add additional measurement error to test scores and therefore likely to reduce test reliability.

9. The ability to assess systematic error is a key feature of generalizability theory. Unlike classical test theory that focuses only on random error, generalizability theory allows the test developer or researcher to segment measurement error into many different facets. Thus, he or she can see how aspects of administration, scoring, or even the test taker can affect test scores. This allows us to estimate the degree to which the results of testing will generalize to other people, places, or times.

References

Cronbach, L. J., & Shavelson, R. J. (2004). My current thoughts on coefficient alpha and successor procedures. *Educational and Psychological Measurement*, 64(3), 391–418. doi:10.1177/0013164404266386

Rotter, J. B. (1966). Generalized expectancies for internal versus external control of reinforcement. *Psychological Monographs*, *80*, 1–28. http://psycnet.apa.org/journals/mon/80/1/1/

7

How Do We Gather Evidence of Validity Based on the Content of a Test?

Chapter Overview

In Chapter 7, we introduce you to the different types of evidence that is used to evaluate whether a proposed interpretation of a test score is valid. We discuss how validity is discussed in the *Standards for Educational and Psychological Testing* (American Educational Research Association [AERA], American Psychological Association [APA], & National Council on Measurement in Education [NCME], 2014). We begin with a brief discussion of validity as defined by the *Standards*. We focus most of our attention on evidence of validity based on an evaluation of the content of the test. We end with an overview of other types of evidence of validity of a test, such as evidence based on the relationship of the test scores to other variables.

Learning Objectives

After completing your study of this chapter, you should be able to do the following:

- Explain what validity is.
- Discuss the five sources of validity evidence described in the *Standards for Educational and Psychological Testing* (AERA, APA, & NCME, 2014).
- Describe the general nature of the traditional terms *content validity*, *criterion-related validity*, and *construct validity*, and explain how these terms are related to the terms used in the *Standards* (AERA, APA, NCME, 2014).
- Explain, at a general level, the appropriate use of various validation strategies.
- Describe and execute the steps involved in ensuring that a test demonstrates evidence of validity based on its content.

- Describe methods for generating validity evidence based on the content of a test.
- Explain the nature and importance of face validity and why it does not provide evidence for interpreting test scores.

Chapter Outline

Sources of Evidence of Validity
  Traditional Views of Validity
  Our Current Views of Validity
  Evidence Based on Test Content
  Evidence Based on Relations With Other Variables
The Appropriate Use of Various Validation Strategies
Evidence of Validity Based on Test Content
  Demonstrating Evidence of Validity Based on Test Content During Test Development
  Demonstrating Evidence of Validity Based on Test Content After Test Development
  Evidence of Validity Based on Test Content Summary
Face Validity
Chapter Summary

Key Concepts

abstract attributes:	Attributes that are more difficult to describe using behaviors because people disagree on which behaviors represent the attribute; examples include personality, intelligence, creativity, and aggressiveness.
competency modeling:	A procedure that identifies the knowledge, skills, abilities, and other characteristics most critical for success for some or all the jobs in an organization.
concrete attributes:	Attributes that can be described in terms of specific behaviors, such as the ability to play the piano.
concurrent evidence of validity:	A method for establishing evidence of validity based on a test's relationships with other variables in which test administration and criterion measurement happen at roughly the same time.
construct:	An attribute, trait, or characteristic that is abstracted from observable behaviors.
construct validity:	An accumulation of evidence that a test is based on sound psychological theory and therefore measures what it is supposed to measure; evidence that a test relates to other tests and behaviors as predicted by a theory.
content areas:	The knowledge, skills, and/or attributes that a test assesses.

content validity:

The extent to which the questions on a test are representative of the material that should be covered by the test.

content validity ratio:

An index that describes how essential each test item is to measuring the attribute or construct that the item is supposed to measure.

convergent evidence of validity:

One of two strategies for demonstrating construct validity showing that constructs that theoretically should be related are indeed related; evidence that the scores on a test correlate strongly with scores on other tests that measure the same construct.

criterion:

The measure of performance that we expect to correlate with test scores.

criterion-related validity:

Evidence that test scores correlate with or predict independent behaviors, attitudes, or events; the extent to which the scores on a test correlate with scores on a measure of performance or behavior.

discriminant evidence of validity:

One of two strategies for demonstrating construct validity showing that constructs that theoretically should be related are indeed related; evidence that test scores are not correlated with unrelated constructs.

face validity:

The perception of the test taker that the test measures what it is supposed to measure.

instructional objectives:

A list of what individuals should be able to do as a result of taking a course of instruction.

job analysis:

A systematic assessment method for identifying the knowledge, skills, abilities, and other characteristics required to perform a job.

practical test:

A test in which a test taker must actively demonstrate skills in specific situations.

predictive evidence of validity:

A method for establishing evidence of validity based on a test's relationships with other variables that shows a relationship between test scores obtained at one point in time and a criterion measured at a later point in time.

test specifications:

The plan prepared before test development that documents the written test or practical exam.

testing universe:

The body of knowledge or behaviors that a test represents.

validity:

Evidence that the interpretations that are being made from the scores on a test are appropriate for their intended purpose.

written test:

A paper-and-pencil test in which a test taker must answer a series of questions.

KEY CONCEPTS CROSSWORD

ACROSS

5. Evidence of validity based on a test's relationships with other variables where test administration and criterion measurement happen at roughly the same time.

6. The perception of the test taker that the test measures what it is supposed to measure.

8. Attributes that can be described in terms of specific behaviors, such as the ability to play the piano.

15. Attributes that are more difficult to describe using behaviors because people disagree on which behaviors represent the attribute; examples include personality, intelligence, creativity, and aggressiveness.

19. Evidence of validity based on a test's relationships with other variables that shows a relationship between test scores obtained at one point in time and a criterion measured at a later point in time.

20. An accumulation of evidence that a test is based on sound psychological theory and therefore measures what it is supposed to measure; evidence that a test relates to other tests and behaviors as predicted by a theory.

21. Evidence of validity showing that scores on a test correlate strongly with scores on other tests that measure the same construct.

22. A procedure that identifies the knowledge, skills, abilities, and other characteristics most critical for success for some or all the jobs in an organization.

DOWN

1. A paper-and-pencil test in which a test taker must answer a series of questions.

2. A test in which a test taker must actively demonstrate skills in specific situations.

3. A systematic assessment method for identifying the knowledge, skills, abilities, and other characteristics required to perform a job.

4. An index that describes how essential each test item is to measuring the attribute or construct that the item is supposed to measure.

7. The extent to which the questions on a test are representative of the material that should be covered by the test.

9. Evidence of validity showing that test scores are not correlated with unrelated constructs.

10. The knowledge, skills, and/or attributes that a test assesses.

11. An attribute, trait, or characteristic that is abstracted from observable behaviors.

12. Evidence that the interpretations that are being made from the scores on a test are appropriate for their intended purpose.

13. The measure of performance that we expect to correlate with test scores.

14. Type of validity evidence showing that test scores correlate with or predict independent behaviors, attitudes, or events; the extent to which the scores on a test correlate with scores on a measure of performance or behavior.

16. The plan prepared before test development that documents the written test or practical exam.

17. The body of knowledge or behaviors that a test represents.

18. Type of objective that lists what individuals should be able to do as a result of taking a course of instruction.

LEARNING ACTIVITIES BY LEARNING OBJECTIVE

The following are some study tips and learning activities you can engage in to support the learning objectives for this chapter.

Learning Objectives	*Study Tips and Learning Activities*
After completing your study of this chapter, you should be able to do the following:	The following study tips and learning activities will help you meet these learning objectives:
Explain what validity is.	• Write your definition of validity. Search the Internet, and document various definitions of validity. Compare your definition with the definitions on the Internet and in this chapter. Be prepared to share your definitions with your classmates and to compare your definitions with theirs.
Discuss the five sources of evidence of validity described in the *Standards* (AERA, APA, & NCME, 2014)	• Using ProQuest Direct or another source from your library, review the five sources of evidence of validity described in the *Standards*. List the names of the five sources of evidence of validity. In your own words, write how to obtain evidence of each source.
Describe the general nature of the traditional terms *content validity*, *criterion-related validity*, and *construct validity*, and explain how these terms are related to the terms used in the *Standards*.	• Use ProQuest or another academic database to search for definitions of content validity, criterion-related validity, and construct validity. Document at least three different definitions for each form of validity. Compare these definitions with the definitions in your textbook and with the way in which the *Standards* defines validity.
Explain, at a general level, the appropriate use of various validation strategies.	• Obtain a test manual. Review the manual and determine what evidence of validity is provided by the test publisher. Be prepared to discuss your findings with your class. • Identify a standardized achievement test and a standardized personality test that interest you. Consult the *Mental Measurements Yearbook*, *Tests in Print*, or other testing resources, and gather as much information as you can about how evidence of the test's validity was obtained. Create a table showing the similarities and differences between the validation strategies. Be prepared to share your findings with your class.
Describe and execute the steps involved in ensuring that a test demonstrates evidence of validity based on its content.	• Construct a test specification table for an exam to assess students' knowledge of the information presented in this chapter. Share your table with your class. Discuss similarities and differences in your tables. Come to a consensus on what test specifications would lead to content-based evidence of validity of an exam.

Describe methods for generating validity evidence based on the content of a test.	• Imagine that you are developing a test to measure the abstract attribute of job satisfaction. Use ProQuest or another academic database to learn how others define job satisfaction. Use what you learn to define your testing universe. Create a test specification table outlining the content areas to be included in your test. Be prepared to share your research and test specification table with your class.
Explain the nature and importance of face validity and why it does not provide evidence for interpreting test scores.	• Review the definition of face validity. Consider two tests that you have previously taken: one that had face validity and one that did not. Write about why one test has face validity and the other does not. • Discuss the pros and cons of a test having face validity. Does face validity affect the accuracy of test scores?

EXERCISES

1. The 2014 *Standards* describe five sources of evidence of validity.

   - Evidence based on test content
   - Evidence based on response processes
   - Evidence based on internal structure
   - Evidence based on relations with other variables
   - Evidence based on the consequences of testing

   The table below includes a description of five types of evidence of validity collected when developing an accounting knowledge test to be used as part of a hiring procedure for accountants. Based on the 2014 *Standards* indicate what source best describes each piece of evidence.

Evidence	Type of Evidence
1. After the test was administered, the test developer analyzed the responses and found that the test was equally difficult for minorities and nonminorities, and that all test items had the same psychometric characteristics for both groups.	
2. After the test was administered and job offers were made, the test developer found that male and females had unequal passing rates, but jobs at the same rate.	
3. The test developer identified the relative importance of accounting knowledge areas required by the job. Then she developed the test ensuring that all knowledge areas were covered and that the number of items in each area was based on its relative importance.	
4. After the test was administered, the test developer interviewed test takers and determined that their answers were based on logical reasoning and retrieval of information from memory. Very little guessing was taking place.	
5. The test developer administered the test to accountants who currently were employed at the organization and also collected performance data for these accountants. She found that accountants who had higher accounting knowledge test scores also had better performance.	

2. You are part of a team that is developing a certification test for human resource professionals. The test will contain multiple sections, and you were assigned to take the lead on determining the number of questions to be included in the employment law section of the test. Based on the results of a job analysis, you are told the employment law section should be 30% of the test. Within the employment law section, the job analysis identified four knowledge areas (with associated laws and guidelines) and identified each area's relative importance in as shown in the table below. If the entire certification test must have 100 questions, how many questions should be

developed for each knowledge area based on the information in the table below? Assume that specific laws and guidelines receive equal weight within its knowledge content area.

Knowledge Area	Relative Importance	Number of Questions
Employment Law (30% of total test)		
Compensation	40%	
Fair Labor Standards Act		
Lilly Ledbetter Fair Pay Act		
Equal Employment Opportunity	40%	
Uniform Guidelines and Employee Selection Procedures		
Age Discrimination in Employment Act of 1967		
Leave and Benefits	10%	
Family and Medical Leave Act of 1993		
Job Safety and Health	10%	
Drug-Free Workplace Act of 1988		
Occupational Safety and Health Act of 1970		
Guidelines and Sexual Harassment		

ADDITIONAL LEARNING ACTIVITIES

Activity 7-1 Validity and Target Practice

Background

In the last chapter, we used target shooting to illustrate reliability. Reliability and validity are related concepts, and we can continue with this example to show how. The two targets shown in Figure 7.1 were used in the last chapter to show low reliability (on the left) and higher reliability (on the right). Remember, we stated that both figures, however, are not indicative of accurate shooting. Validity is often conceptualized as accuracy.

Figure 7.1 Reliability/Precision of Target Shooting

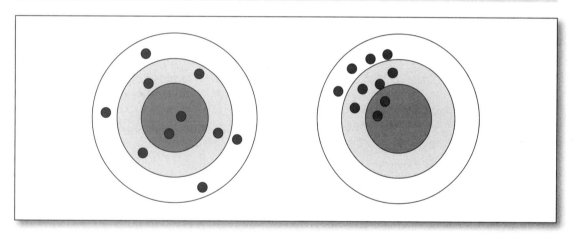

What would a highly consistent and a highly accurate target look like? It would look like the target shown in Figure 7.2.

In the target on the right, all of the shots are in the bull's-eye, hitting where they are supposed to be hitting, so there is good accuracy. For accuracy to occur, all of the shots must be clustered tightly together; therefore, they also have high reliability. There is an often repeated phrase in psychometrics in regards to this phenomenon: Reliability is a necessary, but insufficient, condition for validity. It is impossible to have high accuracy without high consistency, because with low consistency your shots would be scattered all across the target.

Figure 7.2 Target With High Reliability/ Precision and High Validity

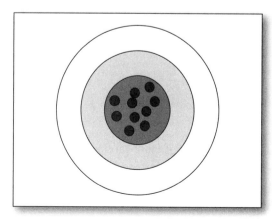

Questions

1. Create a target that illustrates high reliability but low accuracy.

2. Suppose a researcher is using the test–retest method to examine reliability with a two-month period between the shooting trials. Suppose that unknown to the researcher between the two trials, the shooter gets coaching and practices every day. Create two targets that illustrate how practice affects may change the pattern of shots. Explain this in terms of consistency and accuracy.

Activity 7-2 Job Analysis and Content Based Evidence of Validity

Background

Job analysis and its close relative competency modeling are heavily used techniques in test development in organizational settings. A job analysis is a structured process that involves studying a job and identifying (a) the tasks and job activities to be performed in the job, and (b) the knowledge, skills, abilities, and other characteristics required to successful perform the task and job activities. Once this information is known, we can develop a test plan to serve as evidence demonstrating validity based on test content.

A job analysis is a key component of the first two steps of test development:

1. Defining the test universe, target audience, and test purpose.

2. Developing a test plan.

To begin a job analysis, the test developer will typically review previous job analysis studies and other publicly available sources of job information (such as Occupational Information Network and other Federal government resources). He or she will probably talk to some managers and job incumbents. From this information, typically the test developer will construct a survey asking about how important certain tasks, skills, abilities, and so on, are to successful job performance.

Writing good statements for a job analysis survey takes a great deal of practice. This is because each statement must be clear and concise. Each statement must be understood similarly by everyone. While there are no absolute rules for writing job analysis survey statements, there are some best practices. Here we will cover writing task statements.

A task is a specific job activity that demonstrates usage of an occupational skill. A task should have the following characteristics:

- Describe a specific work activity a worker in a specific job may perform
- Consist of one complete activity with a beginning and an end
- Can be performed by one person
- Result in an outcome that contributes to a product or service

In addition, a well-written task statement must include at least an action verb, an object, and object/statement modifiers.

- Action verb (e.g., draft, evaluate, write)
- Object (e.g., letters, software, reports)
- One or more object modifiers that describe the object by indicating what kind of object it is (e.g., *architectural* plans, *new* windows, *technical* reports)
- One or more statement modifiers that describe the statement by indicating why, how, when or where the task is performed (e.g., draft architectural plans *for physical layouts of equipment and space*, evaluate software *to determine its utility for the office*)

A complete statement is of the form: (verb) (object modifier) (object) (statement modifier). Below are two examples.

Examples:

- Manipulate (action verb) attribute (object modifier) geospatial data (object) into formats utilized by production processes (statement modifier).
- Perform tests (action verb) on x-ray machines, explosive detectors, and metal detectors (object) to ensure that the equipment is functioning properly (statement modifier).

Of course, this is not the only way to describe what should be in a task statement. Sometimes it is presented that the task statements should answer several of the questions shown below.

What: What is done or what action is being performed?

Who/what: Who or what is being acted on?

Why: Why is the action occurring (what is the intended outcome)?

How: How is the action being accomplished?

Here is an example:

What is being done?	*Who/what is being acted on?*	*Why is occurring or intended outcome?*	*How is it being accomplished?*
Inspects	engine parts	to detect deformities	by sliding finger on the surface.

The exact approach and amount of detail collected is guided by the unique project or test requirements and what would seem to work well in a given situation. Some types of projects require much greater detail. For example, if you were conducting a job analysis to develop a job knowledge test, you need highly specific and detailed information. Thus, your task statements would be highly detailed and specific.

Some other guidelines for good task statements are as follows:

- Includes only one verb and does not cover two concepts such as "writes and edits"
- Uses an active verb
- Is understandable without further explanation

- Avoids jargon and is understandable by those not in the job (i.e., a judge)
- Defines all acronyms
- Represents the full range of activities performed by a job
- When appropriate, several objects or modifiers can be included in a task statement (types reports, memo, letters, and manuscripts)
- When appropriate, more general objects may be used (inspects *vehicles* rather than *cars and trucks*)

Questions

1. Go to the following website.
http://www.careeronestop.org/Videos/CareerandClusterVideos/career-and-cluster-videos.aspx
CareerOneStop is sponsored by the Department of Labor and it contains a wealth of information on jobs. Once you get to the website, you will see that they have nearly 550 videos about various jobs. Select a job that interests you. After watching the video, write five task statements describing the job.

2. Develop a five-question job interview with each question being related to one of your task statements.

3. Explain how activities in Questions 1 and 2 provide evidence of validity based on content.

PRACTICE TEST QUESTIONS

The following are some practice questions to assess your understanding of the material presented in this chapter.

Multiple Choice

1. A valid test
   a. consistently measures whatever it measures.
   b. consistently measures multiple constructs.
   c. measures only one construct.
   d. allows one to make correct inferences about the meaning of the scores.

2. The current *Standards* (AERA, APA, & NCME, 2014) include discussion of five sources of evidence of validity. Which of the following is one of those sources?
   a. Construct validity
   b. Criterion-related validity
   c. Test content
   d. Face validity

3. Which one of the following is NOT considered a traditional type of validity?
   a. Content
   b. Criterion related
   c. Construct
   d. Alternate forms

4. Demonstrating evidence of validity is often logical rather than statistical for which one of the following?
   a. Face validity and validity evidence based on a test's relationships with a criterion
   b. Face validity and validity evidence based on a test's content
   c. Construct validity and validity evidence based on a test's relationships with a criterion
   d. Validity evidence based on a test's content and based on a test's relationships with a criterion

5. If we demonstrate that a test allows us to identify individuals who are likely to become depressed, we have demonstrated evidence of validity based on the test's
   a. content.
   b. relationship with a criterion.
   c. relationship with a construct.
   d. appearance to the test taker.

6. What type of evidence of validity exists if you took an algebra test that required you to perform a representative sample of algebraic calculations?
   a. Validity based on its content
   b. Validity based on its relationship with a criterion
   c. Validity based on its relationship with a construct
   d. Face validity

7. What type of evidence of validity exists if a test developer finds that the scores on a new test of mathematical achievement correlate with the scores on another test of mathematical achievement?

   a. Validity based on the test's relationship with a criterion

   b. Validity based on the test's relationship with a construct

   c. Validity based on the test's content

   d. Face validity

8. What type of evidence of validity exists if a test developer finds that scores on a new employment test, designed to predict success on the job, correlate with employees' performance appraisal ratings?

   a. Validity based on the test's relationship with a criterion

   b. Validity based on the test's relationship with a construct

   c. Validity based on the test's content

   d. Face validity

9. What type of attribute does a test measures if the attribute can be described in terms of specific behaviors?

   a. Abstract

   b. Nonspecific

   c. Concrete

   d. Specific

10. Which one of the following types of attribute is most difficult to describe in terms of behaviors?

    a. Abstract

    b. Concrete

    c. Nonspecific

    d. Specific

11. Evidence of validity based on a test's content is easiest for tests such as mathematical achievement tests that measure _____ attributes and more difficult for tests such as personality tests that measure _____ attributes.

    a. abstract; concrete

    b. concrete; abstract

    c. nonspecific; specific

    d. specific; nonspecific

12. If test takers perceive a test as appropriate, they are referencing evidence of what?

    a. Face validity

    b. Reliability

    c. Validity based on content

    d. Validity based on relationship with a construct

13. What evidence exists for a writing test that requires a test taker to perform a representative sample of writing activities (for example, writing a poem, writing an essay, writing a term paper)?

    a. Validity based on the test's relationship with a construct

    b. Validity based on the test's relationship with a criterion

    c. Validity based on the test's content

    d. Face validity

14. What two approaches can we use to demonstrate evidence of validity based on a test's relationship with criteria?

    a. Proactive and retroactive

    b. Predictive and nonpredictive

    c. Content and construct

    d. Predictive and concurrent

15. What is the first step to ensuring that a test demonstrates evidence of validity based on its content?

    a. Develop test specifications

    b. Define the testing universe

    c. Determine the content areas

    d. Determine the instructional objectives

16. The content validity ratio for a test item can range from what to what?

    a. −1.00 to 0

    b. 0 to 1.00

    c. −1.00 to 1.00

    d. 1.00 to 10.00

Short Answer

1. How are the traditional concepts of content, criterion-related, and construct validity similar? How are they different?

2. Discuss the five sources of evidence of validity described in the new *Standards* (AERA, APA, & NCME, 2014).

3. How does the 1999 and 2014 treatment of validity in the *Standards* differ from the treatment of validity prior to 1999?

4. What does it mean when we say that validity should be viewed as a unitary concept?

5. In what situations is it appropriate to demonstrate evidence of validity based on test content, relationships with a criterion, and relationships with a construct? When would it be appropriate to collect evidence of more than one type of validity?

ANSWER KEYS

Crossword

ACROSS

5. CONCURRENT—Evidence of validity based on a test's relationships with other variables where test administration and criterion measurement happen at roughly the same time.
6. FACE VALIDITY—The perception of the test taker that the test measures what it is supposed to measure.
8. CONCRETE ATTRIBUTES—Attributes that can be described in terms of specific behaviors, such as the ability to play the piano.
15. ABSTRACT ATTRIBUTES—Attributes that are more difficult to describe using behaviors because people disagree on which behaviors represent the attribute; examples include personality, intelligence, creativity, and aggressiveness.
19. PREDICTIVE—Evidence of validity based on a test's relationships with other variables that shows a relationship between test scores obtained at one point in time and a criterion measured at a later point in time.
20. CONSTRUCT VALIDITY—An accumulation of evidence that a test is based on sound psychological theory and therefore measures what it is supposed to measure; evidence that a test relates to other tests and behaviors as predicted by a theory.
21. CONVERGENT—Evidence of validity showing that scores on a test correlate strongly with scores on other tests that measure the same construct.

DOWN

1. WRITTEN TEST—A paper-and-pencil test in which a test taker must answer a series of questions.
2. PRACTICAL TEST—A test in which a test taker must actively demonstrate skills in specific situations.
3. JOB ANALYSIS—A systematic assessment method for identifying the knowledge, skills, abilities, and other characteristics required to perform a job.
4. CONTENT VALIDITY RATIO—An index that describes how essential each test item is to measuring the attribute or construct that the item is supposed to measure.
7. CONTENT VALIDITY—The extent to which the questions on a test are representative of the material that should be covered by the test.
9. DISCRIMINANT—Evidence of validity showing that test scores are not correlated with unrelated constructs.
10. CONTENT AREAS—The knowledge, skills, and/or attributes that a test assesses.
11. CONSTRUCT—An attribute, trait, or characteristic that is abstracted from observable behaviors.
12. VALIDITY—Evidence that the interpretations that are being made from the scores on a test are appropriate for their intended purpose.
13. CRITERION—The measure of performance that we expect to correlate with test scores.
14. CRITERION-RELATED—Type of validity evidence showing that test scores

22. COMPETENCY MODELING—A procedure that identifies the knowledge, skills, abilities, and other characteristics most critical for success for some or all the jobs in an organization.

correlate with or predict independent behaviors, attitudes, or events; the extent to which the scores on a test correlate with scores on a measure of performance or behavior.

16. TEST SPECIFICATIONS—The plan prepared before test development that documents the written test or practical exam.

17. TESTING UNIVERSE—The body of knowledge or behaviors that a test represents.

18. INSTRUCTIONAL—Type of objective that lists what individuals should be able to do as a result of taking a course of instruction.

Exercises

1.

Evidence	Type of Evidence
1. After the test was administered, the test developer analyzed the responses and found that the test was equally difficult for minorities and nonminorities, and that all test items had the same psychometric characteristics for both groups.	Internal Structure
2. After the test was administered and job offers were made, the test developer found that male and females had unequal passing rates, but jobs at the same rate.	Consequences
3. The test developer identified the relative importance of accounting knowledge areas required by the job. Then she developed the test ensuring that all knowledge areas were covered and that the number of items in each area was based on their relative importance.	Test Content
4. After the test was administered, the test developer interviewed test takers and determined that their answers were based on logical reasoning and retrieval of information from memory. Very little guessing was taking place.	Response Process
5. The test developer administered the test to accountants who currently were employed at the organization and also collected performance data for these accountants. She found that accountants who had higher accounting knowledge test scores also had better performance.	Relations with Other Variables

2.

Knowledge Area	Relative Importance	Number of Questions
Employment Law (30% of total test)		$100 \times .30 = 30$
Compensation	40%	$30 \times .40 = 12$
Fair Labor Standards Act		$12/2 = 6$
Lilly Ledbetter Fair Pay Act		$12/2 = 6$
Equal Employment Opportunity	40%	$30 \times .40 = 12$
Uniform Guidelines and Employee Selection Procedures		$12/2 = 6$
Age Discrimination in Employment Act of 1967		$12/2 = 6$
Leave and Benefits	10%	$30 \times .10 = 3$
Family and Medical Leave Act of 1993		$3/1 = 3$
Job Safety and Health	10%	$30 \times .10 = 3$
Drug-Free Workplace Act of 1988		$3/3 = 1$
Occupational Safety and Health Act of 1970		$3/3 = 1$
Guidelines and Sexual Harassment		$3/3 = 1$

Multiple Choice

1.

Correct Answer: d

Source: Page 183–184

Explanation: A test in and of itself is neither valid nor invalid. Instead, validity concerns the inferences that are made from test scores. Hence, validity is not a property of the test. Rather, validity refers to the consequences and interpretation of test scores for their intended purpose. Furthermore, to establish validity we have to collect different types of evidence to show that are inferences are appropriate.

2.

Correct Answer: c

Source: Page 185–186

Explanation: The *Standards* describe five sources of evidence for validity:

1. Evidence based on test content
2. Evidence based on response processes
3. Evidence based on internal structure
4. Evidence based on relations with other variables
5. Evidence based on the consequences of testing.

3.

Correct Answer: d

Source: Page 184

Explanation: Before the 1999 *Standards*, validity was viewed in three distinct categories: content validity, construct validity, and criterion (related) validity. In contrast, alternative forms is a method for assessing a test's reliability and is not directly related to validity.

4.

Correct Answer: b

Source: Page 186–187 & 205

Explanation: Face validity concerns whether test takers and others view the test as measuring what it is supposed to measure. This is a subjective process and focuses on whether the test "looks" valid to the test taker or others. Also, evidence of validity based on test content involves logically and systematically showing that the test's content is representative of the construct being measured. As a result, neither forms of validity generally involve statistical analyses. However, criterion and construct evidence for validity almost always involve such analyses.

5.

Correct Answer: b

Source: Page 187–188

Explanation: A criterion is an outcome that a test user is interested in predicting. For example, companies are interested in predicting the future performance of applicants, thus the criterion in this example is job performance. Therefore, criterion-related validity evidence seeks to determine the relationship between the test and job performance.

6.

Correct Answer: a

Source: Page 186–187

Explanation: Because the items on the test (i.e., the test content) are representative of the algebraic calculations, we would say that the test has evidence of validity based on its content. While content valid tests are often face valid, remember that face validity refers to if the test "looks valid" and does not refer to what the test actually measures or its content. Thus, in this case, the best answer is evidence based on its content.

7.

Correct Answer: b

Source: Page 188–189

Explanation: This is an example of a specific type of evidence based on the test's relationship with a construct. In this case, because the test correlates with a test measuring a similar or the same construct, we would say that this is convergent evidence of validity.

8.

Correct Answer: a

Source: Page 187–188

Explanation: When a test score predicts a future outcome (often called a *criterion*), we say the test demonstrates evidence of validity based on its relationship with a criterion. This question describes a specific type of evidence called *predictive evidence of validity* because the test scores are significantly related to an important *future* outcome of employee performance, thereby making the test a valid selection tool.

9.

Correct Answer: c

Source: Page 189–190

Explanation: Some tests measure attributes that are relatively easy to observe and are highly specific. In these cases, we say the test is measuring a concrete attribute. These types of attributes are easier to measure and it is easier to collect evidence for their validity.

10.

Correct Answer: a

Source: Page 189–190

Explanation: The textbook defines two types of attributes—concrete and abstract. Concrete attributes are easier to observe. Abstract attributes are much more difficult to describe or measure because it might not be clear exactly what behaviors are most important to be measured. For example, what is leadership? What are the specific behaviors that demonstrate leadership and how will we measure them? Obviously leadership is a vague and abstract concept. Because of this, it is much harder to collect validity evidence for such an abstract attribute.

11.

Correct Answer: b

Source: Page 189–190

Explanation: Both mathematics and achievement are well understood and are easier to define attributes. Therefore, they are concrete in nature. In contrast, personality is much more ambiguous and vague and therefore is best described as an abstract attribute.

12.

Correct Answer: a

Source: Page 205

Explanation: Face validity refers to whether test takers think that the test is measuring what it is supposed to be measuring. While face validity is often an important consideration when choosing a test, it is not a type of psychometric validity. There are many tests that may have significant evidence of validity for intended use, but do not appear face valid to the test takers.

13.

Correct Answer: c

Source: Page 186–187

Explanation: Evidence of validity based on test content requires that the test cover all major aspects of the testing universe (of the construct) in the correct proportion. Thus, if the test taker is performing representative samples of writing activities, then the test content does sample from the construct of writing.

14.

Correct Answer: d

Source: Page 187–188

Explanation: The textbook includes discussion of two specific types of evidence based on

relationships with other variables (criterion). The first is predictive evidence of validity, which refers to when test scores are significantly correlated with an important *future* outcome. The second type is concurrent evidence of validity, which examines if the test scores are related to a criterion that is collected *at the same time*. The key difference between the two is the time when the criterion information is collected.

15.

Correct Answer: b

Source: Page 193

Explanation: The first step in gathering evidence based on test content is to carefully define the body of knowledge or behaviors that a test represents, which is the testing universe. Defining the testing universe often involves reviewing other instruments that measure the same construct, interviewing experts who are familiar with the construct, and researching the construct by locating theoretical or empirical research on the construct. The purpose is to ensure that the test developer clearly understands and can clearly define the construct that he or she will be measuring. Evidence of validity based on test content requires that the test cover all major aspects of the testing universe (the construct(s) being measured) in the correct proportion.

16.

Correct Answer: c

Source: Page 202

Explanation: Content validity ratios are sometimes used to demonstrate content based evidence of validity and are based on a survey of subject matter experts. They can range from between –1.00 and 1.00, where a value of 0.00 means that that 50% of the experts believed a test item to be essential.

Short Answer

1. Prior to the 1999 *Standards for Educational and Psychological Testing* (AERA, APA, & NCME, 2014), experts talked about three types of validity: content validity, criterion-related validity, and construct validity. These three approaches to validity are similar in that they all focus on the appropriateness, meaningfulness, and usefulness of a test and the inferences being drawn from the test scores. They are all slightly different types of evidence, however. Content validity refers to the representativeness between the test and the domain it is intended to measure. Criterion-related evidence refers to the extent to which the scores on the test are related to one or more outcomes. Finally, construct validity indicates the degree to which the test measures the concept or characteristic it is designed to measure.

2. The 2014 *Standards* refers to five sources of validity evidence. The first type is *evidence based on test content*, which examines if the content of the test is representative of the concepts it is intended to measure. The second type is *evidence based on the response process*. This type of evidence involves observing test takers to ensure that the mental processes used to answer questions matches the expected processes required of the test. The third type is *evidence based on the internal structure* of the test. This type of evidence ensures psychometric structure of the test matches the intended structure. The fourth type is *evidence based on relationships with other variables* and determines if the test scores are related to other outcomes that we would expect them to be related to. The fifth and final type is *evidence based on the consequences of testing* and looks at both intended and unintended consequences of testing to ensure unbiased results.

3. The 1999 and 2014 *Standards* differed from previous standards in that the 1999 and 2014 *Standards* strongly supported a unitary view of test validity that characterized validity as the degree to which evidence supports the interpretations of test scores as entailed by the proposed uses of the test. In contrast, older versions of the *Standards* divided the validity into three types of validity: content, criterion, and construct validity.

4. Modern views of validity concern the meaning that is placed on test scores. Put another way, a test with evidence of validity is one in which the interpretation of test scores is consistent with the intended purpose. As a result, validity is a single or unitary concept; there are not different types of validity as inferred by older views of validity.

5. It is always sound practice to collect as much evidence of validity as required to support the assertions that are or will be based on test scores. This often means collecting a variety of types of evidence. Given that that the classical views of content, criterion-related, and construct validity closely align to three of the types of validity evidence that are discussed within the most recent *Standards*, it would be appropriate to collect this type of evidence in many situations when it is practical or feasible to do so.

Reference

American Educational Research Association, American Psychological Association, & National Council on Measurement in Education. (2014). Standards for educational and psychological testing. Washington, DC: American Psychological Association.

8

How Do We Gather Evidence of Validity Based on Test–Criterion Relationships?

Chapter Overview

In Chapter 8, we describe the processes psychologists use to ensure that tests perform properly when they are used for making predictions and decisions. We begin by discussing the concept of validity evidence based on a test's relationships to other variables, specifically external criteria. We also discuss the importance of selecting a valid criterion measure, how to evaluate validity coefficients, and the statistical processes such as linear and multiple regression that provide evidence that a test can be used for making predictions.

Learning Objectives

After completing your study of this chapter, you should be able to do the following:

- Identify evidence of validity of a test based on its relationships to external criteria, and describe two methods for obtaining this evidence.
- Read and interpret validity studies.
- Discuss how restriction of range occurs and its consequences.
- Describe the differences between evidence of validity based on test content and evidence based on relationships with external criteria.
- Describe the difference between reliability/precision and validity.

- Define and give examples of objective and subjective criteria, and explain why criteria must be reliable and valid.
- Interpret a validity coefficient, calculate the coefficient of determination, and conduct a test of significance for a validity coefficient.
- Explain the concept of regression, calculate and interpret a linear regression formula, and interpret a multiple regression formula.

Chapter Outline

Key Concepts

accessibility:	The degree to which a test allows test takers to demonstrate their standing on the construct the test was designed to measure without being disadvantaged by other individual characteristics such as age, race, gender, or native language.
b weight:	In regression, the slope of the regression line, or the expected change in the criterion (Y) for a one-unit change in the predictor (X).
coefficient of determination:	The amount of variance shared by two variables being correlated, such as a test and a criterion, obtained by squaring the validity coefficient.
coefficient of multiple determination:	A statistic that is obtained through multiple regression analysis, which is interpreted as the total proportion of variance in the criterion variable that is accounted for by all the predictors in the multiple regression equation. It is the square of the multiple correlation coefficient, R.

concurrent evidence of validity:	A method for establishing evidence of validity based on a test's relationships with other variables in which test administration and criterion measurement happen at roughly the same time.
criterion:	The measure of performance that we expect to correlate with test scores.
criterion contamination:	When the criterion in a validation study measures more dimensions than those measured by the test.
criterion-related validity:	Evidence that test scores correlate with or predict independent behaviors, attitudes, or events; the extent to which the scores on a test correlate with scores on a measure of performance or behavior.
intercept:	The place where the regression line crosses the y-axis.
linear regression:	The statistical process used to predict one set of test scores from one set of criterion scores.
multiple regression:	The process whereby more than one set of test scores is used to predict one set of criterion scores.
objective criterion:	A measurement that is observable and measurable, such as the number of accidents on the job.
peers:	An individual's colleagues or equals, such as other employees in a workplace or other students in a class or school.
predictive evidence of validity:	A method for establishing evidence of validity based on a test's relationships with other variables that shows a relationship between test scores obtained at one point in time and a criterion measured at a later point in time.
restriction of range:	The reduction in the range of scores that results when some people are dropped from a validity study, such as when low performers are not hired, causing the validity coefficient to be lower than it would be if all persons were included in the study.
slope:	The expected change in Y for every one-unit change in X on the regression line.
subjective criterion:	A measurement that is based on judgment, such as supervisor or peer ratings.
test of significance:	The process of determining what the probability is that a study would have yielded the observed results simply by chance.
universal design:	Development of a test in such a way that accessibility is maximized for all individuals for whom the test was designed.
validity coefficient:	The correlation coefficient obtained when test scores are correlated with a performance criterion representing the amount or strength of the evidence of validity for the test.

KEY CONCEPTS CROSSWORD

ACROSS

1. The correlation coefficient obtained when test scores are correlated with a performance criterion representing the amount or strength of the evidence of validity for the test.

3. A measurement that is based on judgment, such as supervisor or peer ratings.

5. The statistical process used to predict one set of test scores from one set of criterion scores.

9. A measurement that is observable and measurable, such as the number of accidents on the job.

13. The measure of performance that we expect to correlate with test scores.

16. An individual's colleagues or equals, such as other employees in a workplace or other students in a class or school.

17. The coefficient of _____ is the amount of variance shared by two variables being correlated, such as a test and a criterion, obtained by squaring the validity coefficient.

18. Evidence of validity based on a test's relationships with other variables that shows a relationship between test scores obtained at one point in time and a criterion measured at a later point in time.

20. The process whereby more than one set of test scores is used to predict one set of criterion scores.

DOWN

2. When the criterion in a validation study measures more dimensions than those measured by the test.

4. The coefficient of _____ is a statistic that is obtained through multiple regression analysis, which is interpreted as the total proportion of variance in the criterion variable that is accounted for by all the predictors in the multiple regression equation. It is the square of the multiple correlation coefficient, R.

6. Development of a test in such a way that accessibility is maximized for all individuals for whom the test was designed.

7. The reduction in the range of scores that results when some people are dropped from a validity study, such as when low performers are not hired, causing the validity coefficient to be lower than it would be if all persons were included in the study.

8. In regression, the slope of the regression line, or the expected change in the criterion (Y) for a one-unit change in the predictor (X).

10. Evidence of validity showing that test scores correlate with or predict independent behaviors, attitudes, or events; the extent to which the scores on a test correlate with scores on a measure of performance or behavior.

11. The place where the regression line crosses the y-axis.

12. The degree to which a test allows test takers to demonstrate their standing on the construct the test was designed to measure without being disadvantaged by other individual characteristics such as age, race, gender, or native language.

14. The process of determining what the probability is that a study would have yielded the observed results simply by chance.

15. Evidence of validity based on a test's relationships with other variables in which test administration and criterion measurement happen at roughly the same time.

19. The expected change in Y for every one-unit change in X on the regression line.

LEARNING ACTIVITIES BY LEARNING OBJECTIVE

The following are some study tips and learning activities you can engage in to support the learning objectives for this chapter.

Learning Objectives	Study Tips and Learning Activities
After completing your study of this chapter, you should be able to do the following:	The following study tips and learning activities will help you meet these learning objectives:
Identify evidence of validity of a test based on its relationships to external criteria (criterion-related evidence of validity), and describe two methods for obtaining this evidence.	• Make a chart of the similarities and differences between predictive and concurrent methods. • Be sure to include when the criterion is measured and its purpose.
Read and interpret validity studies.	• Select two different tests and find some studies that evaluate their validity. (One source of references for validity studies that you might use is the *Mental Measurement Yearbook.*) • Summarize the study and identify the type of evidence for validity that was used for each test.
Discuss how restriction of range occurs and its consequences.	• Review For Your Information Box 8.2, which describes a validation study that might have failed to find evidence of validity because of a flawed design. • Explain the reasons why restriction of range may have occurred in this study.
Describe the differences between evidence of validity based on test content and evidence based on relationships with other variables.	• Make a chart of the similarities and differences. • Be sure to include the method of validation and method of statistical analysis.
Describe the difference between reliability/precision and validity.	• List the differences between reliability/precision and validity.
Define and give examples of objective and subjective criteria, and explain why criteria must be reliable and valid.	• Study Table 8.1, which includes a number of criteria used in educational, clinical, and organizational settings. • See whether you can add other examples of objective and subjective criteria to the list. • Check your additions with a classmate or your instructor.
Interpret a validity coefficient, calculate the coefficient of determination, and conduct a test of significance for a validity coefficient.	• The correlation coefficient between academic self-efficacy and class grades presented in For Your Information Box 8.5 is .67. Determine whether this validity coefficient is statistically significant at $p < .05$ and at $p < .01$ for a sample size of 10. • Interpret your results. • Calculate the coefficient of determination and interpret the result. • Confirm your calculations and interpretations with your professor.
Explain the concept of regression, calculate and interpret a linear regression formula, and interpret a multiple regression formula.	• Use your calculator to work through the example of making a prediction with linear regression in For Your Information Box 8.5. • Calculate the predicted class grade for someone who scored 53 on the academic self-efficacy test. • Write a short essay that explains the difference between linear regression and multiple regression.

EXERCISES

1. Interpreting Validity Studies. Read the summarized published criterion-related validation studies below. For each summary, identify the following elements:

   (1) Predictor(s)

   (2) Criterion

   (3) Evidence of validity examined

   (4) Validity coefficient and its strength

   (5) Type of reliability/precision

   (6) Reliability coefficient (where given)

   a. College Students' Recent Life Experiences. Researchers administered to 216 undergraduate students (in the same time period) the Inventory of College Students' Experiences and a measure of daily hassles. The total coefficient alpha was .92 for the inventory and .96 for the measure of daily hassles. The inventory correlated with the measure of daily hassles at .76 ($p < .001$). (Adapted from Osman, Barrios, Longnecker, & Osman, 1994.)

   b. The Pilot Personality. Test scores for the Eysenck Personality Inventory and Cattell's 16 Personality Factor Questionnaire were obtained for male army applicants for flyer training. Forms A and B were used for each test, and the correlations between forms for the same test ranged from .39 to .85. Some of the men entered flying school several years after taking the tests. The correlations of the subscales on the two tests with training outcome (pass or fail) averaged approximately .20. (Adapted from Bartram, 1995.)

   c. Computer Aptitude and Computer Anxiety. Researchers gave 162 students enrolled in computer courses a test that measured computer anxiety and another test that measured computer aptitude. Both tests were given at the begining of the course. Student performance in the course was measured by the grades the students earned in the course. Computer aptitude correlated with course grade at .41 ($p < .01$) for one course and at .13 (ns; note that ns stands for "not significant") for the other course. Correlations of computer anxiety and course grade were .01 and .16 (ns). (Adapted from Szajna, 1994.)

2. Objective and Subjective Criteria. A number of criteria are listed in the table below. Decide what type of criterion each is, and mark either "Objective" or "Subjective" in the Type column. Discuss what you think the advantages and disadvantages may be with using each of the criteria.

Criterion	Type
Ratings of training success	
Letters of reference	
Completion of a work sample (pass/fail)	
Ratings based on a work sample	
Annual salary	
Number of alcoholic drinks	
Self-ratings of drug use	
Course grade	
Number of weeks in therapy	
Therapist's estimate of weekly progress	

3. Interpreting Statistics. The following table contains symbols that stand for statistics used in validation studies. Identify each, and explain when to use it and what it means.

Statistic	When to use	What it means
R		
r^2		
R^2		
Y'		
b		
X		
p		
df		

4. A Case for Incremental Validity. Return to the description of the study by Chibnall and Detrick (2003) described in the section on multiple regression. After re-reading the information about this study and reviewing Table 8.2, answer the following questions:

(1) What are the predictors and criteria for this study?

(2) What did the predictors have in common?

(3) What are the strengths and weaknesses of this study?

(4) Would you feel comfortable using the predictors in this study to select men and women for admission to a police academy? Why or why not?

5. Testing the Significance of Validity Coefficients. The table below contains validity coefficients and sample sizes. Complete the table below, identifying the degrees of freedom (*df*), the critical *r*, if the validity coefficient is significant at the .05 level, and coefficient of determination. Which coefficient in the table provides the best evidence of validity? Test the coefficients using a two-tailed test with p < .05. If the degrees of freedom are not listed in the table, use the next lowest degrees of freedom listed.

Validity Coefficient	Size of Sample	df	Critical r From Appendix E	Significant at p < .05?	Coefficient of Determination
.23	40				
.43	10				
.33	50				
.22	1,000				
.50	6				

6. Calculating a Validity Coefficient. Imagine the simulated data in the table below were collected when an organization tested 10 job candidates before they were hired and then evaluated them using supervisor ratings after they had worked for six months. Calculate the validity coefficient for these data. What kind of evidence of validity does it represent? Now suppose that the company had not hired those who scored 60 or below on the employment test. What would the validity coefficient be for the six employees only? Can you explain why the validity coefficient changed?

Candidate	Employment Test	Supervisor Rating (1–5)
Abel	80	2
Bartmann	98	3
Cardoza	95	5
Dixon	55	3

Candidate	Employment Test	Supervisor Rating (1–5)
Everett	70	2
Friedman	75	4
Grass	50	2
Hart	55	1
Isaacs	90	2
Jensen	60	1

ADDITIONAL LEARNING ACTIVITIES

Activity 8-1 Did You Ever Build a Model Plane That Flew?

Background

"Did you ever build a model airplane that flew?" This single question was an excellent predictor of success in flight school in World War II. In fact, this item alone predicted success as well as the entire Air Force Battery (Casio & Aguinis, 2011). Items like this are called *biodata* and are often used in organizational settings. In fact, a common application bank could be considered a form of biodata because it collects information about the applicant's personal history. Biodata is based on the idea of behavioral consistency. For example, if a person had built a model plane that flew this would likely suggest an interest in planes, an understanding of aerodynamics, and so on. Those applicants who built planes that flew would have a better basic understanding entering flight school and would probably show more interest during flight school, which would lead to greater success.

The term *biodata* is a broad term, and therefore there are a lot of variations and an exact definition is difficult. However, Meal (1991) described 10 dimensions of biodata items. One of them is job relevance. Interestingly, biodata items do not always need to be directly related to the job. Below are three questions that vary along this dimension. Suppose that these questions were used as part of a selection system for salespeople.

Job relevant: How many units of cereal did you sell during the last calendar year?

Less job relevant: Are you proficient at crossword puzzles?

Less job relevant: How many books have you read in the last month?

The first question is clearly directly related to a sales job. The other two questions are less relevant, and unless the job is a crossword puzzle maker or book reviewer, they do not seem very job relevant. However, just because they are not directly related to the job does not always mean they will be bad predictors of job success.

Job relevancy is important for items used for employee selection in an organizational setting, but biodata items are developed based on their relationship to an external criterion and not on their connection to job content. Although there are many ways to develop biodata items, one traditional approach is to construct a large number of items that might predict job performance. These items are then administered to a sample of individuals for whom you can obtain job performance data. Using statistical analyses, the questions with the strongest observed correlations to the job performance criterion would be kept and the other items discarded. This approach is sometimes called *dustbowl empiricism* because it lacks any underlying theoretical foundation. However, the developed items can show evidence of validity based on their relationship with an external criterion and therefore be good predictors of job success. Unfortunately, because of the way in which the items are developed, they may lack face validity, and this can result in negative applicant reactions. On the positive side, research has shown that biodata has little adverse impact on minority groups. Thus, like any selection method, biodata has strengths and weakness that employers need to consider before using it as part of an employee selection system.

Questions

1. Create a 10-item biodata measure to be used for police officers.

2. Describe how you could conduct a study to collect validation evidence for your items developed in Question 1.

3. How would you react if you were required to complete a biodata questionnaire when applying for a job and the items did not appear to be related to the job?

Activity 8-2 Criterion Deficiency and Criterion Contamination

Background

When gathering evidence of validity based on test–criterion relationships, inexperienced test developers tend to only focus on the test and pay less attention to the criterion measure. This can be a costly mistake because a criterion-based approach to test validation examines the correlation between the test *and* the criterion. Poorly developed criteria can cause just as many problems as poorly developed tests. Criterion measures are so important that Wayne Casio and Herman Aguinis, two prominent industrial and organizational psychologists, in their book *Applied Psychology in Human Resource Management*, devote an entire chapter solely to criteria.

When working in an applied setting, it is important for the test developer to keep in mind that the organization is not a laboratory and that there are many real-world constraints to criterion development and selection. However, this is not an excuse for using poor criteria. A balance must always be achieved between practicality and rigor. One concern that the test developer will face is criterion deficiency. Criterion deficiency focuses on whether the criteria adequately cover the entire domain of interest. For example, in applied settings it is common to use a measure of job performance as a criterion. Job performance can mean many different things and it can be difficult or impractical to capture all of its components. In addition, for some jobs, accurately measuring job performance can be a challenging task that sometimes includes vague and ambiguous measures.

Another concern when developing criteria is criteria contamination. This occurs when the criterion measure includes variance that is not related to the construct one is interested in measuring. This can be thought of as construct validity of the criterion. For instance, if the dollar amount of sales is the criteria by which you wish to judge sales reps' performance, it is important that most of the variance in the dollar volume of sales is accounted for purely by the skill set of the sales reps. If the territory they work in or particular products that they are responsible for selling also contribute to differences in the dollar amount of sales, the criterion would be considered to be contaminated. When this occurs, the correlation between a test of sales ability and the criterion of dollar volume of sales would be reduced due to the contamination of the criterion.

Questions

1. Suppose you are developing a promotion test for police officers and wish to collect evidence of validity based on the relationship between the test and some criteria. Identify and describe several dimensions of performance that could be part of your criterion measure.

2. What are some practical constraints that you might face when trying to collect the performance information identified in Question 1?

3. Identify possible sources of contamination that may interfere with the accurate measurement of your criterion.

PRACTICE TEST QUESTIONS

The following are some practice questions to assess your understanding of the material presented in this chapter.

Multiple Choice

1. When a test is used to predict future performance, there must be evidence of validity

   a. based on test takers' perceptions.

   b. based on test relationship with a criteria.

   c. using the predictive method.

   d. using the concurrent method.

2. Sarah conducted a study in which she correlated students' scores on the SAT taken in high school with students' grade point averages at the end of the first year of college. Her study was designed to find evidence of what type of validity?

   a. Validity based on test content

   b. Validity using the concurrent method

   c. Validity based on test takers' perceptions

   d. Validity using the predictive method

3. In the study at Brigham Young University, researchers correlated scores on the PREParation for Marriage Questionnaire with measures of marital satisfaction and marital stability. In this study, what were the measures of marital satisfaction and marital stability?

   a. Predictors

   b. Tests

   c. Criteria

   d. Coefficients

4. One problem with studies of validity using the concurrent method is that there may be

   a. no evidence of validity based on test content.

   b. no criterion measure.

   c. restriction of range.

   d. low reliability.

5. Both the predictive method and the concurrent method are ways to establish evidence of what?

   a. Validity based on test-criteria relationships

   b. Validity based on test content

   c. Validity based on the perceptions of the test takers

   d. Both validity and reliability

6. What is a major difference between the predictive method and the concurrent method?

   a. The place where the criterion is measured

   b. The people for whom the criterion is measured

   c. The time when the criterion is measured

   d. The format in which the criterion is measured

7. _____ is a characteristic of the test itself; _____ depends on how the test is used.

   a. Reliability; validity

   b. Validity; reliability

   c. Face validity; content validity

   d. Content validity; face validity

8. Sharon wanted to show evidence of validity for a test that was designed to predict reading readiness for kindergarten children. She chose as her criterion the overall score on a published standardized test of academic

performance that was administered to the children after they completed first grade. When she completed her study, she was dismayed that the validity was much lower than she expected. Which one of the following was most likely responsible for the low validity?

a. Reliability contamination

b. Validity contamination

c. Face validity contamination

d. Criterion contamination

9. When we ask, "What is the probability that our study would have yielded the validity coefficient we found by chance alone?" we are conducting a

a. validation study.

b. reliability study.

c. test of significance.

d. linear regression.

10. Which one of the following helps us interpret a validity coefficient by telling us how much variance the predictor and the criterion share?

a. Reliability coefficient

b. Test of significance

c. Content validity ratio

d. Coefficient of determination

11. The difference between linear regression and multiple regression is the number of

a. predictors.

b. criteria.

c. coefficients of determination.

d. participants.

12. What does the linear regression formula ($Y' = a + bX$) allow us to do?

a. Predict the value of the criterion measure associated with any test score

b. Calculate the predictive validity of a test

c. Provide evidence of validity based on test content

d. Estimate the accuracy of any test score

13. When using test scores for decision making, the test user is ethically and morally responsible for ascertaining that the test shows acceptable evidence of what?

a. Predictive and concurrent evidence of validity

b. Face validity and test taker acceptance

c. Reliability and validity

d. Reliability and face validity

14. Who has the responsibility for preventing test misuse by making test manuals and validity information available before purchase?

a. Test users

b. Test takers

c. Test publishers

d. Test developers

15. When assessing groups that include minorities, it is preferable for the test user to do what?

a. Use unstandardized tests to prevent bias due to test standardization

b. Adjust the scores of minority so majority and minority mean scores are the same

c. Use tests that have norms that include all the minority groups that are being tested

d. Alert minorities to the fact that their scores on the test may be difficult to interpret

16. Which one of the following is used to indicate the incremental validity of a predictor?

a. $R^2\Delta$

b. R^2

c. r

d. b

Short Answer

1. What is meant by evidence of validity based on test–criteria relationships? Describe two research methods for obtaining it.

2. What is the difference between evidence of validity based on test content and evidence of validity based on test–criteria relationships?

3. What are some challenges that organizations face when seeking to obtain predictive evidence of validity for a test?

4. Why is it important to evaluate the quality of the criterion when gathering evidence of validity of a test using the concurrent method?

5. What is the difference between reliability and validity? Give an example.

6. Discuss the difference between objective criteria and subjective criteria. Give examples of each.

7. Why do we conduct tests of significance and calculate the coefficient of determination?

8. What is the relation between correlation and linear regression? How does the process of linear regression help us make predictions?

9. Discuss ethical issues that arise when assessing test takers with diverse cultures, primary languages, races, and/or religions.

10. Describe how multiple regression can be used to determine incremental validity for two predictors.

ANSWER KEYS

Crossword

ACROSS

1. VALIDITY COEFFICIENT—The correlation coefficient obtained when test scores are correlated with a performance criterion representing the amount or strength of the evidence of validity for the test.
3. SUBJECTIVE CRITERION—A measurement that is based on judgment, such as supervisor or peer ratings.
5. LINEAR REGRESSION—The statistical process used to predict one set of test scores from one set of criterion scores.
9. OBJECTIVE CRITERION—A measurement that is observable and measurable, such as the number of accidents on the job.
13. CRITERION—The measure of performance that we expect to correlate with test scores.
16. PEERS—An individual's colleagues or equals, such as other employees in a workplace or other students in a class or school.
17. DETERMINATION—The coefficient of _____ is the amount of variance shared by two variables being correlated, such as a test and a criterion, obtained by squaring the validity coefficient.
18. PREDICTIVE—Evidence of validity based on a test's relationships with other variables that shows a relationship between test scores obtained at one point in time and a criterion measured at a later point in time.
20. MULTIPLE REGRESSION—The process whereby more than one set of test scores is used to predict one set of criterion scores.

DOWN

2. CRITERION CONTAMINATION—When the criterion in a validation study measures more dimensions than those measured by the test.
4. MULTIPLE DETERMINATION—The coefficient of _____ is a statistic that is obtained through multiple regression analysis, which is interpreted as the total proportion of variance in the criterion variable that is accounted for by all the predictors in the multiple regression equation. It is the square of the multiple correlation coefficient, R.
6. UNIVERSAL DESIGN—Development of a test in such a way that accessibility is maximized for all individuals for whom the test was designed.
7. RESTRICTION OF RANGE—The reduction in the range of scores that results when some people are dropped from a validity study, such as when low performers are not hired, causing the validity coefficient to be lower than it would be if all persons were included in the study.
8. b WEIGHT—In regression, the slope of the regression line, or the expected change in the criterion (Y) for a one-unit change in the predictor (X).
10. CRITERION-RELATED—Evidence of validity showing that test scores correlate with or predict independent behaviors, attitudes, or events; the extent to which the scores on a test correlate with scores on a measure of performance or behavior.
11. INTERCEPT—The place where the regression line crosses the y-axis.
12. ACCESSIBILTY—The degree to which a test allows test takers to demonstrate their

standing on the construct the test was designed to measure without being disadvantaged by other individual characteristics such as age, race, gender, or native language.

14. TEST OF SIGNIFICANCE—The process of determining what the probability is that a study would have yielded the observed results simply by chance.

15. CONCURRENT—Evidence of validity based on a test's relationships with other variables in which test administration and criterion measurement happen at roughly the same time.

19. SLOPE—The expected change in Y for every one-unit change in X on the regression line.

Exercises

1. Interpreting Validity Studies

Exercise	(1) Predictor	(2) Criterion	(3) Evidence of Validity Examined	(4) Validity Coefficient	(5) Type of Reliability	(6) Reliability Coefficient
a	Inventory of college students' experiences	Measure of daily hassles	Concurrent	Strong .76 ($p < .001$)	Internal consistency, coefficient alpha	Inventory = .92; daily hassles = .96
b	Eysenck Personality Inventory and 16 Personality Factor Questionnaire	Training outcome (pass/fail)	Predictive	Very weak; average of coefficients approximately .20	Test–retest	Ranges between .39 and .85
c	Computer anxiety and computer aptitude tests	Course grades	Predictive	Computer aptitude = .41 ($p < .01$; moderate) and .13 (ns); Computer anxiety = .01 and .16 (ns)	Not given	Not given

2. Objective and Subjective Criteria

Criterion	Type
Ratings of training success	Subjective
Letters of reference	Subjective
Completion of a work sample (pass/fail)	Objective

Ratings based on a work sample	Subjective
Annual salary	Objective
Number of alcoholic drinks	Objective
Self-ratings of drug use	Subjective
Course grade	Subjective
Number of weeks in therapy	Objective
Therapist's estimate of weekly progress	Subjective

3. Interpreting Statistics

R	Multiple regression coefficient
r^2	Coefficient of determination for linear relationship
R^2	Coefficient of determination for multiple regression coefficient
Y'	The number on the y-axis that a linear regression coefficient predicts
b	b weight for multiple regression equation
X	Raw score
p	Probability
df	Degrees of freedom

4. A Case for Incremental Validity

The predictors in the Chibnall and Detrick (2003) study were the Minnesota Multiphasic Personality Inventory-2, the Inwald Personality Inventory, and the Revised NEO Personality Inventory, and the criterion was the academic performance of police officers. The information in the tables describes the prediction of the first criterion, namely, academic performance.

The predictors are well-known personality tests. From the data in Table 8.2, we can tell that the predictors share variance among themselves and with the predictor. We know this because the contributions of the predictors vary depending on how they are arranged in the multiple regression equation.

The study's strength is that the researchers used well-known predictors with evidence of validity. The study's weaknesses are that the sample contained only 79 participants and that the study, as reported in this textbook, does not provide information on reliability and evidence of validity of the criteria.

However, we would be comfortable using the predictors in this study to select men and women for a police academy in the area in which the study was conducted. The study suggests that the three predictors and demographic variables account for 55% of variance of the predictors and the criterion—assuming the criterion scores are reliable.

5. Testing the Significance of Validity Coefficients

The best evidence of validity is when the coefficient is statistically significant and also accounts for a substantial amount of shared variance. In this case, $r = .33$ for a sample of 52 provides the best evidence of validity.

Validity	Size of Sample	df	Critical r From Appendix E	Significant at p < .05?	Coefficient of Determination
.23	37	35	.3246	No	.0529
.43	10	8	.6319	No	.1849
.33	52	50	.2732	Yes	.1089
.22	1,000	998	.1946	Yes	.0484
.50	6	4	.8114	No	.2500

6. Calculating a Validity Coefficient

Test Taker	X	Y	d_x	d_x^2	d_y	d_y^2	$(d_x)(d_y)$
Abel	80	2	7.2	51.84	−0.5	0.25	−3.6
Bartmann	98	3	25.2	635.04	0.5	0.25	12.6
Cardoza	95	5	22.2	492.84	2.5	6.25	55.5
Dixon	55	3	−17.8	316.84	0.5	0.25	−8.9
Everett	70	2	−2.8	7.84	−0.5	0.25	1.4
Friedman	75	4	2.2	4.84	1.5	2.25	3.3
Grass	50	2	−22.8	519.84	−0.5	0.25	11.4
Hart	55	1	−17.8	316.84	−1.5	2.25	26.7
Isaacs	90	2	17.2	295.84	−0.5	0.25	−8.6
Jensen	60	1	−12.8	163.84	−1.5	2.25	19.2
Sum	728	25		2805.60		14.50	109.0
Mean	72.8	2.5					
Standard deviation (calculated using the formula presented in Chapter 5)	16.75	1.20					
r		.54					

This represents predictive evidence of validity.

Test Taker	X	Y	d_x	d_x^2	d_y	d_y^2	$(d_x)(d_y)$
Abel	80	2	−4.67	21.78	−1.00	1.00	4.67
Bartmann	98	3	13.33	177.78	0.00	0.00	0.00
Cardoza	95	5	10.33	106.78	2.00	4.00	20.67
Everett	70	2	−14.67	215.11	−1.00	1.00	14.67

Test Taker	X	Y	d_x	d_x^2	d_y	d_y^2	$(d_x)(d_y)$
Friedman	75	4	−9.67	93.44	1.00	1.00	−9.67
Isaacs	90	2	5.33	28.44	−1.00	1.00	−5.33
Sum	508	18		643.33		8	25
Mean	84.67	3.00					
Standard deviation (calculated using the formula presented in Chapter 5)	10.35	1.15					
r		.35					

The validity coefficient changed because of restriction of range.

Multiple Choice

1.

Correct Answer: c

Source: Page 211

Explanation: When it is important to show a relationship between test scores and a future behavior, researchers use the predictive method to establish evidence of validity. This method requires that a group of people take the test (the predictor), and their scores are held for a predetermined time period, such as six months. Later researchers collect information on the criterion. If the test scores and the criterion scores are significantly correlated then the test has demonstrated predictive evidence of validity.

2.

Correct Answer: d

Source: Page 211

Explanation: Because Sarah collected test scores (SAT) at one point in time and then at a later point in time collected data on her criterion (first year college grade point average), she used the predictive method. This approach requires a lag time between testing and collection of the criterion measure.

3.

Correct Answer: c

Source: Page 211–212

Explanation: Marital satisfaction and marital stability were measures that were external to the test and were expected to be related to test scores. Therefore, they are criteria. We would use the word criterion if there was a single measure. For example, marital satisfaction is a criterion and marital stability is a criterion, but when we talk about both of them together they are criteria, which is plural.

4.

Correct Answer: c

Source: Page 213–214

Explanation: The concurrent method requires that you collect information on the criterion at the same time as the test scores. Often only those who scored well on the test will be hired, admitted, and so on, and will be the only ones on which the criterion measure can be collected. Given that those selected are expected to be the best performers, the lower end of performance on the criterion is likely to be cut off. Thus, there is likely to be range restriction, which can lower the validity coefficient.

5.

Correct Answer: a

Source: Page 211

Explanation: The textbook describes two methods that can be used to establish evidence of validity based on test–criteria relationships. The first method is the predictive method, which collects criteria data after the test was given (e.g., six months later). The second method is the concurrent method, which collects information on the criteria at approximately the same time as the test is given.

6.

Correct Answer: c

Source: Page 211 & 214

Explanation: The difference between the predictive method and the concurrent method is the time when the criterion is measured. Otherwise they are the same and both are used to establish evidence validity based on the relationship between a test and a criterion.

7.

Correct Answer: a

Source: Page 216–217

Explanation: Reliability refers to the consistency of test results and concerns itself only with the test. Therefore, reliability of the test is a characteristic of the test. In contrast, validity is related to the inferences the test used makes based on test results. Therefore, it is a concerned with how the test is used and not just with the characteristics of the test.

8.

Correct Answer: d

Source: Page 219

Explanation: If the criterion measures more dimensions than those measured by the test, we say that criterion contamination is present. In the question the test measures reading readiness, but the criterion measured the broader construct of academic performance.

9.

Correct Answer: c

Source: Page 220–221

Explanation: Tests of statistical significance evaluate if the relationship between the test and the criterion could have happened simply by chance or sampling error. The statistical test will determine the probability that the relationship is significantly different from zero.

10.

Correct Answer: d

Source: Page 222

Explanation: The coefficient of determination is obtained by squaring the validity coefficient and is often called r^2. It indicates the amount of variance that is shared by the variables. For example, if the correlation between two variables is .50 then .50 x .50 = .25. This means that 25% of the variance is shared between the two variables, and 75% of each variable's variance is unique and not shared with the other variable. This is important because greater amounts of shared variance indicates stronger relationships. A perfect correlation of 1.00 or −1.00 indicates the variables share 100% of their variance and a correlation of 0.00 means the variables are completely unrelated and share 0% of their variance.

11.

Correct Answer: a

Source: Page 227

Explanation: Linear and multiple regression are essentially the same statistical technique. The difference is that multiple regression is more general in the sense that it allows for more than one predictor variable.

12.

Correct Answer: a

Source: Page 223–224

Explanation: In the formula for linear regression Y' is the score on the criterion and X is the score on the test. Therefore, formula allows us to predict the value on the criterion based on any test score.

13.

Correct Answer: c

Source: Page 233–234

Explanation: Decisions based on tests can have far-reaching consequences and therefore test users must make sure that the test is both reliable and valid which is key to ensuring that decisions are fair and unbiased. In contrast, face validity is only the appearance that the test measures what it is supposed to and does not have anything to do with the test's accuracy. Face validity does, however, lead to test taker acceptance. In addition, predictive and concurrent studies are specific types of validity evidence but answer option "a" does not include the key feature of reliability.

14.

Correct Answer: c

Source: Page 234

Explanation: Test publishers are ethically responsible for ensuring that tests are not misused. One way to contribute to this goal is to provide test manuals that contain information about the test's reliability and validity, test users qualifications, administration instructions, norming information, and so on.

15.

Correct Answer: c

Source: Page 233

Explanation: The misapplication of norms can be a serious problem. For example, different groups may interpret test items differently. For example, the original MMPI norms were developed using a largely White rural Midwestern population. When the obtained norms were applied to a more diverse population of individuals, questionable decisions were being made based on the test scores. Therefore, the MMPI was updated and norms created that were more representative of the general population of test takers.

16.

Correct Answer: a

Source: Page 229

Explanation: In linear regression the symbol R^2 is the coefficient of multiple determination showing the amount of shared variance between all the predictors and the criterion. When there is only one predictor in the regression equation, R^2 is the validity for that one predictor. Incremental validity is the increase in validity (R^2) when a second predictor is added to the regression model. Because the symbol Δ is used in statistics to indicate change, when the two symbols are combined the result is $R^2\Delta$ indicating the change in validity or the incremental validity of the second predictor over and above that of the first predictor.

Short Answer

1. Validity evidence based on test–criteria relationships has traditionally been referred to as *criterion-related validity*. This type of validity evidence is obtained by examining the relationship between the test scores and some outcome that is external to the test. For example, test developers may examine the relationship between SAT scores and later college academic performance. If individuals with higher test scores tend to have higher academic performance, then that is an indication of validity. There are two approaches to collecting criterion-related validity evidence. The first is the predictive method. This method requires that the test developer obtain test scores and then at a later point in time collect the criterion measure. The example of using SAT scores to

predict later academic performance is an example of the predictive method. The concurrent method is the second way to collect the data. Using this approach, the test developer collects both the test scores and the criterion measure at the same time. For example, to show evidence of validity the test developer might give an employment test to current employees and correlate the test scores with their performance appraisal data collected at the same time.

2. Evidence of validity based on test content is concerned with demonstrating that the items in the test are representative of the content domain that is being tested. In contrast, evidence of validity based on test–criteria relationships only concerns itself with whether the test predicts external criteria and does not look at the content of the test.

3. Collecting the criterion measure using a predictive method can be difficult for organizations. This is because when the predictive method is used, there is a time period between test administration and the collection of the criterion measure. For example, an organization could give a test to a large group of potential hires, put them through a training program, and then examine their success in the training program. The problem with this approach is that few organizations would like to go through the time and expense of training people who are unlikely to be successful. Therefore, an organization is likely to only train people who score high on the test. As a result, this will likely decrease the amount of variance in the criterion measure by removing people who would likely have been less successful in the training. Statistically, this is called *criterion range restriction* and usually results in a lower validity coefficient.

4. Selection of an appropriate criterion is an important consideration when using the concurrent method for collecting evidence of validity. A common concern is criterion contamination, which occurs when the criterion measures things that are not related to the test. For example, total sales could be used as a criterion when performing a concurrent study for sales ability. However, total sales is affected by many other factors than sales ability. In some circumstances sales region may play a bigger role in total sales than sales ability.

5. Reliability/precision and validity are related concepts and are both important to ensure that test scores are fair, unbiased, and useful. Reliability/precision refers to the consistency of measurement. In contrast, validity refers to the appropriateness and accuracy of the inferences test users make based on test scores. The two concepts are related. Consider a target where all of the shots are left of the bull's-eye. The shots are consistent (reliability), but are not accurate (validity). Now consider a target where all of the shots are centered right on the bull's-eye. Now all of the shots are consistent (reliability) and accurate (validity). Hence reliability/precision is a necessary, but not sufficient condition for validity.

6. There are two types of criteria. The first is objective criteria, which are observable. Examples are number of sick days or total sales. The second type is subjective criteria, which are based on a person's judgment. For example, a peer rating of leadership skills or a teacher's rating of a student's sociability would be subjective criteria.

7. Because tests scores are used to make important decisions, it is essential to know if the obtained relationship between test score and criterion is statistically significant. While tests of significance are judged in a yes or no manner, they also provide information on the probability that the validity coefficient is greater than zero. In contrast, the coefficient of determination lets the test developer know the strength of the relationship between the test and the criterion. It is calculated

by squaring the correlation coefficient between the test and the criterion (r), which is then interpreted as the degree of shared variance between the two. The greater the amount of shared variance the stronger the relationship and the more useful the test is in predicting the criterion.

8. Correlation and regression are similar in that both indicate the degree of relationship between variables and use the same statistical model. The difference is that linear regression can be used to predict the criterion score based on test score whereas correlation does not allow this direct prediction.

9. Ethical issues are a major concern in the validation of tests because test scores are often the basis for important high-stakes decisions. Test developers should make sure that the test treats all individuals fairly without bias regardless of the culture, language, race, or religion. As a result, the 2014 *Standards* have embraced a concept called universal design, which states that tests should be constructed from the outset to ensure accessibility allowing all test takers to demonstrate their standing on the intended construct without being disadvantages by individual characteristics, such as age, race, gender, or native language. The goal is to ensure that only the construct that the test is supposed to measure affects tests scores and no other factor, such as race, ethnicity, age, disability, and so on, plays a role.

10. Researchers use multiple regression when they want to predict a criteria using more than one predictor variable. First the researchers run a regression analysis using only one of the variables and they examine the resulting R^2 to determine the validity for that variable. Next, they run a second regression analysis using both predictors and examine the R^2 once again. The difference between the two indicates the validity of the second predictor over and above the first predictor variable and is referred to as incremental validity. The usefulness of this procedure is that it will allow the researcher to make a decision about whether adding a second predictor will significantly contribute to the prediction of the criteria.

References

Bartram, D. (1995). The predictive validity of the EPI and 16PF for military flying training. *Journal of Occupational and Organizational Psychology, 68*(3), 219–236. doi:10.1111/j.2044-8325.1995.tb00583.x

Casio, W. F., & Aguinis, H. (2011). *Applied psychology in human resource management* (7th Ed.). Boston: Prentice Hall.

Chibnall, J. T., & Detrick, P. (2003). The NEO PI-R, Inwald Personality Inventory, and MMPI-2 in the prediction of police academy performance: A case for incremental validity. *American Journal of Criminal Justice, 27*(2), 233–248. doi:10.1007/bf02885696

Meal, M. A. (1991). A conceptual rationale for the domain and attribute of biodata items. *Personnel Psychology, 44*, 763–792. Retrieved from http://onlinelibrary.wiley.com/journal/10.1111/%28ISSN%291744-6570

Osman, A., Barrios, F. X., Longnecker, J., & Osman, J. R. (1994). Validation of the inventory of college students' recent life experiences in an American college sample. *Journal of clinical psychology, 50*(6), 856–863. doi:10.1002/1097-4679(199411)50:6<856::aid-jclp2270500607>3.0.co;2-c

Szajna, B. (1994). An investigation of the predictive validity of computer anxiety and computer aptitude. *Educational and Psychological Measurement, 54*(4), 926–934. doi:10.1177/0013164494054004008

9

How Do We Gather Evidence of Validity Based on a Test's Relation to Constructs?

Chapter Overview

In Chapter 9, we define and illustrate the terms *psychological construct*, *theory*, and *nomological network*. Because establishing evidence of construct validity involves accumulating and relating all of the psychometric information known about a test, we show how familiar concepts—such as reliability/precision, evidence of validity based on test content, and evidence of validity based on a test's relationships with other variables—are linked together. In addition, we discuss how convergent evidence of validity and discriminant evidence of validity are two other factors used for establishing validity based on a test's relationships with other variables. Finally, we describe experimental methods used to establish evidence of construct validity for a test, including two procedures: exploratory factor analysis and confirmatory factor analysis.

Learning Objectives

After completing your study of this chapter, you should be able to do the following:

- Discuss the concept of a construct, and give examples of theoretical constructs.
- Explain how the current *Standards for Educational and Psychological Testing* (American Educational Research Association [AERA], American Psychological Association [APA], & National Council on Measurement in Education [NCME], 2014) treatment of constructs in testing differs from the more traditional usage of the term *construct validity*.

- Explain and give examples of the three steps of construct explication.
- Explain the process of establishing evidence of validity based on a test's relationship with other constructs.
- Explain how Campbell and Fiske's (1959) multitrait–multimethod matrix provides evidence of validity based on a test's relationship with other constructs.
- Discuss the roles of exploratory and confirmatory factor analysis in establishing validity.

Chapter Outline

The Traditional Notion of Construct Validity
   What Is a Construct?
   Construct Explication
Gathering Evidence of Construct Validity
   Gathering Theoretical Evidence
   Gathering Psychometric Evidence
Factor Analysis
   Exploratory Factor Analysis
   Confirmatory Factor Analysis
   Putting It All Together
Chapter Summary

Key Concepts

behavior:	An observable and measurable action.
confirmatory factor analysis:	A procedure in which researchers, using factor analysis, consider the theory associated with a test and propose a set of underlying factors that they expect the test to contain; they then conduct a factor analysis to see whether the factors they proposed do indeed exist.
construct:	An attribute, trait, or characteristic that is abstracted from observable behaviors.
construct explication:	Three steps for defining or explaining a psychological construct.
construct validity:	An accumulation of evidence that a test is based on sound psychological theory and therefore measures what it is supposed to measure; evidence that a test relates to other tests and behaviors as predicted by a theory.
convergent evidence of validity:	One of two strategies for demonstrating construct validity showing that constructs that theoretically should be related are indeed related; evidence that the scores on a test correlate strongly with scores on other tests that measure the same construct.
discriminant evidence of validity:	One of two strategies for demonstrating construct validity showing that constructs that theoretically should be related are indeed related; evidence that test scores are not correlated with unrelated constructs.

exploratory factor analysis:	A method of factor analysis in which researchers do not propose a formal hypothesis but instead use the procedure to broadly identify underlying components.
factor analysis:	An advanced statistical procedure based on the concept of correlation that helps investigators identify the underlying constructs or factors being measured.
factors:	The underlying commonalities of tests or test questions that measure a construct.
hypotheses:	Educated guesses or predictions based on a theory.
multitrait–multimethod correlation matrix:	A type of correlation matrix used in studies of construct validity that presents all the correlations between a group of different traits, attributes, or constructs, each measured by two or more different measurement methods or tests.
multitrait–multimethod (MTMM) design:	A design for test validation that gathers evidence of reliability, convergent evidence of validity, and discriminant evidence of validity into one study.
nomological network:	A method for defining a construct by illustrating its relation to as many other constructs and behaviors as possible.
state:	A psychological attribute that is temporary.
trait:	A psychological attribute that is an enduring characteristic of a person's personality.

KEY CONCEPTS CROSSWORD

ACROSS

2. A method for defining a construct by illustrating its relation to as many other constructs and behaviors as possible.
5. The underlying commonalities of tests or test questions that measure a construct.
7. Three steps for defining or explaining a psychological construct.
9. An observable and measurable action.
11. Type of factor analysis in which researchers consider the theory associated with a test and propose a set of underlying factors that they expect the test to contain; they then conduct a factor analysis to see whether the factors they proposed do indeed exist.
13. A type of correlation matrix used in studies of construct validity that presents all the correlations between a group of different traits, attributes, or constructs, each measured by two or more different measurement methods or tests.
14. Type of validity evidence showing that test scores are not correlated with unrelated constructs.

DOWN

1. Type of validity evidence showing that constructs that theoretically should be related are indeed related; evidence that the scores on a test correlate strongly with scores on other tests that measure the same construct.
3. Educated guesses or predictions based on a theory.
4. A psychological attribute that is temporary.
6. An advanced statistical procedure based on the concept of correlation that helps investigators identify the underlying constructs or factors being measured.
8. A psychological attribute that is an enduring characteristic of a person's personality.
10. Abbreviation for a type of design for test validation that gathers evidence of reliability, convergent evidence of validity, and discriminant evidence of validity into one study.
11. An attribute, trait, or characteristic that is abstracted from observable behaviors.
12. Type of factor analysis in which researchers do not propose a formal hypothesis but instead use the procedure to broadly identify underlying components.

LEARNING ACTIVITIES BY LEARNING OBJECTIVE

The following are some study tips and learning activities you can engage in to support the learning objectives for this chapter.

Learning Objectives	Study Tips and Learning Activities
After completing your study of this chapter, you should be able to do the following:	The following study tips will help you meet these learning objectives:

Discuss the concept of a construct, and give examples of theoretical constructs.	• Define each of the following constructs and propose some observable behavioral measures for each.
	
	  ○ Artistic talent
	  ○ Intelligence
	  ○ Cooking ability
	
	• Compare your answers with those of your classmates.

Explain and give examples of the three steps of construct explication.	• Using ProQuest or a similar database, find a construct validity study and compare it with the study by Sherer and colleagues (1982). Make a list describing the similarities and differences between the two studies.
Explain the process of establishing evidence of validity based on a test's relationship with other constructs.	• Write a short essay of the steps you would take to establish evidence of construct validity for a test of self-esteem. • What types of evidence for validity that you have learned about might you be able to use to help make the case that the test had construct validity?
Explain how Campbell and Fiske's (1959) multitrait–multimethod matrix provides evidence of validity based on a test's relationships with other constructs.	• Make a list of each type of evidence provided by a multitrait–multimethod matrix, and describe how to locate it in the matrix. • Discuss how each type of correlations in an MTMM matrix provides different information for the evidence for construct validity.
Discuss the roles of exploratory and confirmatory factor analysis in establishing construct validity.	• Compare the purposes of exploratory and confirmatory factor analyses and how they can be used in test development and validation. • Describe in writing their similarities and differences.

EXERCISES

1. Below are six constructs. Define and propose an observable behavioral measure for each construct. Identify which are theoretical constructs.

Construct	Definition and Measurement	Theoretical Construct? (Yes or No)
1. Self-confidence		
2. Decisiveness		
3. Beauty		
4. Aggressiveness		
5. Conscientiousness		
6. Temperature		

2. Defining Various Types of Evidence of Validity. In Section II of the textbook, you learned about the different types of evidence of validity listed below in Column II. Find the definition in Column III that matches each type of evidence. Place your answer in Column I.

I	II	III
	Discriminant evidence of validity	A. The test provides a representative sample of the behaviors in the testing universe.
	Face validity	B. The test scores are related to independent behaviors, attitudes, or events.
	Evidence of validity based on test content	C. Questions on the test appear to the test taker to measure what the test is supposed to measure.
	Evidence of validity based on relationships with external criteria	D. The test demonstrates a relationship between a test and a future behavior or outcome.
	Convergent evidence of validity	E. Test scores are correlated with measures of constructs that are theoretically related to the test's construct.
	Predictive evidence of validity	F. The test is highly correlated with itself.
	Concurrent evidence of validity	G. The test is related to behaviors or events in the present.
	Reliability/Precision	H. The test is not correlated with measures of constructs with which the test has no theoretical relationship.

3. Validating a Measure of Self-Esteem. A psychology professor at Northwest Random College gave his Tests and Measurements class the assignment below. After reading the assignment, answer the questions below.

   - **Assignment:** Design a validation study for a test that measures self-esteem in preadolescents. The test should contain 30 statements to which the test taker responds *true of me* or *not true of me*. In general, the statements should reflect test takers' feelings/perceptions about their academic and athletic skills, physical attractiveness, and relationships with friends and family. The elementary school across the street from the college has agreed to participate in an empirical study by administering the test to its students.

   a. What psychometric information would you need about a test to gather evidence of its validity?

   b. Would you need to administer measures other than the test you are validating? If so, what other measures would you like to administer?

   c. Can you gather all of the information you need in one administration? Explain why or why not.

   d. What statistical procedures would you use to analyze your data?

   e. Describe the specific types of judgments or decisions your study will allow you to make. What types of judgments or decisions will you not be able to make?

   f. Describe any follow-up studies your validation study will require.

4. Interpreting a Multitrait–Multimethod Design. Seligson and colleagues (2003) carried out a validation study of the Brief Multidimensional Students' Life Satisfaction Scale (BMSLSS). In addition to using data from students in Grades 6–8, the researchers conducted another study with 46 high school students from a different school. Table 9.1 below contains the multitrait–multimethod correlation matrix from the second study. Using the information provided in the table, answer the following questions:

   a. Which figures represent convergent evidence of validity? Which pair had the greatest convergent evidence? Which pair had the least?

Table 9.1 Multitrait–Multimethod Matrix for the Brief Multidimensional Students' Life Satisfaction Scale (BMSLSS) and the Multidimensional Students' Life Satisfaction Scale (MSLSS) for the Second Study

	MSLSS					BMSLSS				
	A1	B1	C1	D1	E1	A2	B2	C2	D2	E2
A1										
B1	0.26									
C1	0.36	0.36								
D1	0.62	0.56	0.46							
E1	0.64	0.55	0.54	0.70						
A2	**0.70**	0.34	0.31	0.56	0.66					
B2	0.32	**0.67**	0.31	0.50	0.57	0.52				
C2	0.23	0.26	**0.63**	0.35	0.37	0.28	0.33			
D2	0.47	0.33	0.31	**0.61**	0.42	0.55	0.25	0.40		
E2	0.40	0.44	0.17	0.46	**0.57**	0.35	0.61	0.12	0.20	

MTMM Matrix for High School Students

SOURCE: From Seligson, J. L., Huebner, S., & Valois, R. F. (2003). Preliminary validation of the Brief Multidimensional Students' Life Satisfaction Scale (BMSLSS). *Social Indicators Research, 61,* 121–145. Published by Springer Science and Business Media.

NOTE: A = family, B = friends, C = school, D = living environment, E = self. The numbers in bold are the validity coefficients. The heterotrait–monomethod correlations are underlined. The heterotrait–heteromethod correlations are in italics.

b. Which figures represent discriminant evidence of validity? How do the discriminant coefficients compare with the convergent coefficients?

c. Do these data indicate evidence of construct validity for the BMSLSS? Explain your answer.

ADDITIONAL LEARNING ACTIVITIES

Activity 9-1 Under and Over Construct Specification

Background

A construct is a key concept in psychology. Unlike height or weight, constructs cannot be seen, observed, or directly measured. Instead, constructs can only be inferred from observable behaviors.

The researcher literally "constructs" it (the construct) by the measurements he or she makes (Thorndike & Thorndike-Christ, 2010). Typically, a theoretical construct is diagramed as a circle, while the operationalized measurement of the construct is represented by a square. This is shown in Figure 9.1. In addition, an arrow represents the inference that the underlying construct (or trait) is influencing the measured responses. It would not make sense to have the arrow in the other direction, which would suggest that the measurements are influencing the underlying construct (or trait). All of this is shown in the figure below on the left.

The diagram on the left indicates that there is a single measurement for the construct. Rarely is this the case. Although an overall test score can be computed, tests are generally made up of many items. Researchers want to make this idea more explicit in their diagrams, so it is common to have many boxes for the measurement where each question has its own box. For example, the below right diagram shows that there are four questions that measure the construct.

How many squares or measurements it takes to fully describe a construct is difficult to determine. If there are too many squares or poorly designed questions, then the researcher has overspecified the construct, wasted time and money, and has probably included measurements that are not directly related to the intended theoretical construct. In the language of psychometrics, this overrepresentation is referred to *as construct–irrelevant variance.* This occurs when something unrelated to the construct affects the test scores. For instance, a test measuring knowledge of the history of the U.S. Civil War may be written at a very high reading level, but reading is not the construct of interest. Instead, the intended construct is knowledge of the U.S. Civil War. As a result, individuals with a higher reading level will have higher scores, and individuals with a lower reading level will have lower scores regardless of their knowledge of the U.S. Civil War. Another example of construct irrelevant variance occurs when researchers use raters to collect measurements. Humans are known to have many cognitive biases, and these biases can come into play when making ratings. Consider a job setting where a supervisor rates employees more highly because they are White middle-aged males who attended a

Figure 9.1   Theoretical and Operationalized Psychological Constructs

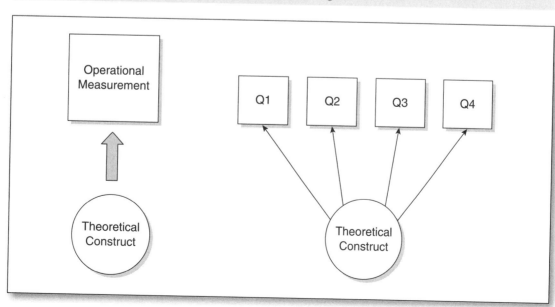

Big 10 university. If the rater is a White middle-aged male who attended a Big 10 university, then this is mostly likely the result of the "similar to me" bias and has absolutely nothing to do with employees' job performance. Although the bias is irrelevant to job performance, it does affect the ratings.

One the other hand, the operationalized squares may underrepresent the construct and there may not be enough of them to fully describe the circle. Consider job performance, which is a broad multidimensional construct. It would be difficult to include every behavior or outcome that may make up job performance. Therefore, researchers try to select a representative sample of "squares" that are the most important in the particular setting and that can be realistically measured given the practical constraints. Sometimes, unfortunately, important behaviors and outcomes are missed and, as a result, the construct is not fully covered by the measurements.

Questions

1. List and describe as many dimensions of performance that represent the construct of job performance for a retail sales clerk.

2. Is it feasible or desirable to measure all of the dimensions that you identified in Question 1?

3. What would be the implication for the construct validity of your measurement of job performance if you only had the resources to measure two dimensions?

Activity 9-2 Culture and Constructs

Background

One concern that test developers and researchers have with construct validity is the degree to which construct-related validity evidence collected in one culture carries over to another culture. Just because there is evidence of validity for a measure created in the United States does not mean that there is corresponding evidence in Mexico or China. There can be problems in translating test questions, and even when there are no translation issues, items can still be interpreted differently or mean different things in different cultures. For example, depression and anxiety are universal human conditions, but in the Cambodian Khmer language, there is no word for it. Instead, they say "thelea tdeuk ceut," which literally means "the water in my heart has fallen" (Singh, 2015). This makes collecting universal construct-related validity evidence difficult and can make diagnosis criteria and treatment even more difficult for those who are not familiar with the language and culture.

There are, however, some constructs that have been studied in great depth, and some have strong construct validity evidence across cultures. Schmitt, Allik, McCrae, and Benet-Martinez (2007) performed a large-scale study of 17,837 individuals from 56 nations and found construct-related validity evidence for the Big Five personality traits (openness, conscientiousness, extraversion, agreeableness, and neuroticism). More specifically, they found that the patterns of relationships among items in the measurement scale were consistent across nations and that the traits were consistently related to external criteria as expected. This does not mean that all nations had the same level of the traits. There are real cultural differences among these groups. For example, East Asian countries score much lower on openness to new experience than Latin American countries. This does not mean that the measurements are faulty or that there is a lack of construct validity. It is simply a reflection of those two cultures. Construct equivalence across cultures examines the relationships of items to ensure that they are the same across groups. If the patterns are the same, then the evidence supports the use of the measure with the different groups.

Questions

1. If one group scores lower than another on a test, is that an indication of lack of construct-related validity evidence? Explain why or why not.

2. The textbook describes a multitrait–multimethod design for investigating and collecting construct-related validity evidence. Describe how this method could be used to investigate the construct validity for a personality assessment across three cultures.

3. The textbook describes four different types of correlations that appear in a multitrait–multimethod matrix. Provide an example for each type of correlation from the investigation that you propose for Question 2.

PRACTICE TEST QUESTIONS

The following are some practice questions to assess your understanding of the material presented in this chapter.

Multiple Choice

1. Why have a number of theorists challenged the strategies of developing evidence of test validity based on content or relationships with other criteria?

   a. Theorists did not believe they got good results.

   b. Strategies were difficult to understand and implement.

   c. Strategies failed to link the testing instrument to a theory.

   d. Strategies were seldom used by test developers.

2. Serena investigated the relationship between influence and sales in her thesis. She collected data on several objective criteria, but she also wanted to use a subjective criterion. Which one of the following would be best for her to use?

   a. Gross monthly sales

   b. Supervisor rating of sales ability

   c. Annual net sales

   d. Number of sales calls

3. For his senior thesis, Mohammed identified the behaviors that relate to self-esteem. He then identified other constructs that may be related to self-esteem. And finally he identified behaviors related to similar constructs, such as self-efficacy, and determined whether these behaviors were related to self-esteem. In his thesis, Mohammed was carrying out the process of construct

   a. investigation.

   b. experimentation.

   c. remuneration.

   d. explication.

4. According to the example in your textbook, gravity is a(n)

   a. subjective criterion.

   b. objective criterion.

   c. theoretical construct.

   d. physical construct.

5. When Susan included a number of educated guesses or predictions in her thesis about aggression, what was she providing?

   a. Traits

   b. Constructs

   c. Factors

   d. Hypotheses

6. Self-efficacy is an example of a(n)

   a. subjective criterion.

   b. objective criterion.

   c. theoretical construct.

   d. physical construct.

7. Which one of the following does NOT provide evidence of construct validity?

   a. Reliability

   b. Convergent correlations

   c. Dragnet empiricism

   d. Evidence based on test content

8. The theory underlying psychological testing suggests that a test

   a. cannot have a stronger correlation with any other variable than it does with itself.

   b. cannot have a stronger correlation with itself than it does with an outside criterion.

   c. must have an equally strong correlation with a criterion as it does with itself.

   d. must have a stronger correlation with a criterion than it does with itself.

9. Which one of the following is NOT provided by the multitrait–multimethod design?

   a. Reliability or precision

   b. Predictive evidence of validity

   c. Convergent evidence of validity

   d. Discriminant evidence of validity

10. If test scores correlate with constructs that the underlying theory says are related, which one of the following types of evidence of validity is being demonstrated?

    a. Predictive

    b. Concurrent

    c. Discriminant

    d. Convergent

11. Hiroshi conducted a study where he delivered a training program designed to raise self-efficacy. He measured training participant self-efficacy before and after the training and found that self-efficacy increased after the training. Which one of the following methods was he using for establishing evidence of construct validity?

    a. Multitrait–multimethod design

    b. Experimental intervention

    c. Nomological network

    d. Construct explication

12. Sherer and colleagues (1982) administered their measure of self-efficacy and a measure of interpersonal competency to 376 students and found a moderate correlation between the two tests. What type of evidence of validity is indicated by the correlation?

    a. Predictive

    b. Face

    c. Convergent

    d. Content

13. John developed a math test for his thesis. He administered the math test with a test of reading ability and was happy when he found that the scores on the two tests were not correlated. What type of evidence of validity does the correlation that John found provide?

    a. Face

    b. Concurrent

    c. Discriminant

    d. Convergent

14. For his senior thesis, Ricardo proposed a set of underlying factors for the construct of altruism. He then administered a test of altruism and used an advanced statistical technique based on correlation to analyze these data. Which one of the following did Ricardo use?

    a. Confirmatory factor analysis

    b. Linear regression

    c. Multitrait–multimethod design

    d. Exploratory factor analysis

15. Yassi carried out a factor analysis in which she broadly looked for underlying theoretical structures in her construct. Which one of the following designs did Yassi use?

    a. Confirmatory factor analysis

    b. Linear regression

    c. Multitrait–multimethod design

    d. Exploratory factor analysis

Short Answer

1. What is construct validity? Is construct validity really a different "type" of validity? Why or why not?

2. What are the steps and activities involved in construct explication?

3. What information constitutes evidence of construct validity? Explain how each type of information provides evidence of construct validity.

4. Draw a diagram of a multitrait–multimethod matrix. Explain where information on reliability, convergent evidence of validity, and discriminant evidence of validity is found.

5. Explain the concepts of a confirmatory factor analysis and an exploratory factor analysis, including their purposes and how they differ.

ANSWER KEYS

Crossword

ACROSS

2. NOMOLOGICAL NETWORK—A method for defining a construct by illustrating its relation to as many other constructs and behaviors as possible.
5. FACTORS—The underlying commonalities of tests or test questions that measure a construct.
7. CONSTRUCT EXPLICATION—Three steps for defining or explaining a psychological construct.
9. BEHAVIOR—An observable and measurable action.
11. CONFIRMATORY—Type of factor analysis in which researchers consider the theory associated with a test and propose a set of underlying factors that they expect the test to contain; they then conduct a factor analysis to see whether the factors they proposed do indeed exist.
13. MULTITRAIT–MULTIMETHOD—A type of correlation matrix used in studies of construct validity that presents all the correlations between a group of different traits, attributes, or constructs, each measured by two or more different measurement methods or tests.
14. DISCRIMINANT—Type of validity evidence showing that test scores are not correlated with unrelated constructs.

DOWN

1. CONVERGENT—Type of validity evidence showing that constructs that theoretically should be related are indeed related; evidence that the scores on a test correlate strongly with scores on other tests that measure the same construct.
3. HYPOTHESES—Educated guesses or predictions based on a theory.
4. STATE—A psychological attribute that is temporary.
6. FACTOR ANALYSIS—An advanced statistical procedure based on the concept of correlation that helps investigators identify the underlying constructs or factors being measured.
8. TRAIT—A psychological attribute that is an enduring characteristic of a person's personality.
10. MTMM—Abbreviation for a type of design for test validation that gathers evidence of reliability, convergent evidence of validity, and discriminant evidence of validity into one study.
11. CONSTRUCT—An attribute, trait, or characteristic that is abstracted from observable behaviors.
12. EXPLORATORY—Type of factor analysis in which researchers do not propose a formal hypothesis but instead use the procedure to broadly identify underlying components.

Exercises

1.

Construct	Definition and Measurement	Theoretical Construct? (Yes or No)
1. Self-confidence	Definition: An individual's belief in their ability. Measurement: Self-ratings by individuals about their perception of their overall abilities.	Yes
2. Decisiveness	Definition: The ability to analyze information and reach conclusions in a timely manner. Measurement: Ratings made by assessors in assessment centers measure the ability to make decisions in a timely manner.	Yes
3. Beauty	Definition: A combination of qualities that is aesthetically pleasing. Measurement: Ratings of pleasing appearances of people in pictures.	Yes
4. Aggressiveness	Definition: The competitive drive to push forward, be assertive, and succeed. Measurement: Coaches' ratings of drive, desire, and competitiveness.	Yes
5. Conscientiousness	Definition: The tendency to be careful, prepared, and self-disciplined. Measurement: Self-report survey with items such as "I am always prepared" and "I am highly ordered."	Yes
6. Temperature	Definition: The intensity of heat. Measurement: Thermometers measure temperature mechanically on two scales: Fahrenheit and Celsius.	Yes

2. Defining Various Evidence of Validity

Evidence of validity based on test content	A. The test provides a representative sample of the behaviors in the testing universe.
Evidence of validity based on relationships with external criteria	B. The test scores are related to independent behaviors, attitudes, or events.
Face validity	C. Questions on the test appear to the test taker to measure what the test is supposed to measure.
Predictive evidence of validity	D. The test demonstrates a relationship between a test and a future behavior or outcome.
Convergent evidence of validity	E. Test scores are correlated with measures of constructs that are theoretically related to the test's construct.

Reliability/Precision	F. The test is highly correlated with itself.
Concurrent evidence of validity	G. The test is related to behaviors or events in the present.
Discriminant evidence of validity	H. The test is not correlated with measures of constructs with which the test has no theoretical relationship.

3. Validating a Measure of Self-Esteem

   a. Necessary information about the test would include its test–retest reliability and KR-20 for scales that represent the four situations that the questions cover. Convergent and discriminant correlations would provide evidence of construct validity. Evidence of validity based on relationships with criteria would not be appropriate because the professor did not ask for a criterion measurement. Evidence of validity based on content would require a list of all possible questions in the domain and a test plan.

   b. Convergent evidence and discriminant evidence of validity require administering tests that measure a similar construct and a different construct respectively.

   c. Except for evidence of test–retest reliability, all of the information can be gathered in one administration.

   d. The data can be analyzed using correlation. A multitrait–multimethod analysis would also be appropriate.

   e. The validation study can establish empirical evidence of construct validity; however, construct validity alone is not recommended for decision making.

4. Interpreting a Multitrait–Multimethod Design

   a. Convergent coefficients appear in bold. The highest is for Family (.70), and the lowest is for Self (.57).

   b. The discriminant coefficients appear in italics, and they are lower than the convergent coefficients.

   c. Yes, the data indicate evidence of construct validity for the BMSLSS because they demonstrate both convergent and discriminant evidence of validity.

Multiple Choice

1.

Correct Answer: c

Source: Page 238–239

Explanation: Using the content and criterion approach for evidence of validity neglected the construct a test was designed to measure. Psychologists, as a group, are very concerned about theory and constructs. Focusing attention on the theories of psychological behavior and linking this to the underlying construct refocuses attention on the basic ideas concerning measurement.

2.

Correct Answer: b

Source: Page 245

Explanation: Objective criteria can be easily seen and can generally be counted. Subjective criteria, on the other hand, are more abstract, are difficult to measure, and often rely on the judgment of people. Based on this "supervisor rating of sales ability" is the only subjective criteria listed.

3.

Correct Answer: d

Source: Page 241

Explanation: Construct explication is the process of relating a construct to a psychological theory and proposing a nomological network of the constructs and behaviors to which the construct is related. This process has three steps. First, identify behaviors that relate to the construct. Second, identify other constructs that may be related to the construct being explained. Third, identify behaviors related to similar constructs and determine whether these behaviors are related to the original construct.

4.

Correct Answer: c

Source: Page 239

Explanation: The textbook used the well-known example of gravity being a theoretical construct. Before Newton, the theory of gravity did not exist. Newton created the theory and then tested his theory by making observations, such as an apple falling to earth. The observations over time have supported this theory, and over time enough evidence has accumulated to strongly support the theory of gravity.

5.

Correct Answer: d

Source: Page 242

Explanation: Hypotheses are educated guesses or predictions about how variables may be related. For example, based on theory or previous empirical work, Susan may have good

reason to hypothesize specific patterns of relations between aggression and other constructs. She can then test this to provide validity evidence based on a test's relationship to other constructs.

6.

Correct Answer: c

Source: Page 239–241

Explanation: The textbook uses self-efficacy as an example of a theoretical construct. It cannot be directly measured. Instead, evidence can be obtained by measuring other observable behaviors.

7.

Correct Answer: c

Source: Page 244

Explanation: Dragnet empiricism is not an acceptable way to provide evidence of construct validity. Construct validity should be based on testable hypotheses within the nomological network. Dragnet empiricism, instead, simply involves collecting evidence based on convenience.

8.

Correct Answer: a

Source: Page 244

Explanation: A correlation ranges from -1.00 to 1.00, where 1.00 indicates a perfect positive correlation. When a variable is correlated with itself, the result is a correlation of 1.00. For all practical purposes, this can only occur when a variable is correlated with itself. Thus, when a test is correlated with any other variable, it will be less than 1.00 and necessarily less than its correlation with itself.

9.

Correct Answer: b

Source: Page 245

Explanation: The multitrait–multimethod design is used for investigating construct validity. Therefore, predictive evidence of validity, which is traditionally called *criterion-related validity*, is not provided by the method. The other three answer options are forms of evidence that can be provided by the multitrait–multimethod design.

10.

Correct Answer: d

Source: Page 249

Explanation: Convergent evidence of validity is a form of evidence that shows the test scores are correlated with scores from similar tests (measuring similar constructs). In contrast, when test scores do not correlate with test scores from unrelated constructs this is called discriminant evidence of validity.

11.

Correct Answer: b

Source: Page 248

Explanation: Experimental interventions in which the test is used as a dependent variable make a substantial contribution to the argument for evidence of construct validity. If the underlying theory predicts that a course of treatment or training will increase or decrease the psychological construct, a significant difference between pretest scores and posttest scores would be evidence of construct validity for the test.

12.

Correct Answer: c

Source: Page 249

Explanation: Convergent evidence of validity occurs when test scores measuring similar constructs are correlated. Thus in this case, with self-efficacy and interpersonal competency

being similar constructs, a correlation was expected and was found.

13.

Correct Answer: c

Source: Page 245

Explanation: John should be happy because one would not expect test scores for dissimilar constructs (such as reading and math ability) to be correlated. By finding that they were not related, he had obtained discriminant evidence of validity, which examines if constructs or measurements that are supposed to be unrelated are, in fact, unrelated.

14.

Correct Answer: a

Source: Page 251

Explanation: Confirmatory factor analysis is a statistical procedure where the researcher considers the theory associated with the test and proposes a set of underlying factors or relationships that he or she expects to see. The researcher then conducts a confirmatory factor analysis to determine if those relationships actually exist.

15.

Correct Answer: d

Source: Page 251

Explanation: Exploratory factor analysis is a statistical technique that does not propose a formal hypothesis, but instead uses the procedure to broadly identify underlying constructs. The key difference between the confirmatory and exploratory approaches to factor analysis is that with confirmatory, the researcher specifies the structure beforehand that he or she expects to see, and with exploratory, the researcher does not propose a structure.

Short Answer

1. The 2014 *Standards* do not use the traditional term of construct validity. The newest *Standards* view validity as a unitary concept that addresses the accuracy and appropriateness of

the inferences that are based on test scores. Therefore, construct validity cannot be a different "type" of validity. However, the more traditional view of construct validity sees it as the test's accuracy of measurement of the underlying theoretical construct the test was designed to measure.

2. Measurement of an abstract construct depends on our ability to observe and measure behavior that is related to the construct. There are three steps for accomplishing this, and the process is referred to *construct explication*. The steps and activities are (1) identify the behaviors that are related to the construct, (2) identify other constructs that may be related to the construct being explained, and (3) identify behaviors related to similar constructs, and determine whether these behaviors are related to the original construct.

3. There are two main approaches to gathering evidence of construct validity. They are gathering theoretical evidence and gathering psychometric evidence. The first step is to gather evidence based on theoretical grounds by reviewing as many studies as possible involving the construct and its relations with other observable and measureable behaviors. The next step is to gather quantitative or psychometric evidence. There are several methods to gather this type of evidence. Reliability is a necessary component of construct validity evidence; if the construct cannot be consistently measured, then it cannot be measured accurately. Convergent and discriminant validity evidence is another approach. Convergent evidence of validity occurs when measures of similar constructs are related. Discriminant evidence of validity occurs when measures of different types of constructs are unrelated. For example, you would expect reading scores from two different tests to be related, but you would not expect them to be related to scores on a math test. There is also the multitrait–multimethod design that collects reliability, convergent, and discriminant evidence at the same time. The underlying theory of a construct can be examined experimentally where the test is used as a dependent variable. Evidence based on content can also provide evidence of construct validity showing that the test content and construct domain overlap. Finally, construct validity evidence can be based on the test's relationship with external criteria that the test should be related to.

4. Refer to Figure 9.4 in your textbook to see the types of evidence that can be found in a multitrait–multimethod matrix. Reliability is found along the main diagonal in parentheses. For example, the reliability of A_1 (extraversion measured by a self-report) is .89. Convergent validity evidence is found along the diagonals between the broken line triangles. For example, construct A (extraversion) is measured by three methods and the convergent validity evidence between Method 1 (self-report) and Method 3 (objective-test) is .56. Evidence of discriminant validity is found in the dashed triangles. The values found in these triangles represent the measurement of different constructs by different methods. Thus, one would expect these values to be the lowest of the matrix and they provide the best evidence of discriminant validity.

5. Factor analysis is an advanced statistical procedure that looks at how items on a test interrelate and is based on their correlations with each other. Using this technique, test developers can examine the underlying concepts or constructs that a test measures. Confirmatory factor analysis is used to determine if a test actually aligns with the underlying hypothesized constructs that the test is supposed to measure. Using this technique, test developers would state what the hypothesized underlying factors and constructs are and statistically test these against the empirically observed relationships found in the test data. If the hypothesized structure aligns with the observed structure, then this is considered convergent evidence of validity. In contrast, exploratory factor analysis is just that—exploratory. The test developer does not specify any expected structure. Instead, he or she uses the technique to explore and uncover the underlying structure found in the observed test data.

References

Campbell, D. T., & Fiske, D. W. (1959). Convergent and discriminant validation by the multitrait-multimethod matrix. Psychological Bulletin, 56, 81–105.

Rogers, R. W. (1982). The Self-Efficacy Scale: Construction and validation. *Psychological Reports, 51,* 663–671.

Schmitt, D. P., Allik, J., McCrae, R. R., & Benet-Martinez, V. (2007). The geographic distribution of Big Five personality traits: Patterns and profiles of human self-description across 56 nations. *Journal of Cross-Cultural Psychology, 38*(2), 173–212. Retrieved from http://jcc.sagepub.com/

Sherer, M., Maddux, J. E., Mercandante, B., Prentice-Dunn, S., Jacobs, B., &

Thorndike, R. M., & Thorndike-Christ, T. (2010). *Measurement and evaluation in psychology and education.* Boston: Pearson.

Singh, M. (2015). Why Cambodians never get "depressed." Retrieved from http://www.npr.org/blogs/goatsandsoda/2015/02/02/382905977/why-cambodians-never-get-depressed

10

How Do We Construct and Administer Surveys and Use Survey Data?

Chapter Overview

In Chapter 10, we have included a dedicated discussion to surveys. We begin by defining what a survey is. We then discuss the popularity of surveys, including some of the most popular survey software. After reviewing a five-phase scientific approach to constructing, administering, and analyzing surveys, we discuss survey reliability and validity.

Learning Objectives

After completing your study of this chapter, you should be able to do the following:

- Describe the similarities and differences between a survey and a psychological test.
- Recognize some of the most popular survey software providers.
- Explain how the scientific method differs from other methods for acquiring information, and describe the five steps associated with the scientific method.
- Apply the five-phase scientific approach to constructing and administering surveys and analyzing their data.
- Describe survey reliability and validity and associated concepts.

Chapter Outline

What Are Surveys?
Survey Software
The Survey Research Method
The Scientific Method of Survey Design
  Preparing for the Survey
  Constructing the Survey
  Administering the Survey
  Coding, Entering, and Analyzing Survey Data
  Presenting the Findings
Survey Reliability/Precision and Validity
  Survey Reliability/Precision
  Survey Validity
Chapter Summary

Key Concepts

bivariate analyses:	Analyses that provide information on two variables or groups.
cluster sampling:	A type of sampling that involves selecting clusters of respondents and then selecting respondents from each cluster.
convenience sampling:	A type of sampling in which an available group of participants is used to represent the population.
database:	A matrix in the form of a spreadsheet that shows the responses given by each participant (row) for each question (column) in the survey.
decennial census survey:	A survey that is administered by the U.S. Census Bureau every 10 years, primarily to determine the population of the United States.
descriptive research techniques:	Techniques that help us describe a situation or phenomenon.
double-barreled question:	A question that is actually asking two or more questions in one.
experimental research techniques:	Research designs that provide evidence for cause and effect.
experts:	Individuals who are knowledgeable about a topic or who will be affected by the outcome of something.
face-to-face surveys:	Surveys in which an interviewer asks a series of questions in a respondent's home, a public place, or the researcher's office.
field test:	An administration of a survey or test to a large representative group of individuals to identify problems with administration, item interpretation, and so on.

focus group:	A method that involves bringing together people who are similar to the target respondents in order to discuss issues related to the survey.
homogeneity of the population:	How similar the people in a population are to one another.
individually administered surveys:	Surveys administered by a facilitator in person for respondents to complete in the presence of the facilitator.
item nonresponse rate:	How often an item or question was not answered.
literature reviews:	Systematic examinations of published and unpublished reports on a topic.
mail surveys:	Surveys that are mailed to respondents with instructions for completing and returning them.
measurement error:	Variations or inconsistencies in the measurements yielded by a test or survey.
multivariate analyses:	Analyses that provide information on three or more variables or groups.
nonprobability sampling:	A type of sampling in which not everyone has an equal chance of being selected from the population.
nonsampling measurement errors:	Errors associated with the design and administration of a survey.
operational definitions:	Specific behaviors that define or represent a construct.
personal interviews:	Surveys that involve direct contact with the respondents in person or by phone.
population:	All members of the target audience.
pretesting:	A method for identifying sources of nonsampling measurement errors and examining the effectiveness of revisions to a question(s) or to an entire survey or test.
probability sampling:	A type of sampling that uses a statistical procedure to ensure that a sample is representative of its population.
random error:	The unexplained difference between a test taker's true score and the obtained score; error that is nonsystematic and unpredictable, resulting from an unknown cause.
response rate:	The number of individuals who responded to a survey divided by the total number of individuals who received the survey.
sample:	A subset of a population used to represent the entire population.
sample size:	The number of people in a sample.
sampling error:	A statistic that reflects how much error can be attributed to the lack of representation of the target population due to the characteristics of the sample of respondents.
scientific method:	A process for generating a body of knowledge that involves testing ideas and beliefs according to a specific testing procedure that can be observed objectively.

self-administered surveys: Surveys that individuals complete themselves without the presence of an administrator.

simple random sampling: A type of sampling in which every member of a population has an equal chance of being chosen as a member of the sample.

stratified random sampling: A type of sampling in which a population is divided into subgroups or strata.

structured observations: Observations that are guided by forms or instructions that instruct an observer in collecting behavioral information, such as using a form to document the play behaviors of children on a playground.

structured record reviews: Forms that guide data collection from existing records, such as using a form to collect information from personnel files.

survey objectives: The purpose of a survey, including a definition of what it will measure.

survey research firms: Companies that specialize in the construction and administration of surveys and analysis of survey data for purposes such as marketing, political opinion assessment, and employee organizational satisfaction.

survey researchers: People who design and conduct surveys and analyze the results.

surveys: Instruments used for gathering information from a sample of the individuals of interest.

systematic sampling: A type of sampling in which every nth (for example, every fifth) person in a population is chosen as a member of the sample.

telephone surveys: Surveys in which an interviewer calls respondents and asks questions over the phone.

univariate analyses: The computation of statistics that summarize individual question responses.

KEY CONCEPTS CROSSWORD

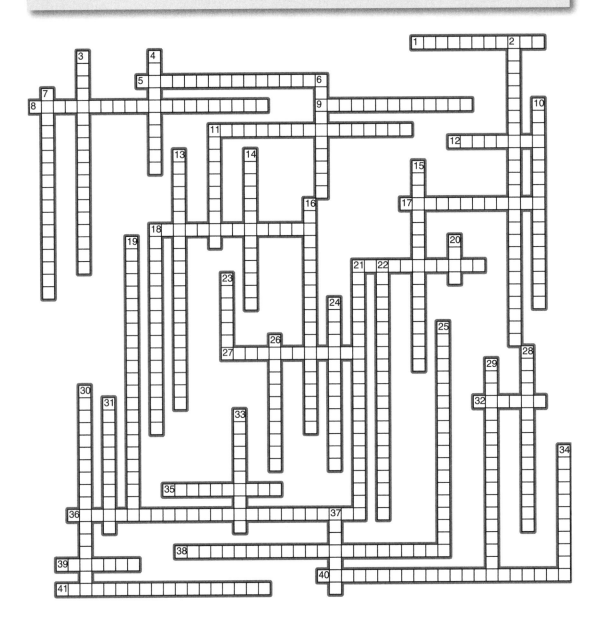

ACROSS

1. Type of sampling that uses a statistical procedure to ensure that a sample is representative of its population.
5. A survey the U.S. Census Bureau administers every 10 years, primarily to determine the population of the United States.
8. Techniques that help us describe a situation or phenomenon.
9. The number of individuals who responded to a survey divided by the total number of individuals who received the survey.
11. A process for generating a body of knowledge that involves testing ideas and beliefs according to a specific testing procedure that can be observed objectively.
12. A matrix in the form of a spreadsheet that shows the responses given by each participant (row) for each question (column) in the survey.
17. Surveys in which an interviewer asks a series of questions in a respondent's home, a public place, or the researcher's office.
18. A statistic that reflects how much error can be attributed to the lack of representation of the target population due to the characteristics of the sample of respondents.
21. The number of people in a sample.
27. The unexplained difference between a test taker's true score and the obtained score.
32. A subset of a population used to represent the entire population.
35. An administration of a survey or test to a large representative group of individuals to identify problems with administration, item interpretation, and so on.
36. Forms that guide data collection from existing records, such as using a form to collect information from personnel files.
38. Specific behaviors that define or represent a construct.
39. Instruments used for gathering information from a sample of the individuals of interest.

DOWN

2. Surveys administered by a facilitator in person for respondents to complete in the presence of the facilitator.
3. Systematic examinations of published and unpublished reports on a topic.
4. A method for identifying sources of non-sampling measurement errors and examining the effectiveness of revisions to a question(s) or to an entire survey or test.
6. Observations that are guided by forms or instructions that instruct an observer in collecting behavioral information, such as using a form to document the play behaviors of children on a playground.
7. Surveys that individuals complete themselves without the presence of an administrator.
10. Surveys in which an interviewer calls respondents and asks questions over the phone.
11. Type of sampling in which every nth (for example, every fifth) person in a population is chosen as a member of the sample.
13. Research techniques that provide evidence for cause and effect.
14. Type of sampling in which every member of a population has an equal chance of being chosen as a member of the sample.
15. Type of sampling in which a population is divided into subgroups or strata.
16. Surveys that involve direct contact with the respondents in person or by phone.
18. The purpose of a survey, including a definition of what it will measure.
19. Errors associated with the design and administration of a survey.
20. Surveys that are mailed to respondents with instructions for completing and returning them.
21. Companies that specialize in the construction and administration of surveys and analysis of survey data for purposes such as marketing, political opinion

40. How often an item or question was not answered.
41. People who design and conduct surveys and analyze the results.

assessment, and employee organizational satisfaction.

22. Analyses that provide information on three or more variables or groups.
23. Type of sampling that involves selecting clusters of respondents and then selecting respondents from each cluster.
24. A type of sampling in which not everyone has an equal chance of being selected from the population.
25. The computation of statistics that summarize individual question responses.
26. Refers to how similar the people in a population are to one another.
28. A question that is actually asking two or more questions in one.
29. Analyses that provide information on two variables or groups.
30. Variations or inconsistencies in the measurements yielded by a test or survey.
31. A method that involves bringing together people who are similar to the target respondents in order to discuss issues related to the survey.
33. All members of the target audience.
34. Type of sampling in which an available group of participants is used to represent the population.
37. Individuals who are knowledgeable about a topic or who will be affected by the outcome of something.

LEARNING ACTIVITIES BY LEARNING OBJECTIVE

The following are some study tips and learning activities you can engage in to support the learning objectives for this chapter.

Learning Objectives	*Study Tips and Learning Activities*
After completing your study of this chapter, you should be able to do the following:	The following study tips will help you meet these learning objectives:
Describe the similarities and differences between a survey and a psychological test.	• Imagine you were talking with a faculty member who had just developed an instrument to measure something. Write down the questions you would ask the faculty member to determine if the instrument was a survey or a test.
Recognize some of the most popular survey software providers.	• Conduct an Internet search looking for online survey software providers using different search phrases. Which survey providers do you see most often using the different search phrases? Create a table with five popular survey software providers. Include the similarities and differences in software capability.
Explain how the scientific method differs from other methods for acquiring information, and describe the five steps associated with the scientific method.	• Review Helmstadter's (1970) six methods for how we acquire information. Identify an example of how you have acquired knowledge using each method. • Think of the scientific method as a process. Write down the five steps associated with this process and the value of each step.
Apply the five-phase scientific approach to constructing and administering surveys and analyzing their data.	• Write down the five steps associated with the scientific method and the corresponding steps for designing surveys. Consider the implications of skipping or not carefully approaching each step. • Brainstorm a purpose statement for a survey. Operationalize your purpose statement. • Find an existing survey (e.g., your college's course evaluation survey, a hotel customer satisfaction survey, a survey used by a faculty member as part of his or her research). What are the survey's strengths? What are its weaknesses?
Describe survey reliability and validity and associated concepts.	• Think back to Chapters 6 through 9, in which we discussed the methods for obtaining evidence of reliability and validity. Consider how you would gather evidence of the reliability and validity of a survey. Give examples.

EXERCISES

1. Read the following anecdote from the beginning of Chapter 10 and document what is wrong with the two survey questions. How could you reword each survey question to make it better?

"I had to complete a course evaluation survey for my Research Methods class. One of the questions on my survey was 'Was the teacher available and responsive to your needs?' Another question was 'How much time did you spend studying for this class?' My teacher said that these were not very good survey questions. Why not?"

2. Read the following three examples. Identify the type of sampling used in each example:

- Your psychology professor constructs a survey to measure college students' attitudes toward the Greek community on your college campus. The professor gets a list of all students from the registrar's office. He divides the students into freshmen, sophomores, juniors, and seniors. He then divides them into males and females. He randomly samples students from each of these groups.
- Your sociology professor constructs a survey to measure females' attitudes toward all-male schools. The professor administers the survey to all of the students in her classes.
- The U.S. Census Bureau constructs a supplement to the decennial census. The decennial census is a census of all people in the United States. The Census Bureau takes all people who responded to the most recent decennial census and uses a computer to select 5,000 to take the supplemental survey.

ADDITIONAL LEARNING ACTIVITIES

Activity 10-1 Science and Pseudoscience

Background

Chapter 10 describes how the design of surveys should be based on the scientific method. Included is a discussion of the generally accepted steps of the scientific method:

1. Identify a problem and form a hypothesis.
2. Design a study to explore the problem and test the hypothesis.
3. Conduct the study.
4. Analyze the research data.
5. Communicate the research findings.

This approach of defining science as a process is consistent with well-known skeptic and promoter of scientific thinking Michael Shermer, founder of the Skeptics Society and Editor-In-Chief of the magazine *Skeptic*. Shermer (2011) stated, "We can demarcate science from pseudoscience less by what science is and more by what scientists do. Science is a set of methods aimed at testing hypotheses and building theories" (para. 7).

Sometimes a full understanding of a topic not only requires knowing what something is, but also knowing what it is not. Approaching a problem or a question from the opposite direction can be useful. Pseudoscience, which is an attempt to appear scientific even though it is not based on scientific method, is the flip side of science and has some particular characteristics that are useful to understand. Some of these characteristics are shown below (Pseudoscience, n.d.).

- Beliefs that are based on authority rather than evidence derived from observation and investigation. Beliefs can also be based on a single individual and personality.
- Pseudoscience makes claims that cannot be observed or tested and, as a consequence, are non-falsifiable.
- Claims are often vague and malleable.
- Claims often rely on myths and legends.
- Pseudoscience makes selective use of anecdotes or intuition and contradictory evidence is dismissed based on grounds other than reason and empirical evidence.
- Opposition is often suppressed.
- There is an over-reliance on confirmation rather than refutation.
- There is a lack of openness, which prohibits the claim being tested by others.

Questions

1. Describe how you would go about justifying the use of a survey that was not developed using the scientific method.

2. Contrast your justification created in Question 1 with a justification that is based on the scientific method.

Activity 10-2 Two Debates Concerning Likert Scales

Background

Since Rensis Likert published his work on survey scales in 1932, there have been two eternal debates. The first debate is the correct pronunciation of Likert. Fortunately, one of the study guide's authors had a professor who worked under Likert at the University of Michigan's Institute for Social Research and can put this debate to rest. Based on inside personal information, it is pronounced LICK-urt not LIKE-ert (a bit of Internet research will confirm this as well). Unfortunately, pronouncing it as Likert himself did will often bring funny looks and corrections from others, but at least you will have the quiet satisfaction of knowing how to pronounce the scale's namesake.

The second debate concerns the number of rating points to use. A Likert item is a statement that the respondent indicates his or her level of agreement using a symmetric bipolar scale. The most-used format is the five-point agree-disagree scale shown below.

1 = Strongly disagree

2 = Disagree

3 = Neither agree nor disagree

4 = Agree

5 = Strongly disagree

When there is an odd number of answer options, as above, there is a midpoint that corresponds to neutral or neither *agree* nor *disagree*. However, when an even number of options is used, there is no longer a midpoint, and respondents are forced to choose a side or position. For this reason, formats that are based on an even number of options are often referred to as *forced-choice*. The most common is the four-point format shown below.

1 = Strongly disagree

2 = Disagree

3 = Agree

4 = Strongly disagree

The use of the middle point gives people an out if they are unsure, but the midpoint could also mean different things to different people. A study by Sturgis, Roberts, and Smith (2014) illustrates this idea. They performed a study where they asked people who chose the middle neutral option an open-ended follow-up question to determine what their answer meant to them. Analyzing the responses, they found that the middle item could mean "I don't have sufficient information,"

"I have no interest," "It doesn't impact me," or "I don't know"—with "I don't know" being the most frequent answer. Thus, responses may mean different things to different people, and this can greatly impact the conclusions derived from survey data.

Not having a middle option may be quite reasonable for some types of questions based on Sturgis et al.'s (2014) research findings, but is this true for all types of questions? For example, in the Sturgis et al. study, one of the questions asked was, "How important or unimportant do you think it is for Britain to be at the forefront of developments in nanotechnology?" (the research was conducted in Great Britain). For this question, many individuals may simply choose the middle point, "neither important nor unimportant," as a convenient "out" rather than saying they do not know and appearing uninformed. In contrast, other questions, such as one asking about job satisfaction, are much less likely to result in the misuse of the middle point by respondents because it is unlikely that they would not know their own level satisfaction.

Questions

1. When you are asked a Likert-type item, do you prefer four- or five-point response options? Why?

2. Have you ever selected the midpoint on a survey question as a way "out" when you did not know or did not care to answer? If yes, what was your reasoning for doing so? How might your response have affected the accuracy of the reported results?

3. Write two questions where a four-point scale might be preferable over a five-point scale based on Sturgis et al.'s (2014) research.

PRACTICE TEST QUESTIONS

The following are some practice questions to assess your understanding of the material presented in this chapter.

Multiple Choice

Choose the one best answer to each question.

1. Psychological tests focus on _____ outcomes, and surveys focus on _____ outcomes.
   a. individual; group
   b. group; individual
   c. individual; individual
   d. group; group

2. The results of psychological tests are usually reported _____, and the results of surveys are often reported _____.
   a. as an overall score; as an overall score
   b. as an overall score; at the question level
   c. at the question level; as an overall score
   d. at the question level; at the question level

3. Surveys are research tools for collecting information to describe and compare which of the following?
   a. People's attitudes
   b. People's attitudes and knowledge
   c. People's attitudes, knowledge, and behaviors
   d. People's attitudes, knowledge, behaviors, and motives

4. If we asked parents to complete a survey to find out how they feel about their children wearing school uniforms, we would be asking them about their
   a. knowledge.
   b. attitude(s).
   c. behavior(s).
   d. motive(s).

5. If we come to believe that Friday the 13th is an unlucky day because of a superstition, we have acquired this knowledge through
   a. intuition.
   b. authority.
   c. tenacity.
   d. rationalism.

6. According to Helmstadter (1970), which one of the following methods of acquiring knowledge is the best for gathering accurate information?
   a. Intuition
   b. Tenacity
   c. Authority
   d. Scientific method

7. How many steps are associated with the scientific method?
   a. Three
   b. Five
   c. Seven
   d. Nine

8. Which one of the following statements is FALSE about surveys?
   a. Constructing surveys is as much a science as it is an art.
   b. In most cases, surveys are experimental research techniques.
   c. Surveys are used to collect important information from individuals.
   d. Surveys gather information about attitudes, knowledge, and behaviors.

9. When constructing a survey, the developer must have knowledge of all of the following EXCEPT

   a. different types of surveys.

   b. different types of survey questions

   c. selecting the appropriate respondents.

   d. how to assemble questions into a survey instrument.

10. Research suggests that when people answer survey questions they go through what stages?

    a. Comprehension, retrieval, and response communication

    b. Comprehension, retrieval, judgment, and response communication

    c. Comprehension, judgment, and response communication

    d. Comprehension, judgment, retrieval, and response communication

11. Which one of the following would you NOT recommend when assembling a survey?

    a. Using shading to prevent respondents from writing in specific sections.

    b. Integrating white space so that the survey looks inviting and is easy to complete.

    c. Printing on one side of the paper so respondents can use the other side for taking notes.

    d. Spiral binding surveys that are very long.

12. Nonsampling errors are errors associated with all of the following EXCEPT the

    a. choice of the individuals to be included in the survey.

    b. design and administration of the survey.

    c. quality of the survey questions.

    d. consistency of the way in which the survey administrators ask follow-up questions.

13. Which one of the following is NOT a purpose of pretesting a survey?

    a. Identifying sources of sampling measurement errors

    b. Examining the effectiveness of question revisions

    c. Indicating the effect of alternative versions of a question or survey

    d. Assessing the final version of a survey for ease of completion

14. Which one of the following is TRUE about simple random sampling?

    a. Every member of a population has an equal chance of being chosen.

    b. Every nth (for example, every fifth) person in a population is chosen.

    c. A population is divided into subgroups or strata.

    d. Clusters are selected and participants are selected from each cluster.

15. When should you use cluster sampling?

    a. When the population is very small

    b. When it is not feasible to list all individuals who belong to a population

    c. When it is impossible to select a random sample from the population

    d. When the population is very homogeneous

16. Which one of the following is FALSE about sample size?

    a. The sample size should be equal to or greater than 30% of the population size.

    b. The sample size can be calculated by knowing the confidence interval and level.

    c. The more dissimilar the members of the population, the larger the sample that is necessary.

    d. The smaller the sample size, the more error the survey results are likely to include.

17. Which one of the following would we NOT use to describe or summarize responses to an individual survey question?

a. Descriptive statistics

b. Frequency distributions

c. Univariate analyses

d. Bivariate analyses

18. Univariate analyses include all of the following EXCEPT

a. frequency counts.

b. percentages.

c. means, modes, and medians.

d. correlations.

19. Bivariate analyses include all of the following EXCEPT

a. correlation coefficients.

b. cross-tabulations.

c. chi-square comparisons.

d. percentages.

Short Answer

1. Describe the similarities and differences between surveys and psychological tests. Give examples.

2. Compare and contrast the methods for acquiring knowledge according to Helmstadter (1970). Give an example of each.

3. How does the scientific method differ from other methods of acquiring knowledge? What steps do we follow when using the scientific method? Describe each step in terms of survey research.

4. List four different types of survey questions. Give an example of each.

5. Explain the importance of reliability and validity when collecting data using surveys. Include definitions of reliability and validity as they apply to surveys.

6. Describe the characteristics that one may considered when selecting a survey software provider or product.

ANSWER KEYS

Crossword

ACROSS

1. PROBABILITY—Type of sampling that uses a statistical procedure to ensure that a sample is representative of its population.

5. DECENNIAL CENSUS—A survey the U.S. Census Bureau administers every 10 years, primarily to determine the population of the United States.

8. DESCRIPTIVE RESEARCH—Techniques that help us describe a situation or phenomenon.

9. RESPONSE RATE—The number of individuals who responded to a survey divided by the total number of individuals who received the survey.

11. SCIENTIFIC METHOD—A process for generating a body of knowledge that involves testing ideas and beliefs according to a specific testing procedure that can be observed objectively.

12. DATABASE—A matrix in the form of a spreadsheet that shows the responses given by each participant (row) for each question (column) in the survey.

17. FACE-TO-FACE—Surveys in which an interviewer asks a series of questions in a respondent's home, a public place, or the researcher's office.

18. SAMPLING ERROR—A statistic that reflects how much error can be attributed to the lack of representation of the target population due to the characteristics of the sample of respondents.

21. SAMPLE SIZE—The number of people in a sample.

27. RANDOM ERROR—The unexplained difference between a test taker's true score and the obtained score.

DOWN

2. INDIVIDUALLY ADMINISTERED—Surveys administered by a facilitator in person for respondents to complete in the presence of the facilitator.

3. LITERATURE REVIEWS—Systematic examinations of published and unpublished reports on a topic.

4. PRETESTING—A method for identifying sources of nonsampling measurement errors and examining the effectiveness of revisions to a question(s) or to an entire survey or test.

6. STRUCTURED—Observations that are guided by forms or instructions that instruct an observer in collecting behavioral information, such as using a form to document the play behaviors of children on a playground.

7. SELF-ADMINISTERED—Surveys that individuals complete themselves without the presence of an administrator.

10. TELEPHONE SURVEYS—Surveys in which an interviewer calls respondents and asks questions over the phone.

11. SYSTEMATIC—Type of sampling in which every *n*th (for example, every fifth) person in a population is chosen as a member of the sample.

13. EXPERIMENTAL RESEARCH—Research techniques that provide that provide evidence for cause and effect.

14. SIMPLE RANDOM—Type of sampling in which every member of a population has an equal chance of being chosen as a member of the sample.

15. STRATIFIED RANDOM—Type of sampling in which a population is divided into subgroups or strata.

16. PERSONAL INTERVIEWS—Surveys that involve direct contact with the respondents in person or by phone.

32. SAMPLE—A subset of a population used to represent the entire population.

35. FIELD TEST—An administration of a survey or test to a large representative group of individuals to identify problems with administration, item interpretation, and so on.

36. STRUCTURED RECORD REVIEWS—Forms that guide data collection from existing records, such as using a form to collect information from personnel files.

38. OPERATIONAL DEFINITIONS—Specific behaviors that define or represent a construct.

39. SURVEYS—Instruments used for gathering information from a sample of the individuals of interest.

40. ITEM NONRESPONSE RATE—How often an item or question was not answered.

41. SURVEY RESEARCHERS—People who design and conduct surveys and analyze the results.

18. SURVEY OBJECTIVES—The purpose of a survey, including a definition of what it will measure.

19. NONSAMPLING MEASUREMENT—Errors associated with the design and administration of a survey.

20. MAIL—Surveys that are mailed to respondents with instructions for completing and returning them.

21. SURVEY RESEARCH FIRMS—Companies that specialize in the construction and administration of surveys and analysis of survey data for purposes such as marketing, political opinion assessment, and employee organizational satisfaction.

22. MULTIVARIATE ANALYSES—Analyses that provide information on three or more variables or groups.

23. CLUSTER—Type of sampling that involves selecting clusters of respondents and then selecting respondents from each cluster.

24. NONPROBABILITY—A type of sampling in which not everyone has an equal chance of being selected from the population.

25. UNIVARIATE ANALYSES—The computation of statistics that summarize individual question responses.

26. HOMOGENEITY—Refers to how similar the people in a population are to one another.

28. DOUBLE-BARRELED—A question that is actually asking two or more questions in one.

29. BIVARIATE ANALYSES—Analyses that provide information on two variables or groups.

30. MEASUREMENT ERROR—Variations or inconsistencies in the measurements yielded by a test or survey.

31. FOCUS GROUP—A method that involves bringing together people who are similar to the target respondents in order to discuss issues related to the survey.

33. POPULATION—All members of the target audience.

34. CONVENIENCE—Type of sampling in which an available group of participants is used to represent the population.

37. EXPERTS—Individuals who are knowledgeable about a topic or who will be affected by the outcome of something.

Exercises

1. Both of these course evaluation questions have difficulties. The first question ("Was the teacher available and responsive to your needs?") is actually asking more than one question—what we refer to as a *double-barreled question*. If a survey respondent replied yes to this question, it would be impossible to tell whether the respondent was saying yes to the teacher being available, responsive, or to both. The same difficulty would exist if the survey respondent replied no to this question. It would have been more appropriate to break this question into two questions such as "Was the teacher available?" and "Was the teacher responsive to your needs?" Although at first glance the second question ("How much time did you spend studying for this class?") might seem like a clear and concise question, it does not clearly define the context or unit of analysis. Is the survey developer interested in how much time students spent studying per day, per week, or over the course of the entire semester? And is the survey developer interested in the number of hours or number of days? A better question would be "On average, how many hours did you spend per week studying for this class?"

2. Each of the three examples uses a different type of sampling. The first uses stratified random sampling, where a population is divided into subgroups (or strata) and a random sample is selected from each stratum. The second example uses convenience sampling, where any available group of participants is used to represent the population. The third example uses simple random sampling, where every member of a population has an equal chance of being chosen as a member of the sample.

Multiple Choice

1.

Correct Answer: a

Source: Page 268

Explanation: Both psychological tests and surveys are used to make important decisions and collect information about individuals. However, surveys are generally used at the group level while psychological tests are used at the individual level. For example, an organization may give a survey to employees to determine their level of job satisfaction. The organization typically does not examine individual responses, but examines the job satisfaction for groups of employees.

2.

Correct Answer: b

Source: Page 268

Explanation: The results of a psychological test are often reported in terms of an overall derived score or scaled scores. On the other hand, the results of surveys are often reported at the question level by providing the percentage of respondents who selected each answer alternative. The distinction between surveys and tests is not always clear, however.

3.

Correct Answer: c

Source: Page 269

Explanation: As the textbook describes, surveys allow us to collect information to describe and compare how people feel about things (attitudes), what they know (knowledge), and what they do (behaviors).

4.

Correct Answer: b

Source: Page 269

Explanation: The key word in the question stem is "feel." This word suggests that the survey is interested in measuring the parents' attitudes about school uniforms. It would be entirely possible, however, to construct a survey that measures their knowledge or behavior as well.

5.

Correct Answer: c

Source: Page 279–280

Explanation: Table 10.1 describes Helmstadter's six methods by which knowledge is obtained. Information acquired through tenacity is based on superstition or habit, leading people to continue believing something we have always believed. For example, people may come to believe that a certain brand is better than others simply because they have always used it.

6.

Correct Answer: d

Source: Page 279–280

Explanation: The scientific method often leads to the most accurate information because it is more systematic and objective than the other methods of acquiring information.

7.

Correct Answer: b

Source: Page 281

Explanation: While there may be some minor disagreement among researchers concerning the exact five steps of the scientific method, they are generally considered to be the following:

1. Identify the question and form a hypothesis

2. Design a study to test the hypothesis

3. Conduct the study

4. Analyze and interpret the data collected during the study

5. Communicate the results

8.

Correct Answer: b

Source: Page 281

Explanation: The correct answer, which is an incorrect statement about surveys, is that surveys are in most cases experimental research techniques. Experimental methods allow us to determine cause and effect and surveys generally do not allow us to do this. Instead surveys are primarily used in a descriptive manner.

9.

Correct Answer: c

Source: Page 284-299

Explanation: Selecting appropriate respondents is not part of constructing a survey. It is a part of the survey process though as appropriate respondents must be identified before the survey can be administered. All of the other answer options are important to know about when constructing a survey.

10.

Correct Answer: b

Source: Page 287

Explanation: Cognitive psychologists and survey researchers have studied how respondents answer survey questions. The research shows that it can be difficult and complex cognitive task. The research suggests that when people answer survey questions, they go through at least four stages:

Comprehension → Retrieval → Judgment → Response Communication

First respondents must comprehend or understand the question, which involves things like having the required vocabulary capabilities and the ability to attend to the entire question. Once they understand the question, they have to retrieve the appropriate information from their memory. After they retrieve the information, they need to determine or judge that the information meets the criteria of the question. Finally, respondents must correctly communicate their response.

11.

Correct Answer: c

Source: Page 293–296

Explanation: Surveys do not require respondents to take notes, so there is no need to print surveys on one side to allow for note taking. All of the other answers options are important considerations when preparing a survey instrument and are more fully described in the textbook section *Preparing the Survey Instrument*.

12.

Correct Answer: a

Source: Page 300–302

Explanation: Pretesting the survey will allow the developer to identify nonsampling measurement errors that may occur. These are errors that are associated with the design and administration of the survey and not the choice of the survey respondents. All of the choices except "a" are nonsampling errors.

13.

Correct Answer: a

Source: Page 297

Explanation: Sampling errors do not come into play when pretesting a survey. They occur when the test is actually administered and are a result of selecting an inappropriate sample, not selecting a large enough sample, or incorrect distribution of the survey.

14.

Correct Answer: a

Source: Page 300

Explanation: When a simple random sampling approach is used, every member of the population has an equal chance of being chosen as part of the sample. Because of this characteristic, it is often assumed that the sample will be representative of the population. However, this is not always the case, and there is always the chance that the sample will vary in key ways from the population.

15.

Correct Answer: b

Source: Page 301

Explanation: Cluster sampling is used when it is not possible to list all of the members who belong to a particular population. It is also often used when the target population is large and has relatively homogenous groups of individuals within the population. Each one of the homogenous groups becomes a cluster. Then clusters can be randomly sampled.

16.

Correct Answer: a

Source: Page 303

Explanation: There is no set percentage of the population that the sample should be. Instead, determining sample size is a complex science that considers many factors, such as desired level of confidence and the homogeneity of the respondent population.

17.

Correct Answer: d

Source: Page 307

Explanation: Descriptive statistics, frequency distributions, and univariate analyses all help us to describe or summarize the main characteristics of the data that are collected by survey questions. However, we use bivariate analyses to provide information on two variables or groups. For instance, a correlation coefficient is a bivariate statistic because it enables us to describe the relationship between two variables.

18.

Correct Answer: d

Source: Page 307

Explanation: Univariate analysis only examines one variable or question at a time. In contrast, a correlation requires two variables and examines the relationship between the two variables. Thus the correlation is considered a bivariate analysis.

19.

Correct Answer: d

Source: Page 307

Explanation: The first three answer options—correlation coefficients, cross-tabulations, and chi-square comparisons—require two variables and are therefore considered bivariate analyses. The only answer option that is not a bivariate analysis is "percentages," which only requires a single variable and is therefore considered a univariate analysis.

Short Answer

1. Surveys allow researchers to collect information so they can understand people and compare people's attitudes, knowledge, and behaviors. The words *survey* and *test* are often confused, but there are differences (and similarities) between the two. First the similarities. Both surveys and tests are used to collect data and make decisions. These decisions can be relatively low stakes and have little impact, or they can be high stakes that have important impact on the lives of individuals or groups of people. For example, a supervisor could survey her employees to determine if they would prefer pepperoni or cheese pizza at a work function, or a government could conduct a survey to determine the unemployment rate, which has broad economic and political impacts. Surveys and tests are different in that tests generally focus on individual outcomes and surveys focus on group outcomes. For example, tests are used to make a decision about a single person, such as whether a college admits a student. Surveys focus on groups, such as how satisfied the owners are with the performance of a certain type of car. Another difference is that surveys often report their results at the individual item level focusing on the percentage of respondents choosing each answer option. Tests, on the other hand, tend to focus on an overall all score.

2. Helmstadter in 1970 identified six methods people use to obtain knowledge. They are tenacity, intuition, authority, rationalism, empiricism, and scientific method. The first three place few demands on information processing and are easy to perform. The last three require more effort.

Below is a brief description of each with an example.

1. Tenacity—Knowledge is accepted because we have accepted it for so long. For example, we use a certain type of toilet paper because we have used it for so long, so it must be the best. And conversely because it is the best we have used it for so long.

2. Intuition—Knowledge is accepted based on a gut feeling or because it appears self-evident, thus there is no process of assessment. For example, the earth appears to us to be flat so we assume it is flat.

3. Authority—Knowledge is accepted based on the status of the source. For example, we believe that the earth is the center of the universe because religious authorities say it is at the center.

4. Rationalism—Knowledge is gained by reaching a conclusion through logical analysis. Logical syllogisms are an example: All men are mortal, Socrates is a man, therefore, Socrates is mortal.

5. Empiricism—Knowledge is gained by reaching a conclusion based on observation and gathering of data. For example, we take a specific type of pill and our headache goes away. Therefore, it must have been the pill that made the headache go away.

6. Scientific method—Knowledge is gained by reaching a conclusion based on a systematic and objective process. Generally, the process involves stating a hypothesis, planning a study, conducting the study and collecting data, analyzing the data, and communicating the findings. An example of the scientific method is the process that is used by most articles published in peer-reviewed psychological journals on measurement and testing.

3. The scientific method tends to be more systematic and objective than the other methods. All attempts are explicitly made to remove personal beliefs, perceptions, biases, values, attitudes, and emotions. Generally, the process involves stating a hypothesis, planning a study, conducting the study and collecting data, analyzing the data, and communicating the findings. Each step is further elaborated below.

1. *Identify a problem and state a hypothesis.* In terms of survey research, this requires the researcher to conduct a literature review, gather people who are knowledgeable about the survey topic, and conduct focus groups.

2. *Design a study to test the hypothesis.* At this step, the survey researcher should know about different types of surveys and questions; should know how to write questions, how to assemble the survey, and how to pretest surveys; and should be able to devise a data analysis plan.

3. *Conduct the study.* Here the survey researcher should understand how to sample respondents and be able to handle all the logistics of survey administration.

4. *Analyze the data.* At this step, the researcher should know how to enter and code data and be able to conduct appropriate statistical analyses.

5. *Communicate the research findings.* For the final stage, the researcher should be able to write reports, prepare presentation materials, and present the results to groups of people.

4. There are many different types of survey questions. Below are some of the most popular types that were described in the textbook.

- Open-ended
- Closed-ended
- Yes/no questions
- Fill in the blank
- Implied no choice
- Single-item choice

- Enfolded
- Free choice
- Multiple choice
- Ranking
- Rating
- Guttman format
- Likert and other intensity scale formats
- Semantic differential
- Paired comparisons and constant referent comparisons

Perhaps the most popular type of survey question is the Likert format. This type of question requires that respondents indicate their amount of agreement or disagreement on a symmetric scale. For example, respondent may be asked to indicate their level of agreement with the statement "Overall I am satisfied with my job" using the following response options 1 = Strongly Disagree, 2 = Disagree, 3 = Neither Disagree Nor Agree, 4 = Agree, 5 = Strongly Agree.

Opened-ended questions are a popular type of survey question. While easy to construct, the answers they elicit can be difficult to code and interpret. An example of an open-ended prompt is "Describe your level of satisfaction with your job."

Another popular survey question type is the multiple-choice format. An example is "What is the biggest driver of you overall job satisfaction?" With the response options of 1 = pay, 2 = coworkers, 3 = type of work, 4 = supervisor. When developing written multiple-choice questions, it can be difficult for the researcher anticipate all of the possible response options. As a result, sometimes a catch-all options such as *other* will be used with an opportunity to write in additional information. While useful, this can introduce the same coding and interpretation issues found with open-ended questions.

A less used type of survey question is the semantic differential. For this type of question, the respondents are asked to choose their position along two bi-polar adjectives. An example is "Circle the number representing your overall job satisfaction."

Dissatisfied 1 2 3 4 5 6 7 8 9 10 Satisfied

5. The psychometric concepts of reliability and validity apply to surveys as well as to tests. A survey must measure what it is intended to measure consistently (reliability) and accurately (validity) if we are to make good decisions with the obtained information. Remember that reliability is a necessary, but not sufficient, condition for a valid test. For example, an unreliable survey cannot be valid because the measurements would be "scattered" all over which necessarily means there is no accuracy. However, a highly reliable survey still can be inaccurate as it can consistently give you erroneous information. All of the previously discussed approaches to reliability that are used with tests, such as test–retest, alternate forms, and spilt-half reliability can be applied to surveys.

When applied to testing, validity refers to whether there is evidence to support the inferences based on tests scores. This same approach applies to surveys. However, for surveys, it is common to focus more heavily on evidence related to construct validity as it is important to know that the survey actually measures the concepts or constructs the researcher is intending to measure.

6. As technology has advanced, many aspects of surveying have been automated. Third-party providers and specialists have emerged to assist survey researchers. There are many firms dedicated to providing survey software so that individuals and companies can design, collect, analyze, and report their own data quickly and easily. While there are many different survey software products available, there are similarities and differences among them. There is no single best survey software, and the choice of software depends on the researcher's specific needs, desires, and constraints. For example, one researcher may need quick, simple software that provides easy to design and implement templates. Another researcher may need to design and implement complex surveys on an ongoing basis. Some individuals may have limited or no funds available, while others may have funding to help support their survey needs. Thus, SurveyMonkey, which allows users to create up to 10 surveys and 100 respondents for free, may be quite sufficient. However, researchers who need to create many surveys and collect data on thousands of individuals may need different software. In this case, the researcher might select one of SurveyMonkey's paid plans (Select, Gold, Platinum, and Enterprise), which has increasing levels of features and support.

Another factor researchers may consider is access to respondents. Some survey software providers help identify and survey respondents who are within the researchers' identified population. One more feature survey researchers might want to consider is the extent of reporting support that is provided. Some software only provides basic reports, while other software allows highly powerful report design and analyses. Finally, some software allows for complex survey administration schemes, such as 360° or multirater surveys. This is a popular survey approach where a focal individual (a supervisor for example) will be rated on important job performance dimensions by subordinates, peers, managers, and even possibly customers.

Reference

Helmstadter, G. C. (1970). *Research concepts in human behavior.* New York: Appleton-Century-Crofts.

Likert, R. (1932). A technique for the measurement of attitudes. *Archives of Psychology*, 140, 1–55. Retrieved from http://psycnet.apa.org/psycinfo/1933-01885-001

Pseudoscience. (n.d.). *The Skeptic's Dictionary.* Retrieved from http://skepdic.com/pseudosc.html

Shermer, M. (2011). What is pseudoscience? Distinguishing between science and pseudoscience is problematic. *Scientific American*, 305(3), 92. Retrieved from http://www.scientificamerican.com/article/what-is-pseudoscience/

Sturgis, P., Roberts, C., & Smith, P. (2014). Middle alternatives revisited: How the neither/nor response acts as a way of saying "I don't know." *Sociological Methods & Research*, 43(1), 15–38. doi: 10.1177/0049124112452527

11

How Do We Develop a Test?

Chapter Overview

In Chapter 11, we discuss the steps for developing psychological tests. We look at the process of constructing a test plan, various formats for writing questions (e.g., multiple choice, true/false), the strengths and weaknesses of different formats, and how test takers' perceptions and preconceived notions can influence test scores. Finally, we present guidelines on how to write test questions and discuss the importance of the instructions that accompany a test.

Learning Objectives

After completing your study of this chapter, you should be able to do the following:

- Describe how to define the test domain, the target audience, and the purpose of the test.
- Develop a test plan, including defining the construct or constructs the test measures, choosing the test format, and specifying how to score the test.
- Differentiate between objective and subjective test questions, and describe the strengths and weaknesses of each.
- Describe the important issues in writing instructions for the test administrator and the test taker.

Chapter Outline

Why Develop a New Test?
Defining the Testing Universe, Audience, and Purpose
   Defining the Testing Universe
   Defining the Target Audience
   Defining the Test Purpose

Developing a Test Plan
    Defining the Construct and the Content to Be Measured
    Choosing the Test Format
    Administering and Scoring the Test
    Developing the Test Itself
Composing the Test Items
    Objective Items
    Subjective Items
    Complex Item Formats
    Response Bias
Writing Effective Items
    Multiple-Choice and True/False Items
    Essay and Interview Questions
    A Comparison of Objective and Subjective Formats
Writing the Administration Instructions
    Administrator Instructions
    Instructions for the Test Taker
    Scoring Instructions
Chapter Summary

Key Concepts

acquiescence:	The tendency of some test takers to agree with any ideas or behaviors presented.
categorical model of scoring:	A test scoring model that places test takers in a particular group or class.
cumulative model of scoring:	A test scoring model that assumes that the more the test taker responds in a particular fashion, the more the test taker exhibits the attribute being measured; the test taker receives 1 point for each "correct" answer, and the total number of correct answers becomes the raw score.
distracters:	The incorrect responses to a multiple-choice question.
essay questions:	Popular subjective test items in educational settings that are usually general in scope and require lengthy written responses by test takers.
faking:	The inclination of some test takers to try to answer items in a way that will cause a desired outcome or diagnosis.
forced choice:	A test item format that requires the test taker to choose one of two or more words or phrases that appear to be unrelated but are equally acceptable.
interview questions:	The traditional subjective test questions in an organizational setting that make up the employment interview.
ipsative model of scoring:	A test scoring model that compares the test taker's scores on various scales within the inventory to yield a profile.

multiple choice:	An objective test format that consists of a question or partial sentence, called a *stem*, followed by a number of responses, only one of which is correct.
objective test format:	A test format that has one response that is designated as "correct" or that provides evidence of a specific construct, such as multiple-choice questions.
performance assessments:	A complex item format requiring test takers to demonstrate their skills and abilities to perform a complex task in a setting as similar as possible to the conditions that will be found when the tasks are actually performed.
pilot test:	A scientific investigation of a new test's reliability and validity for its specified purpose.
portfolio:	A collection of an individual's work products that a person gathers over time to demonstrate his or her skills and abilities in a particular area.
projective technique:	A type of psychological test in which the response requirements are unclear so as to encourage test takers to create responses that describe the thoughts and emotions they are experiencing; three projective techniques are projective storytelling, projective drawing, and sentence completion.
projective tests:	Tests that are unstructured and require test takers to respond to ambiguous stimuli.
random responding:	Responding to items in a random fashion by marking answers without reading or considering the items.
response sets:	Patterns of responding to a test or survey that result in false or misleading information.
sentence completion:	Psychological test item format in which the assessor administers partial sentences, verbally or on paper, and asks the test taker to respond by completing each sentence.
simulation:	A complex item format requiring test takers to demonstrate their skills and abilities to perform a complex task in a setting as similar as possible to the conditions that will be found when the tasks are actually performed.
social desirability:	The tendency of some test takers to provide or choose answers that are socially acceptable or that present them in a favorable light.
stem:	A statement, question, or partial sentence that is the stimulus in a multiple-choice question.
subjective test format:	A test format that does not have a response that is designated as "correct"; interpretation of the response as correct or providing evidence of a specific construct is left to the judgment of the person who administers, scores, or interprets the test taker's response.
test format:	The type of questions on a test.
test item:	A stimulus or test question.
test plan:	A plan for developing a new test that specifies the characteristics of the test, including a definition of the construct and the content to be measured (the testing universe), the format for the questions, and how the test will be administered and scored.
testing environment:	The circumstances under which a test is administered.
true/false:	A test item that asks, "Is this statement true or false?"

KEY CONCEPTS CROSSWORD

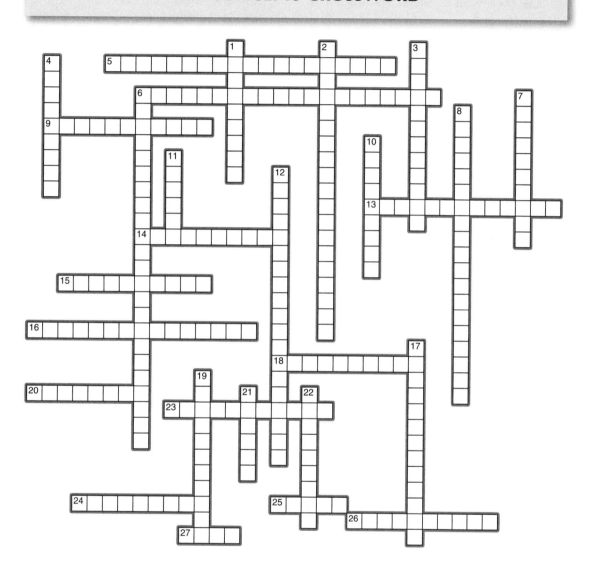

ACROSS

5. The circumstances under which a test is administered.

6. A type of psychological test in which the response requirements are unclear so as to encourage test takers to create responses that describe the thoughts and emotions they are experiencing.

9. A _____ model of scoring places test takers in a particular group or class.

13. A test item format that requires the test taker to choose one of two or more words or phrases that appear to be unrelated but are equally acceptable.

14. The model of scoring that assumes the more the test taker responds in a particular fashion, the more the test taker exhibits the attribute being measured.

15. A complex item format requiring test takers to demonstrate their skills and abilities to perform a complex task in a setting as similar as possible to the conditions that will be found when the tasks are actually performed.

16. An objective test format that consists of a question or partial sentence, called a *stem*, followed by a number of responses, only one of which is correct.

18. Type of test that is unstructured and requires test takers to respond to ambiguous stimuli.

20. A model of scoring that involves comparing the test taker's scores on various scales within the inventory to yield a profile.

23. The incorrect responses to a multiple-choice question.

24. A stimulus or test question.

25. Type of popular subjective test question in educational settings that are usually general in scope and require lengthy written responses by test takers.

26. A scientific investigation of a new test's reliability and validity for its specified purpose.

27. A statement, question, or partial sentence that is the stimulus in a multiple-choice question.

DOWN

1. A plan for developing a new test that specifies the characteristics of the test, including a definition of the construct and the content to be measured (the testing universe), the format for the questions, and how the test will be administered and scored.

2. The traditional subjective test questions in an organizational setting that make up the employment interview.

3. The tendency of some test takers to agree with any ideas or behaviors presented.

4. Type of test format that has one response that is designated as "correct" or that provides evidence of a specific construct, such as multiple-choice questions.

6. A complex item format requiring test takers to demonstrate their skills and abilities to perform a complex task in a setting as similar as possible to the conditions that will be found when the tasks are actually performed.

7. A test format that does not have a response that is designated as "correct," where interpretation of the response as correct or providing evidence of a specific construct is left to the judgment of the person who administers, scores, or interprets the test taker's response.

8. The tendency of some test takers to provide or choose answers that are socially acceptable or that present them in a favorable light.

10. A collection of an individual's work products that a person gathers over time to demonstrate his or her skills and abilities in a particular area.

11. Responding to items in a random fashion by marking answers without reading or considering the items.

12. Psychological test item format in which the assessor administers partial sentences, verbally or on paper, and asks the test taker to respond by completing each sentence.

17. Patterns of responding to a test or survey that result in false or misleading information.

19. The type of questions on a test.

21. The inclination of some test takers to try to answer items in a way that will cause a desired outcome or diagnosis.

22. A test item that asks, "Is this statement true or false?"

LEARNING ACTIVITIES BY LEARNING OBJECTIVE

The following are some study tips and learning activities you can engage in to support the learning objectives for this chapter.

Learning Objectives	Study Tips and Learning Activities
After completing your study of this chapter, you should be able to do the following:	The following study tips will help you meet these learning objectives:
Describe how to define the test domain, the target audience, and the purpose of the test.	• Using a source such as the *Mental Measurements Yearbook* database, look at the various tests that measure intelligence. • Find the definition of each test domain. Are they different or the same? • How many different target audiences do you find? How does the target audience affect the characteristics of each test? • Find the purpose of each test. Are they different or the same?
Develop a test plan, including defining the construct or constructs the test measures, choosing the test format, and specifying how to score the test.	• Test plans in educational settings are based on the material presented for students to learn. Now that you have read and studied this chapter, develop a test plan for this test using a multiple-choice and an essay test format to measure the information learned from this chapter.
Differentiate between objective and subjective test questions, and describe the strengths and weaknesses of each.	• Try writing multiple-choice questions for this chapter, and then write essay questions that measure the same material. Make notes on how the question format affects your ability to measure the construct.
Describe the important issues in writing instructions for the test administrator and the test taker.	• Make a list of types of information that should be covered in the instructions for the test administrator. Make another list of the types of information that should be covered in the instructions for the test taker. Compare your lists with those of a classmate.

EXERCISES

1. Read the description of an item format in Column A. Then write the name of the format in Column B.

Column A: Format Description	Column B: Format Name
A subjective format organizations typically use for hiring employees	
An objective format that gives the respondent a 50% chance of guessing the correct answer	
An objective format developed during World War II to prevent bias in performance ratings	
A subjective format educational institutions use to elicit detailed information from students on a test	
The most familiar objective format	
A subjective format used in early personality tests that relies on the test taker's imagination to provide an answer	

2. Choose a chapter from a textbook other than *Foundations of Psychological Testing: A Practical Approach*—perhaps one you are using in another class—and develop a test plan you can follow to create a knowledge test to assess student understanding of the content. Then write objective and subjective test questions for the chapter following the test plan. (This is not only a good way to practice test development, but also an excellent way to study for an exam.) Exchange your test with a classmate who has done the same, and take each other's test. Finally, compare the tests and discuss their strengths and weaknesses.

3. Consider the following questions: (a) Which test item format(s) do you like best? (b) Is there one test item format by which you prefer to be tested? (c) Are there other test item formats that you do not like? Write a short essay on why you prefer one test format and dislike another. Compare your essay with the essays of your classmates.

4. Form a group of three or four students, and then as a group develop your own college adjustment scale. Construct your own measure of college adjustment using the constructs, definitions, and behaviors for the College Adjustment Scales described in For Your Information Box 11.1. Develop a test plan, define your target audience, compose test items, and write test instructions. Compare your test with the tests of other groups in your class.

ADDITIONAL LEARNING ACTIVITIES

Activity 11-1 Writing Multiple-Choice Questions

Background

Although item writing is often characterized as art and a science, there is surprisingly little empirical evidence supporting common item writing guidelines that are found in textbooks and easily found on the Internet. However, there is an excellent article where the author evaluates evidence for 31 item writing guidelines for multiple-choice test items. The reference is below and the full-text article can easily be found in most university online databases (or through Google Scholar).

Haladyna, T. M., Downing, S. M., & Rodriguez, M. C. (2002). A review of multiple-choice item-writing guidelines for classroom assessment. *Applied Measurement in Education, 15,* 309–334. doi:10.1207/S15324818AME1503_5

This is an excellent article, and it is not filled with tough statistical analyses. Instead, it is very readable and should be required reading for anyone who creates items for tests. Below, 11 of the recommendations found in the article are listed.

1. Avoid trick items.

2. Reduce the reading requirements by using the simplest language possible.

3. Format response options vertically not horizontally.

4. Put the central idea of the question in the stem (not in the answer options).

5. Use positives, not negatives, in the stem.

6. Write as many plausible distractors as you can, but not more.

7. Place options in logical or numerical order.

8. Keep answer options homogeneous in content and grammatical structure.

9. Use *None of the Above* very carefully.

10. Avoid *All of the Above*.

11. Use humor sparingly.

One item-writing topic that is particularly interesting is the number of answer options. Notice that Haladyna et al. (2002) stated that one should write as many plausible distractors (incorrect answers) as possible, and not always write three incorrect answers. Have you ever wondered why nearly every multiple-choice test that you have taken has one correct answer and three incorrect answers? Anyone who has spent time developing incorrect answers knows that three good incorrect answers are very hard to develop. Generally, item writers can create two good incorrect answers, but often the third and last incorrect option takes an inordinate amount of time. One researcher, Rodriguez (2005), decided to investigate if there was any empirical or psychometric reason for using four answer options (one right, and three wrong). He found that most the time at least one of the incorrect answer options does not work from a psychometric perspective. In other words, no one or very few test takers select at least one of the incorrect options. For testing purposes, any option that no one has selected accomplishes nothing. Thus, the test developer has simply wasted the item writer's time and the test taker's time. The extra non-functioning incorrect answer option only increases the amount of reading for the test taker. More required reading means more testing time. If a test only had one correct answer and two incorrect answers, the amount of time per question would be reduced, and more questions could be asked in the same amount of time. The result could be increased content coverage. Furthermore, because we know that reliability is partly determined by test length, test reliability is likely to be increased. Unfortunately, testing companies tend to be conservative, and four options is considered standard for multiple-choice tests. Test takers also usually expect to see multiple-choice tests containing four options. One of this study guide's authors once surveyed test takers after a job knowledge test and found that most rejected the idea of three-option tests, thinking that it would give an advantage to those test takers who did not study. Thus, reducing the number of answer options might decrease the face validity of the test.

Locate and read the Haladyna et al. (2002) article and then answer the questions below.

Questions

1. Write five multiple-choice items following the guidelines presented in the Haladyna et al. article using the material from Chapter 11. Include an answer key, the page number that the material comes from, and an explanation why the incorrect answers are incorrect and the correct answer is correct.

2. Many people who are asked to write test items are content subject matter experts and do not have much experience writing good test items. As a result, test developers often have to spend considerable time editing the test items that the subject matter experts produce. So test developers need to be good editors as well as good item writers to ensure that each question is measuring what it was designed to measure. To get a sense of what that is like, exchange the items you wrote in Question 1 above with another student in the class, edit them, and provide recommendations for improvement. Use the 11 guidelines for writing good items presented above as the basis for your item review.

3. Which of the item recommendations in the Haladyna et al. article have the most research supporting their use?

PRACTICE TEST QUESTIONS

The following are some practice questions to assess your understanding of the material presented in this chapter.

Multiple Choice

1. What is the first step in developing a new test?
   a. Creating a test plan
   b. Examining the suitability of the test format
   c. Adequately sampling behaviors from a specific test domain
   d. Defining the testing universe, audience, and purpose

2. Making a list of the characteristics of persons who will take a test is which part of the test development process?
   a. Defining the purpose
   b. Defining the target audience
   c. Defining the test universe
   d. Developing the test plan

3. A job analysis provides the basis for a test plan in
   a. organizations.
   b. clinical settings.
   c. educational settings.
   d. No Child Left Behind.

4. What do we call the type of questions that a test contains?
   a. Construct explication
   b. Construct operationalization
   c. Behavioral definition
   d. Test format

5. Which one of the following is an objective test format?
   a. Multiple choice
   b. Sentence completion
   c. Interview
   d. Essay

6. Which one of the following models assumes that the more the test taker responds in a particular fashion, the more the test taker exhibits the attribute being measured?
   a. Categorical model of scoring
   b. Ipsative model of scoring
   c. Cumulative model of scoring
   d. Validity model of scoring

7. In a test Alice developed, the test user assigned a diagnosis to the test taker based on the test taker's score. Which one of the following models of scoring was she using?
   a. Categorical
   b. Cumulative
   c. Ipsative
   d. Validity

8. Which one of the following item types is characterized by a question that has a stem that is followed by a number of distracters?
   a. Forced choice
   b. True/false
   c. Essay
   d. Multiple choice

9. For which one of the following formats is scoring easiest?
   a. Essay
   b. Interview
   c. Multiple choice
   d. Sentence completion

10. Eric developed a test that instructed test takers to choose one of two words that appeared to be unrelated but equally acceptable. Which one of the following formats was he using?

    a. Multiple choice

    b. Forced choice

    c. Sentence completion

    d. True/false

11. What one of the following is considered the most often used subjective test in organizations?

    a. Essay

    b. Multiple choice

    c. Interview

    d. Projective drawing

12. Felicia was concerned that the target audience for her test would be more likely to choose the most acceptable answer instead of the truest answer. What was she concerned about?

    a. Acquiescence

    b. Social desirability

    c. Faking

    d. Projection

13. Test developers use reverse scoring to offset the effects of

    a. social desirability.

    b. acquiescence.

    c. faking.

    d. random responding.

14. Random responding is most likely to occur when test takers

    a. lack the necessary skills to take a test or do not wish to be evaluated.

    b. wish to make themselves appear favorably to the test user.

    c. wish to make themselves appear mentally ill or incompetent.

    d. have the tendency to agree with any ideas or behaviors presented.

15. As a rule of thumb, how many more items than called for within the test plan should test developers write?

    a. Three times as many items

    b. Two and one half times as many items

    c. Two times as many items

    d. The same amount of items

16. What does the suggestion in the textbook to "make all test items independent" mean?

    a. Ensure all items are independent of the test universe.

    b. Ensure all items are heterogeneous.

    c. Ensure one item does not provide the answer to another item.

    d. Ensure that all items are reliable and valid.

17. Which one of the following is defined as "Behaviors which are culturally sanctioned and approved but which are improbable of occurrence"?

    a. Social desirability

    b. Items on the Marlowe–Crowne Social Desirability Scale

    c. Response sets

    d. Acquiescence

18. What instrument do test developers use to identify test responses that appeal to people who wish to show themselves in a favorable light?

    a. College Adjustment Scales

    b. Computer-adapted test

    c. Marlowe–Crowne Social Desirability Scale

    d. Multiple-choice test

19. Which one of the following item formats is likely to be used to assess performance capabilities when hiring a commercial airline pilot?

    a. Performance assessment

    b. Simulation

    c. Portfolio

    d. Interview

Short Answer

1. Identify the first four steps of developing a test, and describe what activities are involved in each step.

2. Explain why it is important to follow the test development process. Discuss what you risk by not following this process.

3. Discuss the benefits and drawbacks of using an objective test format. Give three examples of objective test formats.

4. Discuss the benefits and drawbacks of using a subjective test format. Give three examples of subjective test formats.

5. Describe the multiple-choice format. What are its advantages and disadvantages? Include a discussion of scoring a multiple-choice test.

6. Describe the essay format. What are its advantages and disadvantages? Include a discussion of scoring an essay test.

7. Describe three models of scoring tests. Which one is the best format?

8. Describe the three types of complex item formats included in the *Standards for Educational and Psychological Testing* that can be used in specialized testing situations.

ANSWER KEYS

Crossword

ACROSS

5. TESTING ENVIRONMENT—The circumstances under which a test is administered.

6. PROJECTIVE TECHNIQUE—A type of psychological test in which the response requirements are unclear so as to encourage test takers to create responses that describe the thoughts and emotions they are experiencing.

9. CATEGORICAL—A _____ model of scoring places test takers in a particular group or class.

13. FORCED CHOICE—A test item format that requires the test taker to choose one of two or more words or phrases that appear to be unrelated but are equally acceptable.

14. CUMULATIVE—The model of scoring that assumes the more the test taker responds in a particular fashion, the more the test taker exhibits the attribute being measured.

15. SIMULATION—A complex item format requiring test takers to demonstrate their skills and abilities to perform a complex task in a setting as similar as possible to the conditions that will be found when the tasks are actually performed.

16. MULTIPLE CHOICE—An objective test format that consists of a question or partial sentence, called a stem, followed by a number of responses, only one of which is correct.

18. PROJECTIVE—Type of test that is unstructured and requires test takers to respond to ambiguous stimuli.

20. IPSATIVE—A model of scoring that involves comparing the test taker's scores on various scales within the inventory to yield a profile.

DOWN

1. TEST PLAN—A plan for developing a new test that specifies the characteristics of the test, including a definition of the construct and the content to be measured (the testing universe), the format for the questions, and how the test will be administered and scored.

2. INTERVIEW QUESTIONS—The traditional subjective test questions in an organizational setting that make up the employment interview.

3. ACQUIESCENCE—The tendency of some test takers to agree with any ideas or behaviors presented.

4. OBJECTIVE—Type of test format that has one response that is designated as "correct" or that provides evidence of a specific construct, such as multiple-choice questions.

6. PERFORMANCE ASSESSMENTS—A complex item format requiring test takers to demonstrate their skills and abilities to perform a complex task in a setting as similar as possible to the conditions that will be found when the tasks are actually performed.

7. SUBJECTIVE— A test format that does not have a response that is designated as "correct," where interpretation of the response as correct or providing evidence of a specific construct is left to the judgment of the person who administers, scores, or interprets the test taker's response.

8. SOCIAL DESIRABILITY—The tendency of some test takers to provide or choose answers that are socially acceptable or that present them in a favorable light.

23. DISTRACTERS—The incorrect responses to a multiple-choice question.
24. TEST ITEM—A stimulus or test question.
25. ESSAY—Type of popular subjective test question in educational settings that are usually general in scope and require lengthy written responses by test takers.
26. PILOT TEST—A scientific investigation of a new test's reliability and validity for its specified purpose.
27. STEM—A statement, question, or partial sentence that is the stimulus in a multiple-choice question.

10. PORTFOLIO—A collection of an individual's work products that a person gathers over time to demonstrate his or her skills and abilities in a particular area.
11. RANDOM—Responding to items in a random fashion by marking answers without reading or considering the items.
12. SENTENCE COMPLETION—Psychological test item format in which the assessor administers partial sentences, verbally or on paper, and asks the test taker to respond by completing each sentence.
17. RESPONSE SETS—Patterns of responding to a test or survey that result in false or misleading information.
19. TEST FORMAT—The type of questions on a test.
21. FAKING—The inclination of some test takers to try to answer items in a way that will cause a desired outcome or diagnosis.
22. TRUE/FALSE—A test item that asks, "Is this statement true or false?"

Exercises

Column A	Column B
Format Description	Format Name
A subjective format traditionally used by organizations for hiring employees	Traditional interview
An objective format that gives the respondent a 50% chance of guessing the correct answer	True/false
An objective format developed during World War II to prevent bias in performance ratings	Forced choice
A subjective format used by educational institutions to elicit detailed information from students on a test	Essay
The most familiar objective format	Multiple choice
A subjective format used in early personality tests that relies on the test taker's imagination to provide an answer	Projective technique

Multiple Choice

1.

Correct Answer: b

Source: Page 316–317

Explanation: The first step is to define the testing universe, audience, and purpose. The other options listed in the question are part of the development process, but they are not the first step. This passage from *Alice's Adventures in Wonderland* shows why it is so important to take the time to define these aspects of the test first.

> "Would you tell me, please, which way I ought to go from here?"
>
> "That depends a good deal on where you want to get to," said the Cat.
>
> "I don't much care where—" said Alice.
>
> "Then it doesn't matter which way you go," said the Cat.
>
> "—so long as I get somewhere," Alice added as an explanation.
>
> "Oh, you're sure to do that," said the Cat, "if you only walk long enough."

Testing is not a haphazard adventure that one does for fun. It is a structured process and the developer must know where he or she is going right from the start.

2.

Correct Answer: b

Source: Page 317

Explanation: Knowing who the test takers will be is critical to developing a successful test. This must be determined from the start as it will guide and influence the rest of the process. Consider a selection test for administrative law judges and entry-level security guards. These two groups will have vastly different levels of reading ability and the test should be written

accordingly. Or consider a test that will be used in occupational rehabilitation. This is a population that could require a lot of test administration accommodations.

3.

Correct: a

Source: page 321

Explanation: A job analysis is most likely to be conducted when developing an employee selection test for an organization. A job analysis is a structured process that identifies the knowledge, skills, abilities, and other characteristics (KSA&Os) required to perform a job. For test development purposes and because of legal guidelines, it is also common to identify tasks and behaviors that occur on the job. The job analyst then clearly demonstrates that the KSA&Os that have been identified are required to perform one or more job tasks. The most important tasks and KSA&Os are identified and these form the basis for a test blueprint ensuring that the test only covers content that is required for successful job performance.

4.

Correct: d

Source: page 321

Explanation: Test format refers to the type of questions being asked on the test. There are two broad types of questions: objective test questions and subjective test questions. Objective test questions have a single correct answer. Examples include multiple choice and true/false. Subjective tests differ from objective tests in that there is not a single correct answer. For example, an essay question has as many possible answers as there are examinees (if any two responses were identical, it would be attributed to cheating). Because there is no single correct answers, scoring requires judgment and the scorers need to be trained to ensure interrater reliability.

5.

Correct: a

Source: page 321

Explanation: A multiple-choice question requires that the test taker select a single answer that can be demonstrated to be true. This is the key feature of an objective test. In contrast, the other options listed can have more than one possible correct answer. Consider this example. After reading a paragraph of text, the test taker is asked, "Before finding the dollar John was feeling _____." One possible correct answer might be sad. However, synonyms for sad are depressed, gloomy, and miserable—all of which would probably be acceptable answers as well. The characteristic of having more than one possible correct or acceptable answer is the defining characteristic of the subjective test format.

6.

Correct: c

Source: 322

Explanation: The cumulative model is the most common method of scoring, and it assumes that the more the test taker responds in a particular way the more of the attribute he or she has. For example, if one examinee gets 98 out of 100 addition problems correct and another examinee gets only 50 correct, we would assume that the first examinee has a greater knowledge of addition. It is typical to simply add one point for each correct answer. However, different scoring methods are possible. In contrast, ipsative scoring is a forced choice scale that has respondents select one of two equally attractive Items. For example, which of the following two items best describe you? "I like to go to parties" or "I am hard working." This type of scoring is mainly used for personality tests. Categorical scoring is used to place individuals into a specific group and is often used for clinical diagnosis—either you have ADHD or you do not. It is important to note that both

ipsative and categorical models can incorporate a cumulative scoring model.

7.

Correct: a

Source: page 322

Explanation: As described in Question 6, categorical models require that a test taker be placed into a specific category or group and are often used in clinical diagnosis. However, categorical models can also be used in many other settings such as in certification testing. If the test taker surpasses a specific score, then he or she has demonstrated the required level of knowledge to be considered certified in the content domain the test was designed to measure.

8.

Correct: d

Source: page 324

Explanation: A multiple-choice test question is probably the most commonly used question format and as a result is a familiar format to nearly all test takers. The multiple-choice question consists of a stem that states the question or the problem to be answered. The distracters are incorrect answer options. The distracters should be plausible to a person who does not know the correct answer (which is called the *key*). The other options listed have a question stem, but they do not have distracters. One might argue that true/false items have a key and one distractor. In a sense, this is correct. However, distracters should be plausible answers directly related to the question being asked. True/false items do not have this characteristic.

9.

Correct: c

Source: page 324

Explanation: The multiple-choice format is extremely easy to score because there is a single correct answer. As a result, scoring can be done by computer or by untrained individuals. Because of this, scoring is fast and cheap. In contrast, the other options require more complex responses without a single easily identified correct answer. This means that scoring must be done by trained individuals, which takes more time and costs more money.

10

Correct: b

Source: page 325

Explanation: Forced-choice tests are most commonly used in personality assessment. Instead of either selecting the correct answer, constructing a response such as writing an essay, or using a rating scale, the test taker must choose between multiple statements that may appear to be equally appealing. Frequently, these statements describe behavior or personality. For example, test takers may be presented with the following statements and be asked to select the two that are most like them: "I can easily relax"; "I pay attention to details"; "I like to work in a group"; "I have high personal standards."

11.

Correct: c

Source: page 326

Explanation: Interviews are the most commonly used selection tool in organizations. They are considered to be subjective tests. Remember subjective tests do not have a single correct answer, and the test takers response must be interpreted and scored. In a multiple-choice test, there is a single correct answer. Essay and projective drawing are both subjective tests but are not commonly used in organizational settings.

12.

Correct: b

Source: page 329

Explanation: This question addresses types of response biases. It is well known that test takers can intentionally or unintentionally distort how they respond. The textbook covers three types of biases: social desirability, acquiescence, and random responding. Research has shown that some people have a response style or response set that leads them to choose answers that are the most socially acceptable even though their true beliefs might actually be different. This type of response set is called *social desirability*. Acquiescence is another type of response bias that occurs when individuals have a tendency to simply agree with all the statements presented in a test. Research has shown that people may have a natural tendency toward this response bias influenced by cultural norms. Random responding and faking are the third type of response biases. These types of biases occur when the test taker does not want to respond accurately. He or she may simply respond randomly without reading questions, or may intentionally try to present an inaccurate picture of him- or herself. One example would be faking insanity in response to a legal charge.

13.

Correct: d

Source: page 329

Explanation: One way random responding can be detected is by employing a technique called *reverse scoring*. The test developer will ask more than one question that measure the same construct but ask them in opposite ways. For example, one item might be "I am very satisfied with my job" and another item might be "I am very dissatisfied with my job." If the test taker is consistent answering the questions, one would agree with one item and a disagree with the other.

14.

Correct: a

Source: page 331

Explanation: While random responding and faking are closely related types of response biases, they are different concepts. Random responding occurs when the test taker, for some reason, does not want to answer or is incapable of answering the test questions. In contrast, faking occurs when the test taker intentionally distorts answers to present an inaccurate image of him- or herself.

15.

Correct: c

Source: page 331

Explanation: Writing effective test items is both an art and a science, and not every question that is written will be of usable quality. In addition, pretesting or piloting items is a good practice. When the test developer examines the results of pretested items, he or she might find that some questions are too hard, some too easy, while others may display other psychometrically objectionable characteristics. Therefore, a general rule of thumb to follow is to develop twice as many test items as required by the test plan. This will allow the test developer to discard poor items and keep only the best-performing ones.

16.

Correct: c

Source: page 332

Explanation: The textbook lists some suggestions for writing effective test items. One of these suggestions is to make all items independent. This means that one item should not tip off the answer of another item. For example, one item might ask, "Sigmund Freud, the father of psychoanalysis, stated . . ." Then another question on the same test might ask "Who is the father of psychoanalysis?" Obviously, the astute test taker will find the correct answer to the first question in the second question. The result is that the second question will be ineffective in determining whether the test taker possesses the knowledge that the second question was designed to tap.

17.

Correct: b

Source: page 329

Explanation: In the 1960s, two psychologists, Douglas Crowne and David Marlowe, developed a scale that measured the degree to which individuals tend to respond in socially desirable ways. They stated that the items on the test are culturally sanctioned, but highly improbable, behaviors. For example, one item asks if a person *never* hesitates to help someone in trouble. While most people would say this is a desirable characteristic, it is also extremely unlikely that someone would *never* hesitate to help someone in trouble. Stating that you *never* hesitate suggests that you chose that response because it was the most socially acceptable answer. Social desirability has been associated with a high need for approval.

18.

Correct: c

Source: page 329

Explanation: Socially desirable responding has two key characteristics. First, the chosen answer is seen as being socially endorsed or sanctioned. The second characteristic is that test takers wish to present themselves in a highly positive manner. The Marlow–Crowne Social Desirability Scale was developed specifically to detect this type of responding by presenting items that are positive in nature but are unlikely to accurately describe a person.

19.

Correct: b

Source: page 328

Explanation: A simulation is similar to a performance assessment in that it requires test takers to demonstrate their skills and abilities to perform a complex task, such as piloting a plane. However, the tasks are not performed in the actual environment because of safety or cost-related concerns. In this case, it would be cheaper and safer to assess candidates with a simulation than place them in an actual plane. In addition, portfolios and interviews could be part of the selection process, but are unlikely to be useful or collect much information about the performance capabilities of a pilot.

Short Answer

1. Step 1.   Define test universe, target audience, and test purpose.

This step is extremely important, and considerable time should be spent thinking about the universe, audience, and purpose of the test. First, the developer needs to create a working definition of what construct the test is being designed to measure. Second, the developer needs to determine who the audience is (the people who will be tested) because different audiences have different requirements. Next, the developer needs to understand how the scores will be used and for what purpose. All of these factors will greatly influence the rest of the test development project.

Step 2.   Develop a test plan.

In this step the construct is operationalized with a more precise definition. Also, at this step, the developer chooses a test format or the type of questions that will be included (i.e., objective, subjective, projective). How the test will be administered and scored is determined as well. For example, will the test be using a cumulative, categorical, or ipsative model of scoring?

Step 3.   Compose the test items.

Once Steps 1 and 2 are completed, the developer can begin to constructing test items. The developer must make sure that the items developed correspond to the test plan or test blueprint. This includes determining the type of items that need to be developed. Will the items be objective (multiple choice, true/false, forced choice) or subjective (essay, interview, projective, sentence completion)? As a general rule, twice as many items as needed should be developed.

Step 4.   Write administration instructions.

1. Developing instructions for administration is an important and often overlooked aspect of test development. Three sets of instructions need to be developed. The first set is for the test administrator covering such things as time limits, equipment needed, testing script to be read, and the required testing environment. The second set is for the test taker describing what he or she is to do and how to do it. The third set of instructions is for the test scorers. These instructions ensure that different scorers will evaluate answers in a similar manner.

2. Test development is a structured process that necessarily follows specific steps. When a test developer does not follow this process, the test may perform poorly. Test formats are the types of questions that the test will contain. There are two broad types of formats: objective and subjective. Objective items include multiple choice, true/false, and forced choice. Types of subjective items include essay, interview, projective, and sentence completion. Most developers prefer to have a single format for a test. This helps to ensure that changes in format do not confuse test takers. This consistency also makes test development, administration, and scoring easier.

3. An objective test has several benefits. Because there is a single correct answer, they are easy to score, as no judgment is required to determine if the correct answer was given. They are also easier to align with a test plan or test blueprint. Both of these characteristics make it easier to evaluate and document the test. One disadvantage of an objective test format is that test takers may be able to more easily guess the correct answer than with a subjective test. Also, objective tests have been subject to the criticism that they only require recognition of facts and are not effective at evaluating deeper thinking. Another criticism of objective tests is that they stress recall and encourage rote memorization. However, well-developed objective items can overcome all these criticisms.

4. Subjective items allow for wider and more varied responses because the test taker must construct an answer. As a result, fewer cues are presented in the question itself. Proponents of subjective tests say that this format encourages more thinking and abstract reasoning than objective tests. However, because of the varied nature of responses, scoring of projective tests is more difficult and requires interpretation and judgment. This can introduce inconsistencies in scoring which can lower the reliability and validity of the test.

5. Multiple choice is the most used item format and as a result is more familiar to test takers. This type of question has a stem that presents the question or problem to be answered. It also has a key, which is the correct answer option, and distractors, which are incorrect answer options. Care must be taken when writing items to make sure that they are clear and concise. All distractors must be completely incorrect and should not provide any cues to the test taker that could increase the odds of guessing correctly. The major advantage of this type of item is that it is quick, easy, and inexpensive to score. However, because test takers have an opportunity to guess the correct answer, this must be taken into account when interpreting test scores. The effect of guessing on scores can be reduced by following good item writing practices.

6. Essay questions are a popular type of subjective test item that are often found in educational settings. To answer these types of questions, the test taker needs to construct a response. Essay questions allow more freedom in responding than objective items. Because of this some developers believe that it is easier to assess higher cognitive skills such as thinking, analysis, and evaluation using essay questions. Some students (and developers) like this type of item and believe that it also makes it possible for the test taker to demonstrate what they know more effectively than with objective tests. However, there are drawbacks to essay questions such as increased difficulty in scoring. The increased flexibility in responding requires that scorers use judgment when interpreting and assigning scores to answers. The scoring also takes more time, and sometimes money, compared to objective tests.

7. There is no single best model for scoring tests. The scoring model should be selected based on what has been defined as the testing universe, target audience, and test purpose. There are three basic models of scoring. The cumulative model of scoring is the most common and assumes that each "correct" answer is an indication of greater standing on the construct. The categorical model of scoring places each test taker into a distinct mutually exclusive group. Finally, the ipsative model of scoring requires the test taker to select among equally appealing options and there is not necessarily a single correct answer. The ipsative scoring model shows the test taker's individual profile on the measured attribute(s) and does not enable comparisons of one test taker with another. It is important to note that the cumulative model can be used in conjunction with both the categorical and ipsative models of scoring.

8. The *Standards for Educational and Psychological Testing* include a discussion of three types of complex item formats: (1) performance assessments, (2) simulations, and (3) portfolios. The first is performance assessments, which require test takers to demonstrate their skills and abilities to perform complex behaviors and tasks in a setting that is as similar as possible to the conditions that will be found when the tasks are actually performed on the job. In an employment setting, performance assessments are often called *work samples* because require the person to demonstrate his or her ability to perform tasks that have been identified as critical for successful job performance. The second specialized item format is a simulation. Simulations are similar to a performance assessment in that they require test takers to demonstrate their skills and abilities to perform a complex task. However, the tasks are not performed in the actual environment in which the real tasks will be performed, often because of safety or cost-related concerns. The third and final complex item format is a portfolio, which is a collection of work products that a person gathers over time to demonstrate his or her skills and abilities in a particular area. It is important to keep in mind that even though these item formats are complex in nature and may not appear to be tests as most people understand them, they are still evaluated using the same standards as are applied to any other test.

References

Haladyna, T, M., Downing, S. M., & Rodriguez, M. C. (2002). A review of multiple-choice item-writing guidelines for classroom assessment. *Applied Measurement in Education, 15,* 309–334. doi: 10.1207/S15324818AME1503_5

Rodriguez, M. C. (2005). Three options are optimal for multiple-choice items: A meta-analysis of 80 years of research. *Educational Measurement: Issues and Practice, 24,* 3–13. doi:10.1111/j.1745-3992.2005.00006.x

12

How Do We Assess the Psychometric Quality of a Test?

Chapter Overview

In Chapter 12, we continue to describe the test development process by discussing piloting the test and analyzing the items in terms of their difficulty, their ability to discriminate among respondents, and their likelihood of introducing error into the test results. We take a close look at how we determine if a test is equally predictive for different subgroups in the population. We also describe the process of revising the test and gathering evidence of reliability and validity. Finally, we briefly discuss the contents of the test manual.

Learning Objectives

After completing your study of this chapter, you should be able to do the following:

- Explain the importance of conducting a pilot test.
- Describe how a pilot test should be set up, and specify the types of information that should be collected.
- Describe the collection, analyses, and interpretation of data for an item analysis, including item difficulty, item discrimination, interitem correlations, item–criterion correlations, item bias, and item characteristic curves.
- Describe the collection and interpretation of data for a qualitative item analysis.
- Identify and explain the criteria for retaining and dropping items to revise a test.
- Describe the processes of validation and cross-validation.
- Explain the concepts of differential validity, single-group validity, and unfair test discrimination.

- Describe two different kinds of measurement bias.
- Explain the purpose of a cut score, and describe two methods for identifying a cut score.

Chapter Outline

Conducting the Pilot Test
    Setting Up the Pilot Test
    Conducting the Pilot Study
    Analyzing the Results
Conducting Quantitative Item Analysis
    Item Difficulty
    Item Discrimination
    Interitem Correlations
    Item–Total Correlations
    Item–Criterion Correlations
    The Item Characteristic Curve
    Item Bias
Conducting Qualitative Item Analysis
    Questionnaires for Test Takers
    Expert Panels
Revising the Test
    Choosing the Final Items
    Revising the Test Instructions
Validating the Test
    Cross-Validation
    Measurement Bias
    Differential Validity in Tests of Cognitive Ability
    Test Fairness
    Testing for Validity Equivalence
Developing Norms and Identifying Cut Scores
    Developing Norms
    Identifying Cut Scores
Compiling the Test Manual
Chapter Summary

Key Concepts

acculturation:	The degree to which an immigrant or a minority member has adapted to a country's mainstream culture.
cross-validation:	Administering a test another time following a validation study to confirm the results of the validation study; because of chance factors that contribute to random error, this second administration can be expected to yield lower correlations with criterion measures.

cut scores:	Decision points for dividing test scores into pass/fail groupings.
differential validity:	When a test yields significantly different validity coefficients for subgroups.
discrimination index:	A statistic that compares the performance of those who made very high test scores with the performance of those who made very low test scores on each item.
empirically based tests:	Tests in which the decision to place an individual in a category is based solely on the quantitative relationship between the predictor and the criterion.
generalizable:	When a test can be expected to produce similar results even though it has been administered in different locations.
intercept bias:	A type of measurement bias in which the intercept of the regression line that is used to predict a criterion of interest is not the same for all demographic groups used in the regression (e.g., men and women).
interitem correlation matrix:	A matrix that displays the correlation of each item with every other item.
item analysis:	The process of evaluating the performance of each item on a test.
item bias:	Differences in responses to test questions that are related to differences in culture, gender, or experiences of the test takers.
item characteristic curve (ICC):	The line that results when we graph the probability of answering an item correctly with the level of ability on the construct being measured; the resulting graph provides a picture of both the item's difficulty and discrimination.
item difficulty:	The percentage of test takers who answer a question correctly.
item-response theory (IRT):	A theory that relates the performance of each item to a statistical estimate of the test taker's ability on the construct being measured.
measurement bias:	When the scores on a test taken by different subgroups in the population (e.g., men, women) need to be interpreted differently because of some characteristic of the test not related to the construct being measured.
phi coefficient:	A statistic that describes the relationship between two dichotomous variables.
pilot test:	A scientific investigation of a new test's reliability and validity for its specified purpose.
qualitative analysis:	When test developers ask test takers to complete a questionnaire about how they viewed the test and how they answered the questions.
quantitative item analysis:	A statistical analysis of the responses that test takers gave to individual test questions.
single-group validity:	When a test is valid for one group but not for another group, such as valid for Whites but not for Blacks.
slope bias:	A type of measurement bias in which the slope of the regression line used to predict a criterion is not the same for all demographic groups used in the regression (e.g., men and women).
subgroup norms:	Statistics that describe subgroups of the target audience, such as race, sex, and age.
subtle questions:	Questions that have no apparent relation to the test purpose or criterion.

KEY CONCEPTS CROSSWORD

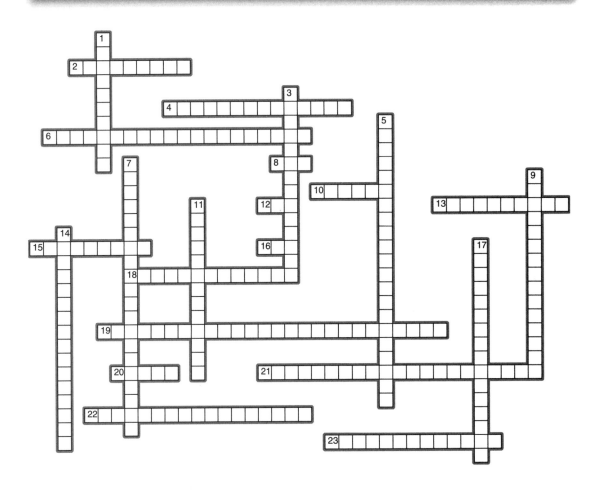

ACROSS

2. Type of correlation matrix that displays the correlation of each item with every other item.
4. Statistics that describe subgroups of the target audience, such as race, sex, and age.
6. A statistic that compares the performance of those who made very high test scores with the performance of those who made very low test scores on each item.
8. Abbreviation referring to the line that results when we graph the probability of answering an item correctly with the level of ability on the construct being measured; the resulting graph provides a picture of both the item's difficulty and discrimination.
10. Type of question that has no apparent relation to the test purpose or criterion.
12. Abbreviation for the theory that relates the performance of each item to a statistical estimate of the test taker's ability on the construct being measured.
13. A scientific investigation of a new test's reliability and validity for its specified purpose.
15. Differences in responses to test questions that are related to differences in culture, gender, or experiences of the test takers.
16. Type of coefficient/statistic that describes the relationship between two dichotomous variables.
18. The process of evaluating the performance of each item on a test.
19. A statistical analysis of the responses that test takers gave to individual test questions.
20. Type of measurement bias in which the slope of the regression line used to predict a criterion is not the same for all demographic groups used in the regression (e.g., men and women).
21. When a test yields significantly different validity coefficients for subgroups.
22. Type of test in which the decision to place an individual in a category is based solely on the quantitative relationship between the predictor and the criterion.
23. The degree to which an immigrant or a minority member has adapted to a country's mainstream culture.

DOWN

1. Decision points for dividing test scores into pass/fail groupings.
3. A type of measurement bias in which the intercept of the regression line that is used to predict a criterion of interest is not the same for all demographic groups used in the regression (e.g., men and women).
5. When a test is valid for one group but not for another group, such as valid for Whites but not for Blacks.
7. When test developers ask test takers to complete a questionnaire about how they viewed the test and how they answered the questions.
9. The percentage of test takers who answer a question correctly.
11. When a test can be expected to produce similar results even though it has been administered in different locations.
14. When the scores on a test taken by different subgroups in the population (e.g., men, women) need to be interpreted differently because of some characteristic of the test not related to the construct being measured.
17. Administering a test another time following a validation study to confirm the results of the validation study; because of chance factors that contribute to random error, this second administration can be expected to yield lower correlations with criterion measures.

LEARNING ACTIVITIES BY LEARNING OBJECTIVE

The following are some study tips and learning activities you can engage in to support the learning objectives for this chapter.

Learning Objectives	*Study Tips and Learning Activities*
After completing your study of this chapter, you should be able to do the following:	The following study tips and learning activities will help you meet these learning objectives:
Explain the importance of conducting a pilot test.	• Make a list of problems that could arise if a clinical practitioner, a human resources department, or a college (choose one) used a new test without carrying out a pilot test and validity studies. Compare your list with that of a classmate.
Describe how a pilot test should be set up, and specify the types of information that should be collected.	• Set up conditions for pilot-testing one of the tests that you developed as an activity for Chapter 11.
Describe the collection, analyses, and interpretation of data for an item analysis, including item difficulty, item discrimination, interitem correlations, item-criterion correlations, item bias, and item characteristic curves.	• Reread the section "Conducting Quantitative Item Analysis," and make a chart that shows each statistic used in an item analysis, its definition, and its sign and formula where appropriate (e.g., p = items correct/total items).
Describe the collection and interpretation of data for a qualitative item analysis.	• Review Table 12.2. Are there other questions you would add to this list? Which areas would you want to explore in a focus group? Which would you ask in a paper-and-pencil test?
Identify and explain the criteria for retaining and dropping items to revise a test.	• Review Table 12.3. Carefully analyze the information on each item. Do you agree with the authors about which items work best? If not, discuss the criteria for choosing items with a classmate or your instructor.
Describe the processes of validation and cross-validation.	• Make a chart that shows the similarities and differences among the pilot test, the validation study, and the cross-validation study.
Explain the concepts of differential validity, single-group validity, and unfair test discrimination.	• Using a search engine such as Google, research the concepts of differential validity, single-group validity, and unfair test discrimination. See whether the information you find corroborates the information in this textbook.
Explain the purpose of a cut score, and describe two methods for identifying a cut score.	• Make a chart of the advantages and disadvantages of having a cut score for a classroom test, an employment test, and a clinical diagnostic test.

EXERCISES

1. The following data are from a pilot study for a math test. Interpret the data, and decide which items you would retain to make a 10-item test. Note that all questions are intended to be homogeneous, and analyses for bias showed none of the items as biased.

Item Number	Average Interitem Correlation	Difficulty	Discrimination Index
1	.40	.90	10
2	.38	.50	60
3	.05	.50	19
4	.30	.48	−2
5	.50	.50	50
6	.01	.98	0
7	.60	.60	48
8	.00	.10	10
9	.55	.49	40
10	.30	.61	−5
11	.44	.51	80
12	−.10	.66	7
13	.40	.55	75
14	.77	.43	−10
15	.71	.71	60
16	.33	.56	40
17	.00	.2	15
18	.22	.35	60
19	.55	.43	70
20	.04	.40	16

2. The following are the raw data for 10 questions from the pilot study for another math test. Calculate the difficulty and discrimination index for each item. Score the test using the cumulative method. Contrast the top third with the bottom third for the discrimination index. Correct answers are marked 1, and incorrect answers are marked 0.

Test	Item 1	Item 2	Item 3	Item 4	Item 5	Item 6	Item 7	Item 8	Item 9	Item 10	Score
1	1	1	0	1	1	0	1	1	0	1	
2	0	0	0	1	0	0	0	0	1	1	
3	0	0	1	1	0	0	1	1	0	1	
4	0	0	0	0	0	0	1	0	0	1	
5	1	1	0	1	0	0	1	1	1	1	
6	1	1	1	1	1	1	1	1	1	1	
7	1	0	1	1	0	1	0	1	0	1	
8	1	1	1	1	1	1	1	1	0	1	
9	0	1	1	1	1	1	1	1	1	1	
10	0	0	0	1	0	1	1	1	1	1	
11	0	0	0	1	0	0	0	0	0	0	
12	0	1	1	1	1	1	1	1	1	1	
13	1	1	1	1	1	1	1	1	1	1	
14	0	1	0	1	0	1	1	1	1	1	
15	1	1	1	1	0	1	0	1	1	1	
16	0	1	0	1	0	0	0	0	0	0	
17	0	0	0	0	0	0	0	0	0	0	
18	1	1	1	0	0	1	1	1	0	0	
p											
D											

3. Design a Pilot Test. Following are descriptions of three situations in which a test has been developed. Read each situation, and then design a pilot test. Answer the following questions about each pilot test:

a. Who will take the test?

b. What information will you gather, and how will you gather it?

c. What should the testing environment be like?

d. Who should administer the test?

e. Do you foresee any problems that need to be investigated during the pilot test?

Situation 1. The admissions office at your college has developed a test for incoming students. The purpose of the test is to identify students who may have difficulty in adapting to campus life at your college. The college accepts students of both traditional and nontraditional ages with varying cultural and socioeconomic backgrounds. The 50-item test has a multiple-choice format that can be scored using an electronic scan system. The admissions office plans to include the test in its application package and will ask prospective students to return the test with their applications.

Situation 2. Dr. Query has a local clinical practice for individuals who show signs of depression. She has noticed that some of her clients do better when they participate in group interventions, and others make more progress when she sees them individually. She has developed a 20-minute intake interview that can be conducted by a graduate assistant or caseworker in her office. The purpose of the interview is to identify the type of treatment (group or individual) that is likely to work best for each client.

Situation 3. AAAA Accounting prepares individual and corporate tax returns. The company has developed a test to measure knowledge of federal income tax law that it wants to use to hire tax preparers. The test has 400 items, 100 of which require calculations. The test will be administered in the company's offices when prospective employees apply to be tax preparers.

4. Which Statistic Should I Use? This chapter described a number of statistics that are used for quantitative item analysis. The table below contains a research question in Column A. In Column B, write in the appropriate statistic(s) that answers the research question. Note: More than one statistic may answer some questions.

A. Research Question	B. Appropriate Statistic(s)
1. Does this item measure the same construct as other items?	
2. Is this item easier for men than for women?	
3. Does this item provide information that helps predict a criterion?	
4. How difficult is this item?	
5. If I drop this item from the test, will it increase or decrease internal reliability?	

(Continued)

(Continued)

A. Research Question	B. Appropriate Statistic(s)
6. How did the people who did well on this test do on this item?	
7. Is this item of sufficient difficulty, and does it discriminate between high and low performers on the test?	
8. Is this test biased against a minority group?	
9. How well does the answer on this item correlate with the individual's overall test score?	

5. What's the Difference? This chapter describes three data collection studies: the pilot test, the validation study, and the cross-validation study. What are the differences among these studies? What are the similarities? Address issues such as the following: Who are the test takers? What is done with the data? What decisions might be made with the data?

6. What Went Wrong With the Firefighter Exam? Carefully review In the News Box 12.1, which describes the testing problems that faced the City of Chicago after it administered an exam to select potential firefighters. Do you think the problem was with the test itself, the cut score, or both? Would conducting a validation study have averted some of these problems? If so, how?

ADDITIONAL LEARNING ACTIVITIES

Activity 12-1 Sensitivity Review

Background

The textbook discusses expert panels as a method to collect qualitative information to improve tests during the development processes. One way that test developers do this is by the use of sensitivity panels, which examine tests for content that may offend or disturb test takers or that may be unfair to certain groups of test takers.

It is important to note the difference between bias and fairness. Bias is a psychometric concept, and its detection is based on empirical statistical analyses. In contrast, fairness is a social concept about what is right and what is wrong. As a result, there is more than one definition of fairness, and the detection of unfair (and insensitive) items is based on human judgment. Even though fairness and sensitivity are not psychometric concepts, they still must be considered and incorporated into all phases of test development and use. For example, the 2014 *Standards for Educational and Psychological Testing* states,

> Test content or situations that are offensive or emotionally disturbing to some test takers may impede their ability to engage with the test should not appear in the test unless the use of the offensive or disturbing content is need to measure the intended construct. Examples of this type of content are graphic descriptions of slavery or the Holocaust when such descriptions are not specifically required by the construct. (AERA, APA, & NCME, 2014, p. 55)

In an effort to meet this standard, test development companies train their item writers on how to avoid content that may be offensive or emotional to test takers. In addition, they regularly assemble fairness and sensitivity panels to review test items. These panels are tasked with ensuring that tests are as free as possible from unnecessary distractions and barriers that could affect the scores of test takers. While the reviews consider all test takers, they often focus on item characteristics that could be offensive or otherwise understood differently because of an individual's disability, ethnic group, gender, native language, race, religion, sexual orientation, or socioeconomic status.

We used the phrase *as free as possible* above because it is an extremely difficult task to offend no one. Also, even the most innocuous contexts could evoke an emotional reaction. For example, a reading passage about the weather could cause a strong emotional reaction from a test taker who recently lost his or her home in a tornado. For another example, a passage about dancing might be offensive to certain religious groups.

Test developers do the best job they can when they perform fairness and sensitivity reviews. Not only must a test be unbiased, but it must also appear to test takers to be fair and sensitive. Unfortunately, research has shown that reviewers perform no better than chance at identifying biased items, that they cannot identify which items will be nonequivalent across languages, and that reviewers have low to modest agreement when identifying potentially insensitive or otherwise poor items (Golubovich, Grand, Ryan, & Schmitt, 2014). Furthermore, research shows that equal numbers of "biased" items are found to benefit and hurt any specific group (minority or majority). Thus, the overall effect of biased items is that they balance out with no overall effect on test performance. Therefore, the utility of sensitivity reviews seems limited.

It would be impossible to list everything that could offend or insult a test taker. Luckily there is good information available online about the guidelines that major test developers use to write and review items. Several are listed below.

ETS Guidelines for Fairness Review Assessments

https://www.ets.org/Media/About_ETS/pdf/overview.pdf

ETS Standards for Quality and Fairness Chapter 4 - Fairness

https://www.ets.org/s/about/pdf/standards.pdf

ETS International Principles for Fairness Review of Assessments

https://www.ets.org/s/about/pdf/fairness_review_international.pdf

ACT Fairness Reports

http://www.act.org/research-policy/research-reports/

Locate and read one of the documents listed above. Then identify any potentially insensitive or unfair content in the questions below, explaining why and propose how the question could be rewritten.

Questions

1. Frankie, a male nurse, ordered 0.125 mg pills. How many pills should Frankie give to the patient if the required dosage is 0.25 mg?

2. At her high school basketball game, Ebony made five free throws, five baskets, and two three-pointers. How many total points did she score?

3. If an average of 3.5 people per square mile were seriously injured or killed in a hurricane, about how many people were injured in a city of 75 square miles?

4. If each borough has 75 gas stations, and there are five boroughs in the city, how many gas stations are in the city?

5. In America, each state has two senators. How many senators are there in total?

Activity 12-2 Adverse Impact

Background

Test developers must not only understand measurement bias and fairness from a psychometric perspective, but they must understand it from a legal perspective too. There is a very important document for employee selection testing. It is called the *Uniform Guidelines on Employee Selection Procedures*. This document was first published in 1978 by four U.S. federal government agencies (Equal Employment Opportunities Commission, Department of Justice, Department of Labor, and the Civil Service Commission, now the Office of Personnel Management).

To understand why this document is important, a little background information is helpful. When Congress enacted the Civil Rights Act of 1964, federal agencies became responsible for implementing, monitoring, and enforcing compliance with the Act. The result was that between 1966 and 1978, many government agencies had independently published separate guidelines on employment testing and selection. Obviously, having separate guidelines was quite unwieldy, so the four agencies got together to create a set of "uniform guidelines" on which they could all agree. The result was the *Uniform Guidelines on Employee Selection Procedures*. In 1979, same four agencies issued a set of 93 questions and answers regarding the guidelines.

People are often confused as to what constitutes an "employee selection procedure." As you will see, the phrase is interpreted more broadly than you might expect. Section 2.B of the guidelines states:

B. Employment decisions.

These guidelines apply to tests and other selection procedures which are used as a basis for any employment decision. Employment decisions include but are not limited to hiring, promotion, demotion, membership (for example, in a labor organization), referral, retention, and licensing and certification, to the extent that licensing and certification may be covered by Federal equal employment opportunity law. Other selection decisions, such as selection for training or transfer, may also be considered employment decisions if they lead to any of the decisions listed above.

Many people mistakenly believe that the guidelines only apply to written tests, but this is not the case. Under the formal definition presented above, many different types of personnel actions taken by organizations can be construed as an employment decision and therefore they are subject to the Guidelines.

There is one other important aspect of the Uniform Guidelines to note. The Uniform Guidelines are not a law and do not have the rule of law. Instead, as their name implies, they are guidelines to be used by organizations to help them when they make employment decisions. While they are not law, the Uniform Guidelines have been given "great deference" by the courts so it is important to know about them.

The Guidelines define and identify discrimination through a concept known as *adverse impact*. The origin of this concept comes from a famous case, *Griggs v. Duke Power*, where the Supreme Court focused on the fact that a minority group was disqualified by a selection procedure "at a substantially higher rate" than the majority group. However, the court did not say what a "substantially higher" disqualification rate meant in practice. Therefore, it was difficult for organizations to use the Court's decision for guidance in hiring. The Uniform Guidelines attempted to remedy this problem by defining what "substantially" meant in practice. According to the Uniform Guidelines,

> *A selection rate for any race, sex, or ethnic group which is less than four-fifths (4/5) (or eighty percent) of the rate for the group with the highest rate will generally be regarded by the Federal enforcement agencies as evidence of adverse impact, while a greater than four-fifths rate will generally not be regarded by Federal enforcement agencies as evidence of adverse impact. (§ 4.D)*

Because this definition was a little confusing to many people, the questions and answers that were published later included 22 questions dealing just with the concept if adverse impact.

Here is a simple example taken from the Q&As that demonstrate how adverse impact is calculated based on the definition presented above.

Suppose an employer gave a selection test to 120 applicants. Of these, 80 were White and 40 were Black. Based on test results, 48 of the White applicants were hired, and 12 of the Black applicants where hired. This means that 60% (48 out of 80) of the White applicants were hired. Another way of saying the same thing is that the selection ratio of White applicants was .60. For the Black applicants, 12 out of 40, or 30% were hired. Therefore, section ratio of Black applicants was .30.

If 30% of the Black applicants were hired and 60% of the White applicants were hired, intuitively you can probably see that the selection ratio for Black applicants (.30) is only one half of the selection ratio of the White applicants (.60). Mathematically, we would calculate this by dividing the smaller selection ratio (.30) by the larger ratio (.60). When we make this calculation we see that .30/.60 = .50. This tells us that selection rate for Black applicants was only 50% of the rate for White applicants. Clearly, Black applicants were hired at much lower rate than White applicants.

Under the Uniform Guidelines, adverse impact is indicated when one group is selected at a rate of less than 80% (or 4/5th) of the rate of another group. In our example, the Black applicants were selected at 50% of the rate for White applicants. Because 50% is less than the required 80%, the selection procedure is said to result in adverse impact against Black applicants.

In order for there to have been no adverse impact, the selection ratio for Black applicants would have had to have been at least 80% (4/5th) of the selection ration for White applicants. In our example, this would be equal to (.80 * .60) or .48. In words, 48% of the Black applicants would have had to been hired for there to have been no adverse impact.

All of this is shown in the table below.

Applicants	Hires	Selection Ratio/Percent Hired
80 White	48	48/80 = .60 or 60%
40 Black	12	12/40 = .30 or 30%
Lowest selection rate/Highest selection rate = .30/.60 = .50 or 50%		

50% < 80% therefore there is adverse impact.

Because the selection ratio for Black applicants is less than 80% of the rate of White applicants, the selection procedure disadvantaged the Black applicants.

There is nothing special about this "4/5ths rule." In fact, its use seems to be based on the "Goldilocks principle." Barrett (1998) describes that its inclusion in the Uniform Guidelines was based on guidelines developed by the Technical Advisory Committee on Testing and published by the State of California Fair Employment Practice Commission (FEPC) in 1971. He recounts a discussion regarding the rule in one of the committee member's living room that 85% seemed too high and 75% seemed too low. Apparently 4/5ths or 80% was just right.

The 4/5ths rule was never intended to be a hard and fast rule. The Uniform Guidelines actually call it a "rule of thumb." It was really meant as a trigger to indicate when greater scrutiny using more rigorous statistical methods would be needed. Practitioners, however, pay close attention to the 4/5ths rule.

Also, just because the 4/5ths rule has not been violated does not automatically mean that no discrimination has taken place. The rule merely places a numerical basis for drawing an initial inference about discrimination in the form of adverse impact. There may still be unlawful discrimination even if the rule is not violated.

Questions

Calculate and determine if there is adverse impact for each of the scenarios below. Show your work and explain your answers.

1. One hundred people applied for a job. Of these, 78 were White and 22 were Asian. After a series of written tests, 53 White applicants and 13 Asian applicants were hired.

2. There are 153 applicants who interviewed for a job. Of the 30 Asian applicants, 15 were hired, and of the 123 White applicants, 45 where hired.

PRACTICE TEST QUESTIONS

The following are some practice questions to assess your understanding of the material presented in this chapter.

Multiple Choice

1. Marie designed a self-esteem test for preschool children. Her instructions to the administrator required that the test questions be read orally. The children were instructed to circle a printed face on the answer sheet (variations of a face smiling or frowning) to indicate their answers. Because Marie could not find any preschoolers to use in her pilot study, she administered the test to fifth graders instead. What is wrong with what Marie did?

   a. Preschoolers' self-esteem cannot be measured.

   b. Tests should not be administered orally to preschoolers.

   c. The test takers in her pilot study were not the same as her target audience.

   d. Nothing was wrong with what Marie did.

2. When Isaac conducted an item analysis of the data from his pilot study, he first calculated for each item the percentage of test takers who got the item right. In this analysis, what was he measuring?

   a. Item difficulty

   b. Item discrimination

   c. Item reliability

   d. Item bias

3. Items for which the p value falls in the range of .90 to 1.00 are usually considered

   a. too difficult.

   b. about right.

   c. too easy.

   d. too biased.

4. When analyzing the data from her pilot study, Lucretia compared the performance on each item of those who achieved very high test scores with the performance on each item of those who achieved very low test scores. What was she calculating?

   a. Item difficulty

   b. Item discrimination

   c. Item reliability

   d. Item bias

5. Which one of the following is TRUE about items for which the D value is around 0.00?

   a. They do not discriminate well among test takers.

   b. They are too easy for test takers.

   c. They are too difficult for test takers.

   d. They are biased against low performers.

6. The interitem correlation matrix provides important information for identifying what?

   a. Items that are too easy

   b. Items that are too difficult

   c. Items that do not discriminate among test takers

   d. The test's internal consistency

7. Which one of the following contrasts the probability of answering an item correctly with the level of ability on the construct being measured?

   a. The p value

   b. The D value

   c. The item characteristic curve (ICC)

   d. The interitem correlation matrix

8. What is the preferred method for determining item bias?

   a. Item discrimination index

   b. Item characteristic curve (ICC)

   c. Item difficulty level

   d. Interitem correlation matrix

9. Who would be the most appropriate person to put on an expert panel for conducting a qualitative analysis of a school test?

   a. A parent of a child who was tested in the pilot study

   b. A member of the school board

   c. An expert on the constructs being measured

   d. An outside objective party who has no knowledge of the test

10. Which one of the following items would be best to drop from a test?

    a. $p = .4$, $D = 90$

    b. $p = .5$, $D = 70$

    c. $p = .6$, $D = 50$

    d. $p = .9$, $D = -1$

11. Which one of the following does NOT need to be included in the test manual?

    a. The test itself

    b. Evidence of reliability

    c. Evidence of validity

    d. A description of the target audience

12. Which one of the following correctly describes the most likely relationship between a validity coefficient found in an initial validation study and the validity coefficient that will be found when the study is cross validated?

    a. The cross-validated validity coefficient will be lower than the coefficient found in the original study.

    b. The cross-validated validity coefficient will be the same as coefficient found in the original study.

    c. The cross-validated validity coefficient will be higher than coefficient found in the original study.

    d. The cross-validated validity coefficient will be unrelated to the coefficient found in the original study.

13. When Erica conducted the validation study for her test, she found that the validity coefficient for "men only" was not statistically significant; however, the validity coefficient for "women only" was statistically significant. These results suggest that the test has evidence of what type of validity?

    a. Discriminant evidence of validity

    b. Single-group validity

    c. Multiple-group validity

    d. No evidence of validity

14. What are statistics that describe subgroups of the target audience called?

    a. Norms

    b. Subgroup norms

    c. Differential norms

    d. In-group norms

15. When we use tests for making selection decisions, which one of the following is the score at which the decision changes from hire to do not hire?

    a. The normative score

    b. The standard error of measurement

    c. The cut score

    d. The maximum score

16. Which one of the following coefficients is the result of correlating two dichotomous (having only two values) variables?

    a. Validity coefficient

    b. Reliability coefficient

    c. Phi coefficient

    d. Correlation matrix

17. The strength and direction of the relationship between the way test takers responded to an item and the way they responded to all of the items on a test as a whole is described by what coefficient?

    a. Item–total correlation coefficient

    b. Phi coefficient

    c. Item–criterion correlation coefficient

    d. Reliability coefficient

18. According to your textbook, what did researchers Rojdev, Nelson, Hart, and Fercho (1994) conclude about the Minnesota Multiphasic Personality Inventory-1 (MMPI-1) and MMPI-2?

    a. They measure different constructs.

    b. They have significantly different validity coefficients.

    c. They have significantly different reliability estimates.

    d. They are equivalent.

19. An analysis shows that differential validity exists for a test. The regression equation for male students is $Y' = 4.50 + .024x$ and the regression equation for female students is $Y' = 4.50 + .155x$. What type of bias exists?

    a. Slope bias

    b. Intercept bias

    c. Differential item functioning

    d. Fairness bias

20. Which one of the following concepts is associated with social issues rather than statistical or scientific issues?

    a. Slope bias

    b. Differential validity

    c. Measurement bias

    d. Test fairness

Short Answer

1. What is the purpose of a pilot test? When and how should one be conducted?

2. What are the implications of not conducting a pilot test?

3. If you were going to conduct a quantitative item analysis, what statistics would you calculate and why?

4. What is the purpose of a qualitative item analysis? How is one conducted?

5. Discuss the process of revising the test after the pilot study. What process would you use to determine the final test?

6. Discuss the process of validation and cross-validation. What are the outcomes of the validation study?

7. When does a test discriminate unfairly? Include discussions of differential validity and single-group validity.

8. What is a cut score? When is it necessary for a test to have a cut score? What are two methods for determining a cut score?

9. What is the purpose of a test manual? What information should the test manual contain?

ANSWER KEYS

Crossword

ACROSS

2. INTERITEM—Type of correlation matrix that displays the correlation of each item with every other item.
4. SUBGROUP NORMS—Statistics that describe subgroups of the target audience, such as race, sex, and age.
6. DISCRIMINATION INDEX—A statistic that compares the performance of those who made very high test scores with the performance of those who made very low test scores on each item.
8. ICC—Abbreviation referring to the line that results when we graph the probability of answering an item correctly with the level of ability on the construct being measured; the resulting graph provides a picture of both the item's difficulty and discrimination.
10. SUBTLE—Type of question that has no apparent relation to the test purpose or criterion.
12. IRT—Abbreviation for the theory that relates the performance of each item to a statistical estimate of the test taker's ability on the construct being measured.
13. PILOT TEST—A scientific investigation of a new test's reliability and validity for its specified purpose.
15. ITEM BIAS—Differences in responses to test questions that are related to differences in culture, gender, or experiences of the test takers.
16. PHI—Type of coefficient/statistic that describes the relationship between two dichotomous variables.
18. ITEM ANALYSIS—The process of evaluating the performance of each item on a test.

DOWN

1. CUT SCORES—Decision points for dividing test scores into pass/fail groupings.
3. INTERCEPT BIAS—A type of measurement bias in which the intercept of the regression line that is used to predict a criterion of interest is not the same for all demographic groups used in the regression (e.g., men and women).
5. SINGLE-GROUP VALIDITY—When a test is valid for one group but not for another group, such as valid for Whites but not for Blacks.
7. QUALITATIVE ANALYSIS—When test developers ask test takers to complete a questionnaire about how they viewed the test and how they answered the questions.
9. ITEM DIFFICULTY—The percentage of test takers who answer a question correctly.
11. GENERALIZABLE—When a test can be expected to produce similar results even though it has been administered in different locations.
14. MEASUREMENT BIAS—When the scores on a test taken by different subgroups in the population (e.g., men, women) need to be interpreted differently because of some characteristic of the test not related to the construct being measured.
17. CROSS-VALIDATION—Administering a test another time following a validation study to confirm the results of the validation study; because of chance factors that contribute to random error, this second administration can be expected to yield lower correlations with criterion measures.

19. QUANTITATIVE ITEM ANALYSIS—A statistical analysis of the responses that test takers gave to individual test questions.

20. SLOPE—Type of measurement bias in which the slope of the regression line used to predict a criterion is not the same for all demographic groups used in the regression (e.g., men and women).

21. DIFFERENTIAL VALIDITY—When a test yields significantly different validity coefficients for subgroups.

22. EMPIRICALLY BASED—Type of test in which the decision to place an individual in a category is based solely on the quantitative relationship between the predictor and the criterion.

23. ACCULTURATION—The degree to which an immigrant or a minority member has adapted to a country's mainstream culture.

Exercises

1. Items recommended to retain for a 10-item test are indicated by boldface.

Item Number	Average Interitem Correlation	Difficulty	Discrimination Index
1	.40	.90	10
2	**.38**	**.50**	60
3	.05	.50	19
4	.30	.48	−2
5	**.50**	**.50**	50
6	.01	.98	0
7	**.60**	**.60**	48
8	.00	.10	10
9	**.55**	**.49**	40
10	.30	.61	−5
11	**.44**	**.51**	80

(Continued)

(Continued)

Item Number	Average Interitem Correlation	Difficulty	Discrimination Index
12	−.10	.66	7
13	.40	.55	75
14	.77	.43	−10
15	.71	.71	60
16	.33	.56	40
17	.00	.2	15
18	.22	.35	60
19	.55	.43	70
20	.04	.40	16

2. Here are the calculations for the cumulative score for each test taker, item difficulty, and discrimination index.

Test Taker	Item 1	Item 2	Item 3	Item 4	Item 5	Item 6	Item 7	Item 8	Item 9	Item 10	Score
1	1	1	0	1	1	0	1	1	0	1	7
2	0	0	0	1	0	0	0	0	1	1	3
3	0	0	1	1	0	0	1	1	0	1	5
4	0	0	0	0	0	0	1	0	0	1	2
5	1	1	0	1	0	0	1	1	1	1	7
6	1	1	1	1	1	1	1	1	1	1	10
7	1	0	1	1	0	1	0	1	0	1	6
8	1	1	1	1	1	1	1	1	0	1	9
9	0	1	1	1	1	1	1	1	1	1	9
10	0	0	0	1	0	1	1	1	1	1	6
11	0	0	0	1	0	0	0	0	0	0	1
12	0	1	1	1	1	1	1	1	1	1	9
13	1	1	1	1	1	1	1	1	1	1	10
14	0	1	0	1	0	1	1	1	1	1	7
15	1	1	1	1	0	1	0	1	1	1	8
16	0	1	0	1	0	0	0	0	0	0	2

Test Taker	Item 1	Item 2	Item 3	Item 4	Item 5	Item 6	Item 7	Item 8	Item 9	Item 10	Score
17	0	0	0	0	0	0	0	0	0	0	0
18	1	1	1	0	0	1	1	1	0	0	6
p	.44	.61	.50	.83	.33	.56	.67	.72	.50	.78	
D	67	83	83	33	83	100	50	83	67	50	

3. A quantitative item analysis will at minimum always include a measure of item difficulty (p value) to determine that each item is neither too easy nor too hard and a measure of item discrimination (either the D index or item-total correlations) to make sure that each item differentiates between high- and low-ability test takers. If the discrimination index or item-total correlation is negative, the item may be confusing the more able test takers or indicate that the correct answer has been miskeyed.

Although not specifically discussed in this chapter, an item analysis will also always include an estimate of internal consistency, usually coefficient alpha (see Chapter 6) and descriptive statistics such as the mean and standard deviation of all test scores (see Chapter 5).

Depending on the circumstances, the item analysis may also include item–criterion correlations, interitem correlations, and an analysis of the percentage of test takers who choose each distracter to ensure that each one in functioning properly.

4. Which Statistic Should I Use?

A. Research Question	B. Appropriate Statistic(s)
1. Does this item measure the same construct as other items?	interitem correlation, item–total correlation
2. Is this item easier for men than for women?	p value, multiple regression, ICCs
3. Does this item provide information that helps predict a criterion?	Item–criterion correlation
4. How difficult is this item?	p value, ICCs
5. If I drop this item from the test, will it increase or decrease internal reliability?	interitem correlation, item–total correlation
6. How did the people who did well on this test do on this item?	Item–total correlation
7. Is this item of sufficient difficulty, and does it discriminate between high and low performers on the test?	p value, discrimination index, ICCs, item–total correlation
8. Is this test biased against a minority group?	multiple regression
9. How well does the answer on this item correlate with the individual's overall test score?	Item–total correlation

Multiple Choice

1.

Correct Answer: c

Source: Page 343

Explanation: A pilot test is a scientific investigation of the evidence supporting the reliability and validity of test scores. Because validity concerns the inferences from test scores, it is important to pilot test using a sample similar to the target audience. If the pilot test sample and target audience sample are not similar, then it is difficult to conclude that the test is appropriate for the target audience.

2.

Correct Answer: a

Source: Page 344

Explanation: Item difficulty is defined as the percentage of test takers who respond correctly to a test item. An item's difficulty is calculated by dividing the number of people who answered the question correctly by the total number of people who answered the question. Typically, the resulting value is not multiplied by 100 as is done when calculating a percentage; thus the value ranges from 0.00 to 1.00. In a sense, it is really a measure of the item's easiness because higher values indicate more people got the item right and it is therefore easier.

3.

Correct Answer: c

Source: Page 345

Explanation: Based on how item difficulty is calculated, higher values mean more people responded correctly. Therefore a value of .90 would mean that 90% of the people who answered the question did so correctly and a value of 1.00 would mean that everyone who answered the question got it correct. Thus,

questions with item difficulties in this range would be considered easy.

4.

Correct Answer: b

Source: Page 345–346

Explanation: Item discrimination compares the item performance of individuals who achieved high scores on the test with the item performance of those who achieved low scores on the test. Typically test developers will take the top 1/3 of test scorers and the bottom 1/3 of test scorers and use the formula shown below.

$$U = \frac{\text{Number in Upper Group who responded correctly}}{\text{Total number in Upper Group}} \times 100$$

$$L = \frac{\text{Number in Lower Group who responded correctly}}{\text{Total number in Lower Group}} \times 100$$

$$D = U - L$$

Test developers look for items that have high positive D values. In contrast, negative numbers indicate that those who scored low on the test overall responded to the item correctly and that those who scored high on the test responded incorrectly. Low positive numbers suggest that nearly as many people who had low scores responded correctly as did those who had high scores. Each of these situations indicates that the item is not discriminating between high scorers and low scorers.

5.

Correct Answer: a

Source: Page 346

Explanation: Using the formula shown above in Question 4, it is clear that when an item has a D value of 0.00, the same percentage of test takers in the lower scoring group answered the item correctly as those in the higher scoring group. Therefore, there is no difference between high and low scorers on the item and the item does not discriminate between the two groups.

6.

Correct Answer: d

Source: Page 346

Explanation: The interitem correlation matrix provides important information about the test's internal consistency. Each item that measures the same construct should be correlated with other items that measure the same construct. Conversely, items that measure different constructs should not be correlated with each other. Typically, items that are not correlated with other items as expected are removed from the test, which increases the test's internal consistency.

7.

Correct Answer: c

Source: Page 348

Explanation: The item characteristic curve or ICC is derived from a complex statistical procedure called item response theory (IRT). An ICC describes the relationship between a test taker's ability and the probability of answering a test item correctly. ICCs provide rich information to the test developer concerning an item's difficulty and discrimination.

8.

Correct Answer: b

Source: Page 350

Explanation: Although there are a variety of methods for detecting item bias, which is defined as occurring when an item is easier for one group than another group, the ICC is the preferred approach. This is because when ICCs are used the test developer can easily compare the probability of answering the question correctly when both group membership and ability level are considered. The problem with the simple measure of item difficulty that has been

used in the past is that it does not consider possible group differences in ability level.

9.

Correct Answer: c

Source: Page 355

Explanation: While parents and school board members may have a large interest in a test's quality, they are not likely to know much about measurement or about the intended test construct. Therefore, experts on the construct being measured are most likely to provide useful information about improving the test.

10.

Correct Answer: d

Source: Page 356–357

Explanation: A negative discrimination (D) value indicates that lower scoring individuals were more likely to answer the question correctly than high scoring individuals. In addition, a difficulty value (p) of .9 means that 90% of the question takers correctly answered the question, which shows it was extremely easy. Thus, of the answer options provided, answer d is the worst performing question.

11.

Correct Answer: a

Source: Page 372–374

Explanation: Evidence of reliability, validity, and of the target audience are key pieces of information that would allow a test user to make an informed judgment about administering a test. Test users and administrators do not need to have prior knowledge of every test item. Providing widespread and easy access to the test would compromise test security.

12.

Correct Answer: a

Source: Page 359

Explanation: Cross-validation is a method for providing evidence of validity by applying a regression equation calculated on one sample of test takers to a second sample of test takers. The key to answering this question correctly is understanding the concept of *shrinkage* in regression. Statistically, applying a regression equation derived on one group of people to predict the performance of a different group of people will usually result in a lower validity coefficient than was obtained on the original group. It is typical that when the regression weights obtained from one sample are applied to another sample the R^2 value will become smaller.

13.

Correct Answer: b

Source: Page 360

Explanation: Single group validity occurs when the test is valid for one group of test takers, but not for other groups of test takers. In this case, it was valid for men, but not for women. This is an indication of measurement bias.

14.

Correct Answer: b

Source: Page 371

Explanation: Norms are used to compare test scores of similar test takers and aid in test score interpretation. When tests are given to large groups of individuals it is often possible to calculate norms that describe very specific subgroups based on characteristics such as race, sex, and age. These group specific norms are called *subgroup norms*.

15.

Correct Answer: c

Source: Page 371

Explanation: A cut score is a specific score where a decision changes based on test results. For example, an organization may decide that those who score 65 and above on a job knowledge test pass and those score less than 65 fail. Setting valid and legally defensible cut scores can be a challenging task for the test developer.

16.

Correct Answer: c

Source: Page 346

Explanation: Phi coefficients are a statistic that indicates the relationship (correlation) of two dichotomous variables, which are variables that are scored using only two options such as correct (1) and incorrect (0). They are interpreted identically to the well-known Pearson product-moment correlation.

17.

Correct Answer: a

Source: Page 347

Explanation: An item–total correlation correlates the relationship between answering a question correctly/incorrectly and the total test score obtained. Item–total correlations are expected to be greater than 0.00, as this indicates that higher scoring individuals tended to answer the item correctly more than lower scoring individuals. If a question has an item–total correlation of less than 0.00, then this means that lower scoring individuals tended to perform better on the item than higher scoring individuals, which is an indication of a problem with the item.

18.

Correct Answer: d

Source: Page 369

Explanation: Rojdev et al. (1994) compared evidence of validity based on relationships with other external variables of the MMPI-1 and MMPI-2. It is important to conduct such studies when updating or revising a test because test users need to know if different forms of a test are comparable in terms of validity.

19.

Correct Answer: a

Source: Page 363

Explanation: Differential validity occurs when two regression equations describe the test results better than a single overall regression equation. In this case, the question states that the test exhibited differential validity and two equations are given. The type of bias can be determined by examining the regression equations. Because both equations have the same *y*-intercept (4.50) and different slopes (.024 for males and *.155* for females), the test shows slope bias.

20.

Correct Answer: d

Source: Page 368

Explanation: The issue of test fairness often comes up when the issue test validity is discussed. It is important to understand that fairness is based on societal values rather than statistics.

Short Answer

1. A pilot test is a critical part of any test development effort. Pilot tests are conducted to ensure that tests are reliable and valid for their intended purpose. Because test scores are used to make important decisions that can have substantial individual and institutional impact, not conducting a pilot test could be considered unethical. As described in the textbook, just as it would be unsafe to carry passengers on an airplane that has not been tested, as it would be improper to use test scores that have not been shown to be reliable and valid.

The size and complexity of a pilot test depends on the intended purpose of the test. For example, high-stakes tests will require a much larger and sophisticated pilot test than a low-stakes test. It is also important that the pilot test closely mimic the situation that the test will be used to ensure comparability of results and generalizability. After the test has been administered as a pilot, test developers will analyze the results both at the item and test levels. They will be looking at characteristics such as difficulty, discrimination, bias, criterion relationships, and so on. The test developers can also examine the test in a qualitative manner by asking test takers' their experiences while taking the test and conducting interviews and focus groups with subject matter experts. Once this information is obtained, the test developer can then revise and improve the test.

2. Depending on the situation, not conducting a pilot test could be considered unethical. For example, using a test to assess the mental health of a parent in a child custody hearing that has not undergone a pilot test and shown to be reliable and valid would be highly troubling.

3. There are several important quantitative statics to examine during a pilot test. The *item difficulty* is the percentage of test takers who answer a question correctly. This statistic can help weed out overly easy or overly hard test questions. *Item discrimination* is another important statistic. This statistic indicates the relationship between success on the test overall and success on a test question. A question with a 0.00 discrimination means that there is no relationship between test score and success on the question. In other words, the question does not help in discriminating high from low performers. Positive values indicate that better performing individuals perform better on the question. Negative values indicate that there is a problem with the test question because low performers are more likely to get the question correct than are high performers. *Interitem correlations* show how the test questions interrelate and provide important construct related validity evidence allowing test developers to remove items that do not contribute to the measurement of the intended construct(s). *Item–total correlations* provide additional information on the

questions' discrimination. *Item–criterion correlations* show whether the each test question contributes to the prediction of an external criterion, allowing the test developer to use only item that prove to be valuable in the prediction of important outcomes. *Item characteristics curves* (ICC) from Item Response Theory are a useful to examine the difficulty, discrimination, and bias of test questions. Finally, *item bias* is an important consideration. While there are a lot of statistics that examine item bias, the ICC is the preferred method.

4. Qualitative item analyses provide rich and useful information concern test items that might be missed only using quantitative analyses. For example, a qualitative interview can explore how test takers react emotionally to questions, can illustrate cognitive strategies that test takers use to answer test questions, or determine if test takers understand the administration instructions. To collect qualitative information test developers can interview and conduct focus groups with test takers or with subject matter experts.

5. Using quantitative and qualitative information collected during a pilot test to revise a test is a major part of the development process. Because test developers nearly always develop more items than needed, they can use the pilot test results to weed out poorly performing items, thereby improving the overall functioning of the test. Or they may choose to revise and rewrite poorly performing items. However, this can be dangerous because the item is unlikely to be pilot tested again, and there is no guarantee that the item will work as intended. In addition, test developers may need to revise the administration instructions so there is no confusion. This helps to ensure the test measures the desired construct and not the ability to understand test instructions.

6. Because the pilot test is a single administration, the test may predict differently when administered and used in a different setting. Cross-validation helps to evaluate this potential. Typically, the data obtained in a pilot test are divided into two data sets. Using one data set, called the *screening sampled*, a statistical regression model is developed. Then this model is applied to the second data set, called the *validation sample*, and is used to predict values on the criterion. These predicted values are then compared to the actual criterion values obtained in the validation sample. Finally the predicted and actually criterion scores are correlated to tell you how closely the scores align.

7. The *Standards* clearly state that mean group differences in test scores is not an indication of test or measurement bias. This is because in some cases, different groups do have different group means on the construct being measured. Although there are different models of bias, the most common model used is predictive bias. This occurs when a separate regression lines for each group would predict better than a single overall regression line. This is an indication that the test predicts differently for the groups.

8. A cut score is a decision point. At or above a cut score one decision would be made and below the cut score a different decision would be made. Most commonly, the decision on a test is pass/fail. Thus, for a certification test, individuals at or above the cut score would pass and become certified, and those below the score would fail. It is important to have a cut score when a test user must make a dichotomous decision such as pass/fail, hire/don't hire, pathological/not pathological, and so on. Identifying cut scores can be a difficult task, but there are well-accepted approaches. One approach is to use a panel of judges to estimate the number of items that a minimally qualified person is likely to answer correctly. A second approach is to use an external criterion such as job

performance. A regression model would be developed using test score to predict job performance. The point at which job performance became unacceptable would be identified, and then whatever test score corresponded to this value on the regression line would be taken as the cut score.

9. A test manual is a critical component of the test development process. This document gives test users the ability to evaluate the test in terms of reliability, validity, and potential usefulness for their particular application. What is included in the test manual depends on the development process, but some common and important elements include reliability evidence, validity evidence, norms, and information on interpreting test scores. Basically the manual should document the validation and test development process in detail and in its entirety.

References

Adoption of Questions and Answers To Clarify and Provide a Common Interpretation of the *Uniform Guidelines on Employee Selection Procedures*. 44 *Federal Register* 11, 996–12,009 (1979).

AERA, APA, & NCME. (2014). *Standards for educational and psychological testing*. Washington, DC: American Educational Research Association.

Barrett, R. S. (1998). Challenging the myths of fair employment practices. Westport, CT: Quorum Books/Greenwood Publishing Group.

Golubovich, J., Grand, J. A., Ryan, A. M., & Schmitt, N. (2014). An examination of common sensitivity review practices in test development. *International Journal of Selection and Assessment, 22*, 1–11. doi:10.1111/ijsa.12052

Griggs v. Duke Power Company (1971), 401 U.S, 424.

Rojdev, R., Nelson, W. M., III, Hart, K. J., & Fercho, M. C. (1994). Criterion-related validity and stability: Equivalence of the MMPI and the MMPI-2. *Journal of Clinical Psychology, 50*, 361–367.

Uniform Guidelines on Employee Selection Procedures. 43 *Federal Register* 38290–38315 (1978).

13

How Are Tests Used in Educational Settings?

Chapter Overview

In Chapter 13, we begin with an overview of the types of decisions educational professionals make in educational settings based on the results of psychological tests. We discuss educational professionals as test users and specific practice standards educational professionals are expected to follow. Following a discussion of exactly how tests are used in the classroom, we highlight how tests are used in educational settings to make selection and placement decisions, counseling and guidance decisions, and curriculum/administrative policy decisions. We end with a discussion of norm- and criterion-referenced tests and authentic assessment in educational settings.

Learning Objectives

After completing your study of this chapter, you should be able to do the following:

- Describe the types of decisions educational administrators, teachers, and other educational professionals make using psychological test results.
- Explain why educational administrators, teachers, and other educational professionals are test users and why they need to follow professional practice standards.
- Explain the professional practice standards specific to those who use tests in educational settings.
- Explain the differences between norm-referenced and criterion-referenced tests.
- Describe authentic assessment and the perceived advantages and disadvantages of authentic assessment.

Chapter Outline

Key Concepts

authentic assessment:	Assessment that measures a student's ability to apply in real-world settings the knowledge and skills he or she has learned.
criterion-referenced tests:	Tests that involve comparing an individual's test score with an objectively stated standard of achievement, such as being able to multiply numbers.
diagnostic assessment:	Assessment that involves an in-depth evaluation of an individual to identify characteristics for treatment or enhancement.
formative assessments:	Assessments that help teachers determine what information students are and are not learning during the instructional process.
high-stakes test:	A test on which student performance significantly affects educational paths or choices.
norm-referenced tests:	Tests that determine how well an individual's achievement compares with the achievement of others and that distinguish between high and low achievers; standardized tests that have been given to a large representative group of test takers from which scores have been used to create norms.
placement assessments:	Assessments that are used to determine whether students have the skills or knowledge necessary to understand new material and to determine how much information students already know about the new material.
portfolio:	A collection of an individual's work products that a person gathers over time to demonstrate his or her skills and abilities in a particular area.
summative assessments:	Assessment that involves determining what students do and do not know; these are typically used to assign earned grades.

KEY CONCEPTS CROSSWORD

ACROSS

3. Tests that involve comparing an individual's test score with an objectively stated standard of achievement, such as being able to multiply numbers.
4. Assessment that involves determining what students do and do not know; these are typically used to assign earned grades.
7. Assessment that measures a student's ability to apply in real-world settings the knowledge and skills he or she has learned.
8. A collection of an individual's work products that a person gathers over time to demonstrate his or her skills and abilities in a particular area.

DOWN

1. Tests that determine how well an individual's achievement compares with the achievement of others and that distinguish between high and low achievers; standardized tests that have been given to a large representative group of test takers from which scores have been used to create norms.
2. Assessment that helps teachers determine what information students are and are not learning during the instructional process.
5. Test on which student performance significantly affects educational paths or choices.
6. Assessment that involves an in-depth evaluation of an individual to identify characteristics for treatment or enhancement.
8. Assessment that is used to determine whether students have the skills or knowledge necessary to understand new material and to determine how much information students already know about the new material.

LEARNING ACTIVITIES BY LEARNING OBJECTIVE

The following are some study tips and learning activities you can engage in to support the learning objectives for this chapter.

Learning Objectives	Study Tips and Learning Activities
After completing your study of this chapter, you should be able to do the following:	The following study tips will help you meet these learning objectives:
Describe the types of decisions educational administrators, teachers, and other educational professionals make using psychological test results.	• Review Table 13.1, which includes a summary of the types of decisions educators make based on psychological test results. Think of all the tests you have ever taken in an educational setting. For each test, suggest some types of decisions individuals in educational settings may have made using your test scores. • Call and speak to one of your college or university's undergraduate or graduate admissions counselors. Ask the counselor what tests he or she uses to make admissions decisions and how he or she uses the tests as part of the selection process. • Make an appointment with a college career counselor. Ask the counselor to share with you how he or she uses tests to help students explore potential career opportunities. Ask whether you can experience the process. • Call the department of education in your state. Ask to speak to someone who can tell you more about how the results of tests are used to make administrative policy decisions. See whether you can find out how the education system has used the results of tests administered in the school systems in your state to make program, curricular, or administrative policy decisions.
Explain why educational administrators, teachers, and other educational professionals are test users and why they need to follow professional practice standards.	• Reflect on the material presented in Chapter 3 about what constitutes a test user. Explain to another person what makes educational administrators, teachers, and other educational professionals test users. • Review the standards specific to educational professionals as test users. Identify three consequences of educational professionals not following professional practice standards. Consider the consequences to test takers, educational institutions, and society as a whole.
Explain the professional practice standards specific to those who use tests in educational settings.	• Imagine you were asked to make a presentation to administrators and teachers in your local school district about the proper use of tests in educational settings. Prepare a slideshow presentation to include not only some best practices for test use, but the specific standards administrators and teachers should be familiar with and why knowing and following the standards is critical.
Explain the difference between norm-referenced and criterion-referenced tests.	• Imagine you were interviewing an expert who recently developed a standardized test for use in high school educational settings. Write down the questions you would ask to determine if the test she developed was norm-referenced or criterion-referenced without using the terms "norm" or "criterion." Write down what you would listen for to determine the test was norm or criterion-referenced.
Describe authentic assessment and the perceived advantages and disadvantages of authentic assessment.	• Contact one of your college or university's admissions counselors. Ask the counselor whether the school requires applicants to submit test scores. If not, ask whether the school allows applicants to submit portfolios in lieu of test scores. If so, ask the counselor to share the criteria for submission and evaluation of portfolios.

EXERCISES

1. After conducting research on each test shown in the table below, indicate if the test is a norm-referenced test or a criterion-referenced test. Find three other tests that are of interest to you. Indicate if each test is a norm-referenced or criterion-referenced.

Test	Norm-Referenced or Criterion-Referenced?
1. SAT	
2. Praxis Teacher Certification Tests	
3. ACT	
4. Georgia High School Graduation Tests	
5. Stanford Achievement Test	
6. California High School Exit Examination	

2. For each testing example shown in the table below, indicate the type of decision, who typically makes the decision, and the type of test typically used.

Testing Example	Type of Decision	Who Typically Makes the Decision	Type of Test Typically Used
A test is given to determine if a system-wide math program should be continued.			
A student is given a test to help her decide what career she may want to pursue.			
A classroom test to determine a student's final grade.			
A student is given a test to determine if he should be placed in a remedial writing class.			

ADDITIONAL LEARNING ACTIVITIES

Activity 13-1 SAT Test Prep and Coaching

Background

Critics of standardized testing often point out that test prep and coaching are huge industries, with costs often running into the thousands for students and parents. Furthermore, critics argue that there is unequal access to test prep and coaching, with the poorest students being at a disadvantage. Proponents of standardized testing argue that despite the claims of test prep companies, gains in scores attributable to the test prep and coaching is minimal (Powers & Rock, 1999). Furthermore, most reported gains can be attributed to practice and familiarization, neither of which require an expensive training class, as many standardized tests, such as the ACT and SAT, have information and practice tests freely available from the test publishers. Additionally, proponents contend that well-designed programs, which are extensive and exhaustive, do actually result in student learning. As a result, well-designed test prep and coaching programs should result in slight score increases.

In 2014, the College Board announced that it would redesign the SAT for 2016. The Board also announced a partnership with the well-known educational website, the Kahn Academy. This is the first time that the College Board has worked with and shared information with an outside entity about the test. Their collaboration will result in free online programmed instruction for students, as is described the College Board's website. Offered will be

- personalized online practice;
- an unprecedented view into the design of the SAT; and
- free access—anytime, anywhere.

College Board President David Coleman said in an interview, "The College Board cannot stand by while some test-prep providers intimidate parents at all levels of income into the belief that the only way to secure their child's success is to pay for costly test preparation and coaching" (Herold, 2014, para. 4). The president indicated that the arrangement will not involve any exchange of money between the two organizations. The Kahn Academy, a not-for-profit organization, stated on their website that they are "For free. For everyone, Forever. No ads, no subscriptions. We are a not-for-profit because we believe in a free, world-class education for anyone, anywhere" (Khan Academy, 2014, para. 6)

This agreement between the two organizations will help address the inequity of high quality test preparation being available to some, but not readily available to others. Thus, the playing field should be leveled allowing more equal access and help to ensure that SAT success is based on merit and hard work.

Find the Kahn Academy SAT prep site, explore the components, and then answer the questions below.

Questions

1. What content exists on website and what exercises are available?

2. Do you believe that having high-quality test prep material available will help ease criticisms of the SAT? Why or why not?

3. The Kahn Academy has test prep material for graduate level entrance exams as well as undergraduate entrance exams. Imagine you are planning on proceeding to graduate school. Would you use these materials rather than paying for a test prep course? Why or why not?

Activity 13-2 Constructed Response as an Alternative to Multiple-Choice

Background

One common criticism of standardized testing in educational settings is that it relies too heavily on multiple-choice tests, emphasizing recall and recognition rather than higher-order thinking skills. As a result, other test formats are at times suggested, such as short answer and essay. These other formats are called *constructed response tests* because the test taker must construct a response rather than selecting an answer from a set of predetermined response options. However, these types of tests come with their own set of challenges. Constructed responses must be graded in a way that is much different from multiple-choice questions. Grading these types of questions requires more time and, sometimes, money. And it is not an easy task to consistently and fairly score hundreds, thousands, or, in the case of the SAT and ACT, millions of constructed responses.

Consider Todd Farley, who worked for 15 years developing and grading constructed responses for major standardized testing efforts. In 2009, he wrote an exposé book describing his experiences. His first grading task involved a situation where a state department of education decided to have 10-year-olds draw a bike safety poster rather than having them answer multiple-choice questions to demonstrate their knowledge of bike safety. Mr. Farley sat through the rater training on how to apply the scoring rubric, which was pretty simple. The scoring rule was that if the poster clearly demonstrated a bike safety rule, one of which was wearing a helmet, then the drawing would receive full credit. If it did not, then it would receive no credit. The training had the raters practice scoring individually and then discuss their ratings to ensure consistency and a common understanding. Then off he went to score his assigned posters. His very first poster showed

> a young cyclist, a helmet tightly attached to his head, flying his bike in a fantastic parabola up and over a canal filled with flaming oil, his two arms waving wildly in the air, a gleeful grin plastered on his mug. A caption below the drawing screamed, "Remember to Wear Your Helmet!" (p. 6)

His initial response was "huh?" The poster clearly demonstrated the bike safety rule of wearing a helmet, but the nothing about the poster indicated safe bike riding. After calling over the team leader and discussing the poster with her, he gave the poster full credit because of the helmet.

Questions

1. How would you have graded the poster above?

2. How would you have improved the scoring rubric?

3. Should a scoring rubric be strictly adhered to, or is the intent and context important in determining fair, consistent, and accurate grades? Why or why not?

PRACTICE TEST QUESTIONS

The following are some practice questions to assess your understanding of the material presented in this chapter.

Multiple Choice

1. Which one of the following types of decisions is frequently made by teachers using teacher-made tests?
   a. Placement
   b. Diagnostic
   c. Counseling
   d. Curriculum

2. If teachers use psychological tests to determine whether students have the knowledge necessary to learn new material, they are using the tests as what type of assessment?
   a. Diagnostic
   b. Formative
   c. Placement
   d. Summative

3. Teachers use what type of assessment to answer the question, "On which learning tasks are the students progressing satisfactorily?"
   a. Diagnostic
   b. Formative
   c. Placement
   d. Summative

4. Teachers use what type of assessment to answer the question, "Which students have mastered the learning tasks to such a degree that they should proceed to the next course or unit of instruction?"
   a. Diagnostic
   b. Formative
   c. Placement
   d. Summative

5. What was the first vocational test developed in 1927?
   a. Graduate Record Examination (GRE)
   b. Kuder Preference Record (KPR)
   c. Strong Vocational Interest Blank (SVIB)
   d. Jackson Vocational Interest Survey (JVIS)

6. Periodically throughout a school year, teachers may use psychological tests as what type of assessment?
   a. Summative
   b. Formative
   c. Placement
   d. Diagnostic

7. If a teacher suspects a student may be having learning difficulties, the teacher may suggest that the student's learning abilities be evaluated using what type of assessment?
   a. Summative
   b. Formative
   c. Placement
   d. Diagnostic

8. Which one of the following is FALSE about the SAT?

   a. The SAT consists of three sections.

   b. The SAT has a guessing penalty.

   c. The SAT is an achievement test.

   d. Math makes up 50% of the score.

9. Which one of the following is FALSE about the ACT?

   a. The ACT has questions on trigonometry.

   b. The ACT measures science reasoning.

   c. The ACT is an achievement test.

   d. Math questions make up 50% of the test.

10. What tests involve comparing an individual's test score with an objectively stated standard of achievement?

   a. Authentic assessments

   b. Standardized tests

   c. Norm-referenced tests

   d. Criterion-referenced tests

11. If you had to provide three examples of a norm-referenced test, which one of the following would you NOT provide?

   a. ACT

   b. SAT

   c. Stanford Achievement Test

   d. Authentic assessment

12. Which one of the following is TRUE about authentic assessment?

   a. Authentic assessment is most valuable for measuring application of learning.

   b. Authentic assessment is a norm-referenced test.

   c. Authentic assessment is more reliable than criterion-referenced and norm-referenced tests.

   d. Authentic assessment often includes more than one measure of performance.

Short Answer

1. Describe the types of decisions educators make based on the results of psychological tests.

2. How do educators use test scores to make curriculum and administrative policy decisions? Provide examples.

3. Explain why educators are test users and why they need to follow the test user guidelines discussed in Chapter 3.

4. Compare and contrast how teachers use psychological tests in the classroom before, during, and after instruction. Give examples of each.

5. Provide some examples of how psychological tests can benefit student motivation, retention and transfer of learning, self-assessment, and instructional effectiveness.

6. Describe how tests are used by educational institutions to make selection and placement decisions. Include a discussion of some of the most common tests used for selection.

7. Describe how tests are used by educational institutions to make counseling and guidance decisions.

8. What are the similarities and differences between the ACT and the SAT? If you have well-developed math skills and an extensive vocabulary, on which test (the ACT or the SAT) might you perform better? Why?

9. What are the similarities and differences between norm-referenced and criterion-referenced tests? Provide an example of each.

10. Why would someone want to or choose to use authentic assessment?

ANSWER KEYS

Crossword

ACROSS

3. CRITERION-REFERENCED—Tests that involve comparing an individual's test score with an objectively stated standard of achievement, such as being able to multiply numbers.
4. SUMMATIVE—Assessment that involves determining what students do and do not know; these are typically used to assign earned grades.
7. AUTHENTIC—Assessment that measures a student's ability to apply in real-world settings the knowledge and skills he or she has learned.
8. PORTFOLIO—A collection of an individual's work products that a person gathers over time to demonstrate his or her skills and abilities in a particular area.

DOWN

1. NORM-REFERENCED—Tests that determine how well an individual's achievement compares with the achievement of others and that distinguish between high and low achievers; standardized tests that have been given to a large representative group of test takers from which scores have been used to create norms.
2. FORMATIVE—Assessment that helps teachers determine what information students are and are not learning during the instructional process.
5. HIGH-STAKES—Test on which student performance significantly affects educational paths or choices.
6. DIAGNOSTIC—Assessment that involves an in-depth evaluation of an individual to identify characteristics for treatment or enhancement.
8. PLACEMENT—Assessment that is used to determine whether students have the skills or knowledge necessary to understand new material and to determine how much information students already know about the new material.

Exercises

1.

Test	Norm-Referenced or Criterion-Referenced
SAT	Norm-Referenced
Praxis Teacher Certification Tests	Criterion-Referenced
ACT	Norm-Referenced
Georgia High School Graduation Tests	Criterion-Referenced
Stanford Achievement Test	Norm-Referenced
California High School Exit Examination	Criterion-Referenced

2.

Testing Example	Type of Decision	Who Typically Makes the Decision	Type of Test Typically Use
A test is given to determine if a system-wide math program should be continued.	Administrative	Specialist Or Administrator	Standardized
A student is given a test to help her decide what career she may want to pursue.	Counseling and guidance	Specialist Or Administrator	Standardized
A classroom test to determine a student's final grade.	Grading	Teacher	Teacher Made
A student is given a test to determine if he should be placed in a remedial writing class.	Placement	Specialist Or Administrator	Standardized

Multiple-Choice

1.

Correct Answer: b

Source: Page 383 & 393

Explanation: Teachers use tests to understand a student's strengths and difficulties. In addition, it is important to note that these tests tend to be teacher made and are not constructed by professional test developers. In contrast, the other answer options are used by a specialist.

2.

Correct Answer: c

Source: Page 383 & 392

Explanation: Teachers will often use psychological tests as placement assessments which determine the extent to which students possess the knowledge, skills, and abilities necessary to understand new material and how much of the material to be taught that students already know.

3.

Correct Answer: b

Source: Page 383 & 392

Explanation: Throughout the school year, teachers may administer tests as formative assessments. Formative assessments help teachers determine what information students are and are not learning during the instructional process. Formative assessments allow teachers to identify areas that students need help with and decide whether it is appropriate to move to the next unit of instruction. These assessments are not used to assign grades; instead, teachers use formative assessments to make immediate adjustments to their own curriculum and teaching methods. That is, teachers can use the results of formative assessments to adjust the pace of their teaching and the material they are covering. Formative assessments are different from diagnostic assessments, in that teachers use tests to determine what information students are and are not learning. In contrast, teachers use diagnostic assessments tests to assess students' learning abilities.

4.

Correct Answer: d

Source: Page 383 & 395

Explanation: Teachers use summative assessments at the end of instruction to determine what students do and do not know and to assign grades. For example, teachers use midterms and final exams to assess the students' level of knowledge and learning and then assign grades using the results. Sometimes students confuse formative and summative assessment, but there are differences. When an assessment is formative, the results are used to direct future instruction. In contrast, when an assessment is used as a summative assessment, the test is often used as a final evaluation to determine grades.

5.

Correct Answer: c

Source: Page 402

Explanation: E. K. Strong developed the first vocational test in 1927, called the Strong Vocational Interest Blank. Updated versions are still used today under the name Strong Interest Inventory.

6.

Correct Answer: b

Source: Page 383 & 392

Explanation: During the course of instruction, teachers my use formative assessments to determine what information students are and are not learning. The assessments provide information allowing teachers to gauge student learning. They can then adjust their teaching as needed.

7.

Correct Answer: d

Source: Page 383 & 393

Explanation: When students have problems with learning, teachers may suggest evaluating the student's learning abilities using a more focused diagnostic assessment. Diagnostic tests are generally quite long, but do allow for more accurate evaluation of learning difficulties.

8.

Correct Answer: c

Source: Page 399

Explanation: The SAT is an *aptitude* test that measures skills students have learned in school. In contrast, the ACT is a content-based *achievement* test that measures what students have learned in school.

9.

Correct Answer: d

Source: Page 399

Explanation: The math portion of the ACT makes up 25% of the total score. In contrast, the math portion of the SAT makes up 50% of the total score for that college admission test.

10.

Correct Answer: d

Source: Page 405

Explanation: All of the tests described in Chapter 13 can be considered either norm-referenced or criterion-referenced tests. Norm-referenced tests are standardized tests in which a test taker's score is compared with the scores of a group of test takers who previously took the test. Criterion-referenced tests, on the other hand, are tests that compare a test taker's scores with an objectively stated standard of achievement, such as the learning objectives for this chapter. With criterion-referenced tests, an individual's performance is based on how well he or she has learned a specific body of knowledge or skills or on how well the individual performs compared with some pre-determined standard of performance.

11.

Correct Answer: d

Source: Page 405

Explanation: The ACT, SAT, and Stanford Achievement Test are all norm-referenced tests because scores are interpreted in comparison to other test takers. In contrast, the focus of authentic assessment is on assessing a student's ability to perform real-world tasks by applying the knowledge and skills he or she has learned.

12.

Correct Answer: a

Source: Page 406

Explanation: Authentic assessment is very valuable for measuring the application of learning. This is because the focus of authentic assessment is on assessing a student's ability to perform real-world tasks. It requires that students apply the knowledge and skills they have learned. Authentic assessment relies on more than one measure of performance, is criterion referenced, and relies on human judgment.

Short Answer

1. There are eight types of decisions that educators make based on the results of psychological tests. Each is listed below.

Instructional decisions: Decisions made by classroom teachers based on tests typically constructed by teachers themselves. The decisions determine instructional strategies such as pace of course.

Grading decisions: Decisions made by classroom teachers based on tests typically constructed by teachers themselves. As the title describes, these decisions are used to determine grades and assessments using assessments such as quizzes, midterms, and so on.

Diagnostic decisions: Decisions made by classroom teachers based on tests typically constructed by teachers themselves. The assessment information is used to understand the student's strengths and weakness. For example, does the student know single digit multiplication?

Selection decisions: Decisions made by a specialist or administrator based on standardized tests. Assessments are used to make group, program, or institutional decisions such as selection into a gifted program.

Placement decisions: Decisions made by a specialist or administrator based on standardized tests. These decisions use assessment to determine the placement of individuals such as should the student be placed in a remedial, standard, or advancement mathematics course.

Counseling and guidance decisions: Decisions made by a specialist or administrator based on standardized tests. These types of decisions occur when students are given assistance and help in selecting things such as a career or program of study.

Program and curriculum decisions: Decisions made by a specialist or administrator based on standardized tests. These types of decisions are made when specialists or administrators use test scores to make broad program or curricular decisions such as adding or dropping an educational program.

Administrative policy decisions: High-level decisions made at the district, state, or national level by a specialist or administrator based on standardized tests. The decisions often involve aspects of education such as budgets or program implementation at a broad level.

2. Administrators are responsible for making broad system-wide improvements and their decisions, which are often informed by test and assessment information, have policy, curricular, and budgetary implications. For example, recently many school districts have implemented pay-for-performance programs for teachers that at least partially link teacher pay to student performance on standardized tests. Administrators may also use test information to assess curriculum at the end of the year to decide if programs need to be added, dropped, or modified.

3. Teachers are test users because they use test information as input to decisions. Any time decisions are made on the basis of test scores, the users should adhere to the testing standards described in Chapter 3. It would be irresponsible and unethical to make important decisions using tests for which the reliability and validity were unknown or unsubstantiated.

4. Teachers make a variety of decisions before, during, and after instruction. At each stage, they may ask slightly different questions and make different decisions, but the goal is always to make accurate decisions. For example, during instruction, the teacher may ask what skills and knowledge the students possess and then make placement decisions. During instruction, the teacher may ask what the students are learning and where students need help. Thus, they are making formative and diagnostic decisions at this point. After instruction, the teacher may ask what the students have learned and what grade they should receive, and as a result are making summative assessments.

5. Tests can aid in the instructional process in several ways. First, tests can influence student motivation by increasing the desire to study and by providing feedback on what the student did correctly and incorrectly on the test. Second, tests can increase retention and transfer of learning to real situations. Test questions can be written in such a way that requires students to apply what they have learned to different situations and repeated exposure to test questions can in recall and memorization. Third, tests can promote student self-assessment and self-awareness by providing students objective and accurate information that they can then act on for improvement. Fourth, test can be used to determine instructional effectiveness, thus allowing teachers to improve their methods or tailor teaching strategies to the students' needs.

6. Educational institutions are faced with making many selection and placement decisions. For example, colleges and universities may receive many more student applications than they can admit. Thus, they need a fair and objective method to screen out individuals who are not likely to succeed and admit those who are likely to perform well. At the undergraduate level, the two most common tests used for selection are the ACT and SAT. However, there have been recent efforts to rely less on a single test for admission. Student portfolios of work have been used as an alternative to standardized tests, but these can be difficult to implement and hard to ensure that they adhere to testing standards. Once students are accepted, colleges and universities often use tests to make decisions regarding placement of students into classes. For example, it is common to give incoming freshmen writing and math tests to determine placement into an appropriate level class.

7. Nearly all colleges and universities have a career services office that helps students in many ways. One activity they perform is providing counseling and guidance to students on potential careers. Before offering counseling and guidance, they may use one of several tests that give students feedback on their skills and interests. This information is then used to provide a list of

majors and careers that best match student interests and skills. Some commonly used assessments are the Campbell Interest and Skill Survey, Strong Interest Inventory, and the Self-Directed Search.

8. The ACT and the SAT are the two main undergraduate college admissions tests used in the United States. Colleges and universities on the West and East Coasts tend to require the SAT while those in the Midwest tend to require the ACT. The two tests are predictors of college success, but there are differences. The SAT is an aptitude test that measures skills students have learned in school. In contrast, the ACT is a content-based achievement test and measures what students have learned in school. While on the SAT has three sections relating to reading and writing, math, and an optional writing test, the ACT has five sections including English, math, reading, science, and an optional writing test. The SAT places more emphasis on math with that section counting as 50% of the total score, while on the ACT only 25% of the total score is determined by math. In terms of language, the SAT measures more vocabulary than the ACT, but it does not test for grammar, which the ACT does test for. When taking the SAT students should understand that the test is not entirely multiple choice and that there is a penalty for guessing. The ACT is entirely multiple choice, and there is no guessing penalty. Therefore, if you had well-development math skills and a highly developed vocabulary, you should perform better on the SAT rather than the ACT because math is more heavily weighted on the SAT and it also includes a vocabulary section which is not included in the ACT.

9. Both norm-reference and criterion-referenced tests can be used as input into educational decisions. In a norm-referenced test, test takers' scores are compared to the other test takers and the scores are interpreted based on their relationship to the other scores. In contrast, a criterion-referenced test compares scores to an objectively defined standard of achievement, and there is no comparison to other test takers. Examples of norm-referenced tests are the ACT and SAT. If you scored 500 on the SAT math test then you scored better than 50% of the test takers. On the other hand, most certification and licensing tests are criterion-referenced tests and passing is based on passing a specific score, which indicates that the test taker possesses the requisite knowledge and skills to be successful.

10. Authentic assessment is a form or assessment where students are asked to perform tasks that are real world in nature and demonstrate the application of specific knowledge and skills. Proponents of authentic assessment believe students acquire their knowledge to perform a task or produce a product and therefore assessment should focus on the capability to actually perform the task or produce the product. Therefore, authentic assessment is a good choice when there is a need to demonstrate a skill rather than just knowing about it. For example, being able to successfully draw blood rather than just knowing the steps.

References

Farley, T. S. (2009). *Making the grades: My misadventures in the standardized testing industry.* Sausalito, CA: PoliPointPress.

Herold, B. (March 12, 2014). College board enlists Khan Academy for SAT prep. *Education Week.* Retrieved from http://www.edweek.org/ew/articles/2014/03/12/24satside.h33.html

Khan Academy. (2014). About. Retrieved from https://www.khanacademy.org/about

Powers, D. E., & Rock, D. A. (1999). Effects of coaching on SAT I: Reasoning test scores. *Journal of Educational Measurement, 36,* 93–118. Retrieved from http://onlinelibrary.wiley.com/journal/10.1111/%28ISSN%291745-3984

14

How Are Tests Used in Clinical and Counseling Settings?

Chapter Overview

In Chapter 14, we begin with an overview of the many ways tests are used in clinical and counseling settings, such as in psychotherapists' offices, hospitals, and counseling centers—anywhere clients are treated for mental health problems or problems in daily living. We then review the kinds of tests, and the specific tests, that are used. Following a discussion of how psychological testing is used in the assessment of three common conditions (autism spectrum disorders, depression, and Alzheimer's disease), we review the technical issue of incremental validity and the meaning of evidence-based assessment. We end with a discussion of the product of test use—providing feedback to clients and preparing a written report about the results of psychological testing.

Learning Objectives

After completing your study of this chapter, you should be able to do the following:

- Explain the work of clinical and counseling psychologists and other mental health counselors.
- Describe how mental health practitioners use psychological tests to diagnose mental health problems, plan treatment programs, monitor client progress, and assess treatment outcomes.
- Identify the different kinds of psychological tests used in clinical and counseling settings.
- Discuss how psychological tests are used in the diagnosis of autism spectrum disorders, depression, and Alzheimer's disease.
- Define evidence-based assessment.
- Explain the two final products of psychological testing in clinical and counseling settings.

Chapter Outline

The Work of Clinical and Counseling Psychologists
Mental Health Diagnosis
Tests Used in Clinical and Counseling Settings
  Structured Interviews
  Behavior Rating Scales
  Symptom Checklists and Symptom-Based Self-Report Tests
  Comprehensive, Clinically Oriented Self-Report Tests
  Performance-Based, or Projective, Clinically Oriented Personality Tests
  Cognitive and Memory Testing
  Neuropsychological Testing
  Specialized Forensic Testing
Case Examples of How Tests Are Used in Clinical and Counseling Settings
  Joanne
  Jesse
  Juan
Psychological Testing in Depth: Assessing Autism, Depression, and Alzheimer's Disease
  Autism Spectrum Disorders
  Depression
  Alzheimer's Disease
Incremental Validity and Evidence-Based Assessment
The Psychological Testing Report and Client Feedback
Chapter Summary

Key Concepts

autism spectrum disorders:	Developmental disabilities that affect communication and social interaction and involve restricted interests and stereotyped, repetitive patterns of behavior.
comorbid disorders:	The presence of mental health problems in addition to depression.
evidence-based practice:	"The integration of the best available research with clinical expertise in the context of patient characteristics, culture, and preferences" (APA, 2014, para. 2).
evidence-based treatment methods:	Treatment methods with documented research evidence that the methods are effective for solving the problems being addressed.
obsessive compulsive disorder:	A mental disorder characterized by repetitive, intrusive ideas or behavior.
projective drawings:	A psychological test in which the assessor directs the test takers to draw their own pictures.
semistructured interviews:	An interview that contains predetermined questions, but the format also allows the assessor to ask some open-ended questions and follow-up questions to clarify the interviewee's responses.
structured clinical interviews:	An interview that has a predetermined set of questions in which the assessor assigns numbers or scores to the answers based on their content.

KEY CONCEPTS CROSSWORD

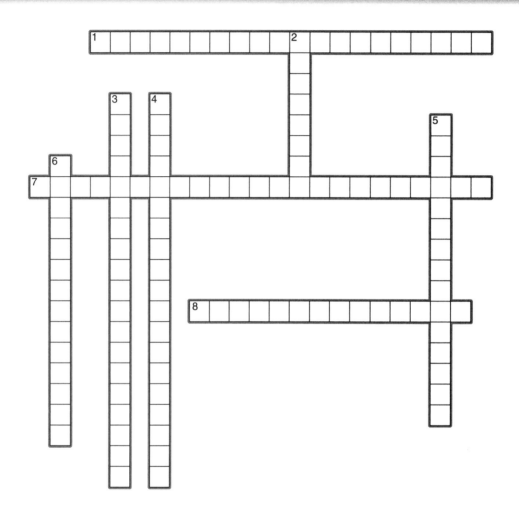

ACROSS

1. A mental disorder characterized by repetitive, intrusive ideas or behavior.
7. What psychologists do when they integrate their clinical expertise with available research.
8. Type of interview that contains predetermined questions, but the format also allows the assessor to ask some open-ended questions and follow-up questions to clarify the interviewee's responses.

DOWN

2. The presence of a disorder or mental health problem in addition to depression.
3. A psychological test in which the assessor directs the test takers to draw their own pictures.
4. A type of interview that has a predetermined set of questions in which the assessor assigns numbers or scores to the answers based on their content.
5. Developmental disorders that affect communication and social interaction and involve restricted interests and stereotyped, repetitive patterns of behavior.
6. Treatment methods with documented research.

LEARNING ACTIVITIES BY LEARNING OBJECTIVE

The following are some study tips and learning activities you can engage in to support the learning objectives for this chapter.

Learning Objectives	Study Tips and Learning Activities
After completing your study of this chapter, you should be able to do the following:	The following study tips and learning activities will help you meet these learning objectives:
Explain the work of clinical and counseling psychologists and other mental health counselors	• Interview a counselor or clinical psychologist about his or her work. Ask about the types of tests used in the practice and why they are used. Share your findings with your classmates or instructor.
Describe how mental health practitioners use psychological tests to diagnose mental health problems, plan treatment programs, monitor client progress, and assess treatment outcomes.	• Do an Internet search to find examples of how psychological tests are used in health care settings. Consider accessing sites such as the Association of Test Publishers. Share your findings with your classmates or instructor.
Identify the different kinds of psychological tests used in clinical and counseling settings.	• Search the *Mental Measurement Yearbook*, *Tests in Print*, test publisher websites, or the Internet to find examples of tests used in clinical and counseling settings. Make a list of five tests, what the tests measure, and how the tests are used in clinical or counseling settings. Share your findings with your class or instructor
Discuss how psychological tests are used in the diagnosis of autism spectrum disorders, depression, and Alzheimer's disease.	• Interview a psychologist or counselor who treats patients with autism spectrum disorders, depression, and/or Alzheimer's disease to discover which tests he or she uses in practice and why. Then, interview a parent or teacher of a child diagnosed with an autism spectrum disorder to find out how testing was used in the diagnosis or treatment of the child. Report your findings to your class or instructor.
Define evidence-based assessment.	• Do an Internet search to find actual examples of how evidence-based assessment has been used in clinical or counseling settings. Report your findings to your class or instructor.
Explain the two final products of psychological testing in clinical and counseling settings.	• Imagine you sought treatment from a clinical psychologist. Think about what information you would like to know if the psychologist administered a test to you. What information would you want your feedback about your test results to include? • Document some of the pros and cons of including specific feedback about test results in a clinical and counseling setting.

EXERCISES

1. The table below contains four clinical and counseling scenarios. For each scenario, identify what type of psychologist (clinical, counseling, forensic, neuropsychologist) is most likely to be involved.

Scenario	Type of Psychologist
1. A child with epilepsy is referred to a psychologist for evaluation to make treatment recommendations to improve functioning.	
2. A psychologist gives the Test of Memory Malingering to determine between a legitimate memory and a memory that is being faked.	
3. A psychologist gives the Million Clinical Multiaxial Inventory for diagnostic purposes.	
4. A patient is administered the Y-BOCS to determine if she has obsessive compulsive disorder.	

2. Using the symptoms and information in the first column, identify what condition is likely to exist.

Symptoms	Condition
1. Richard, age 67, has suffered a gradual loss of memory, thinking, and speaking skills. This has further resulted in anxiety, agitation, and depression.	
2. Frank, at the age of three, was assessed by a pediatrician using the Ages and Stages Questionnaire; the assessment showed delayed verbal and nonverbal communication skills and repetitive rocking behavior.	
3. Juanita has experienced repetitive intrusive thoughts and behaviors. A clinician gives her the Y-BOCS measure.	
4. A clinician asks Sandy about her sleep, appetite, mood, and suicidal feelings. She also has her complete the BDI-II.	
5. Since adolescence Jake, who is now 42, has been inflexible, has had a pattern of unstable relationships, and has been impulsive. Because of his chronic interpersonal difficulties, he is depressed and has anxiety. In addition, his behavior has differed substantially from the cultural norms.	

ADDITIONAL LEARNING ACTIVITIES

Activity 14-1 Self-Diagnosis with Online Tests and Assessments

Background

It is easy to find "psychological" tests online. Some are psychometrically sound, and you can find them at academically respected websites. Others are not psychometrically sound, and you will find them at other websites. For example, Stanford Medicine at their WellMD website has a webpage called Test Yourself. At this site, you will find links to popular online screening tests for anxiety, PTSD, and depression. Another example, *Psychology Today*, which is a popular magazine and not a scientific publisher of psychological findings, has a prominent "Tests" section. At the *Psychology Today* website, you can find tests on a wide variety of constructs, some of which are low-stakes fun tests such as the "Adventurousness Test." However, they also have other tests that assess clinical disorders such as anxiety and depression.

There is probably little potential for damage with online tests that are presented in a fun way and do not assess clinical constructs (such as the Adventurousness Test). However, when the tests purport to measure psychological and psychiatric conditions, such as depression or PTSD, there are potential problems even if the tests are psychometrically sound. For example, there can be potentially serious effects when people receive distressing feedback without appropriate follow-up counseling and guidance. Interestingly, a post by Srini Pillay, MD at *Psychology Today* warns about self-diagnosis with such online tests (Pillay, 2010). For example, people can easily miss subtleties that a trained individual could easily identify. In addition, there are common cognitive biases that can prevent a person from seeing themselves accurately and disorders such as delusional disorder that can cause people to misrepresent themselves.

Pillay stated that one of the greatest dangers of self-diagnosis of psychological problems is that a medical disease may be missed. He provides the example of self-diagnosing yourself as having panic disorder and missing hyperthyroidism or an irregular heartbeat. Another problem is comorbid conditions. These are conditions that commonly occur together. Pillay provides the example that if you had insomnia, inattention, and depression, you may believe that you have a sleep disorder, ADD, and major depression; however, depression can account for all of those symptoms.

If you believe you have a problem or are having symptoms causing distress, you should see a professional for diagnosis and treatment. Self-education can be beneficial, but self-diagnosis can be dangerous.

Questions

1. Have you ever taken a fun online psychological test such as a personality test? How about a test for a clinical psychological disorder? If yes, what tests did you take and why?

2. What are some risks and possible benefits by providing psychology tests online?

3. Integrating your learning from Chapter 3 and Chapter 14, what are some ethical issues that a psychologist might face if he or she put a psychological test online with open access?

Activity 14-2 Forensic Psychology

Interest in forensic psychology has surged in the last few years. This may be partially attributable to popular television shows that portray criminal profiling, but this is an erroneous view of forensic psychology (Ward, 2013). In reality, forensic psychology is the application of clinical psychology in legal settings. The most frequent activity of forensic psychologists is the psychological assessment of individuals who are involved with the legal system. After performing assessments, forensic psychologists write reports and may give testimony in court. Thus, the forensic psychologist must have a strong background in both testing and assessment and in the legal system. To become a forensic psychologist, you must obtain a PhD or PsyD from an American Psychological Association–accredited school and have two years of supervised professional experience. Licensing varies from state to state and there is most likely a licensing examination as well.

Because testing is a major component of the job, forensic psychologists must know and use many different types of assessments. Archer, Buffington-Vollum, Stredny, and Handel (2006) looked at what tests are most likely to be used by surveying forensic psychologists. For example, they found that the most commonly used multiscale inventory was the Minnesota Multiphasic Personality Inventory, which was used at least once by 129 of the 131 responding forensic psychologists. The table below shows the most used tests by test type.

Type of Test	Test
Multiscale inventory for adults	Minnesota Multiphasic Personality Inventory
Clinical scale	Beck Depression Inventory-II
Unstructured personality tests	Rorschach
Cognitive and achievement tests	Wechsler Intelligence scale
Neuropsychology test	Trail Making Tests A and B
Risk assessment/psychopathy	Psychopathy Checklists

Sex offender risk	Static 99
Competency or sanity	MacAruthur Competence Assessment Tool
Malingering	Structured Interview of Reported Symptoms
Child-related forensic issues	Minnesota Multiphasic Personality Inventory-Adolescent

Questions

1. Research one of the tests listed in the table above. Briefly describe the test.

2. Explain how well the popular television portrayal of forensic psychology aligns with the description of forensic psychology described above.

PRACTICE TEST QUESTIONS

The following are some practice questions to assess your understanding of the material presented in this chapter.

Multiple Choice

1. Which one of the following mental health jobs requires a medical degree?
   a. Clinical psychologist
   b. Counseling psychologist
   c. Social worker
   d. Psychiatrist

2. What is it called when clinical psychologists use treatment methods that are based on documented research evidence that are effective for solving the problems being addressed?
   a. Psychotherapy
   b. Evidence-based treatment
   c. Behavioral-based therapy
   d. Clinical assessment and treatment

3. What is the most current edition of the *Diagnostic and Statistical Manual of Mental Disorders?*
   a. 2nd edition
   b. 3rd edition
   c. 4th edition
   d. 5th edition

4. Which one of the following is an example of a semi-structured interview?
   a. Millon Clinical Multiaxial Inventory
   b. Minnesota Multiphasic Personality Inventory 2
   c. Yale-Brown Compulsive Scale
   d. The Posttraumatic Stress Disorder Checklist-Civilian

5. Which one of the following typically requires an informant, usually a parent or teacher, to rate a client in regard to very specific behaviors?
   a. Rating scales
   b. Semi-structured interviews
   c. Symptom checklists
   d. Minnesota Multiphasic Personality Inventory 2

6. What test was originally published in 1940s and is still widely used in clinical settings?
   a. Personality Assessment Inventory
   b. Millon Clinical Multiaxial Inventory
   c. Minnesota Multiphasic Personality Inventory
   d. Clinical Assessment Tool

7. The Exner scoring system is used with which projective technique?
   a. Thematic Apperception Test
   b. Rorschach
   c. Kinetic Family Drawing
   d. Draw-A-Person

8. What type of mental health worker focuses on the relationship between brain functioning and behavior?

   a. Clinical psychologist

   b. Psychiatric nurse

   c. Forensic psychologist

   d. Neuropsychologist

9. Which one of the following is a screening tool clinicians often use for autism?

   a. Ages and Stages Questionnaire

   b. Bayley Scales of Infant and Toddler Development

   c. Millon Clinical Multiaxial Inventory

   d. Autism Spectrum Screener

10. In 2010, the Centers for Disease Control found approximately what percentage of adults in the United States met the diagnostic criteria for a depressive disorder?

   a. 5%

   b. 9%

   c. 12%

   d. 17%

11. Which one of the following conditions is a progressive illness associated with a gradual loss of memory, thinking, and speaking skills and often has behavioral and emotional symptoms, such as anxiety, agitation, and depression?

   a. Parkinson's Disease

   b. Alzheimer's Disease

   c. Stroke

   d. Dementia

12. What term is used when two mental conditions co-occur at the same time?

   a. Combined diagnoses

   b. Dissimulation

   c. Comorbid

   d. Duel diagnoses

Short Answer

1. Compare and contrast the work of clinical and counseling psychologists with other mental health workers.

2. What is evidence-based assessment?

3. How are psychological tests used in the diagnosis of depression?

4. What is the controversy surrounding projective testing? Give examples of three kinds of projective tests.

5. What are the two final products of psychological testing in most clinical and counseling contexts?

ANSWER KEYS

Crossword

ACROSS

1. OBSESSIVE COMPULSIVE—A mental disorder characterized by repetitive, intrusive ideas or behavior.
7. EVIDENCE-BASED PRACTICE— What psychologists do when they integrate their clinical expertise with available research.
8. SEMISTRUCTURED—Type of interview that contains predetermined questions, but the format also allows the assessor to ask some open-ended questions and follow-up questions to clarify the interviewee's responses.

DOWN

2. COMORBID—The presence of a disorder or mental health problem in addition to depression.
3. PROJECTIVE DRAWINGS—A psychological test in which the assessor directs the test takers to draw their own pictures.
4. STRUCTURED CLINICAL—A type of interview that has a predetermined set of questions in which the assessor assigns numbers or scores to the answers based on their content.
5. AUTISM SPECTRUM—Developmental disorders that affect communication and social interaction and involve restricted interests and stereotyped, repetitive patterns of behavior.
6. EVIDENCE-BASED—Treatment methods with documented research evidence that the methods are effective for solving the problems being addressed.

Exercises

1.

Scenario	Type of Psychologist
A child with epilepsy is referred to a psychologist for evaluation to make treatment recommendations to improve functioning.	Neuropsychologist
A psychologist gives the Test of Memory Malingering to determine between a legitimate memory and a memory that is being faked.	Forensic Psychologist
A psychologist gives the Million Clinical Multiaxial Inventory for diagnostic purposes.	Clinical or Counseling Psychologist
A patient is administered the Y-BOCS to determine if she has obsessive compulsive disorder.	Clinical or Counseling Psychologist

2.

Symptoms	Condition
1. Richard, age 67, has suffered a gradual loss of memory, thinking, and speaking skills. This has further resulted in anxiety, agitation, and depression.	Alzheimer's disease
2. Frank, at the age of three, was assessed by a pediatrician using the Ages and Stages Questionnaire; the assessment showed delayed verbal and nonverbal communication skills and repetitive rocking behavior.	Autism spectrum disorders
3. Juanita has experienced repetitive intrusive thoughts and behaviors. A clinician gives her the Y-BOCS measure.	Obsessive compulsive disorder
4. A clinician asks Sandy about her sleep, appetite, mood, and suicidal feelings. She also has her complete the BDI-II.	Depression
5. Since adolescence Jake, who is now 42, has been inflexible, has had a pattern of unstable relationships, and has been impulsive. Because of his chronic interpersonal difficulties, he is depressed and has anxiety. In addition, his behavior has differed substantially from the cultural norms.	Borderline personality disorder

Multiple-Choice

1.

Correct Answer: d

Source: Page 414–415

Explanation: Psychiatrists are medical doctors who have a medical degree, and who completed a four-year residency with at least a minimum of three years working with patients with mental disorders. The other occupations do not require a medical degree.

2.

Correct Answer: b

Source: Page 415

Explanation: Mental health professionals use varied approaches to treatment, depending on their training, preferences, the client populations they serve, and the setting they work in. Most use evidence-based treatment methods—treatment methods with documented research evidence that the method is effective for solving the problems being addressed. However, evidence-based methods are not available for every client in every situation.

3.

Correct Answer: d

Source: Page 417

Explanation: The DSM, a handbook published by the American Psychiatric Association and now in its fifth edition, contains descriptions, symptoms, and criteria for diagnosing over 300 mental disorders. The DSM-5 is the authoritative book professionals use to diagnose of mental health problems. Medical and mental health professionals and all other parties involved in the diagnosis and treatment of mental health conditions use the DSM to help them diagnose mental disorders.

4.

Correct Answer: c

Source: Page 419

Explanation: The Yale-Brown Compulsive Scale is known as the gold standard measure of obsessive compulsive disorder. The clinician is guided to ask the client a range of detailed questions about specific obsessive thoughts and compulsive behaviors, notes the current and past presence of each, and rates the severity of the symptoms based on specific criteria. Clinician ratings rely on the patient's report, observations, and reports of others.

5.

Correct Answer: a

Source: Page 420

Explanation: Rating scales typically require an informant, usually a parent or teacher, to rate a client in regard to very specific behaviors. In contrast, checklists are most often self-report tests that clients complete themselves.

6.

Correct Answer: c

Source: Page 421

Explanation: The MMPI was first published in the 1940s and was revised (MMPI-2) in 1989. The PAI was first published in 1991 and the MCMI-III was first developed in the late 1970s. The Clinical Assessment Tool is a made up assessment that does not exist.

7.

Correct Answer: b

Source: Page 423

Explanation: The Exner Comprehensive system was developed in the 1980s based on a synthesis of a number of competing scoring systems and research that collected normative data for children and adults. In the Exner system, the client's Rorschach responses are coded and tabulated, resulting in summary scores that are relevant to various aspects of personality functioning, such as self-perception, coping strategies, quality of thought processes, and emotional responsiveness.

8.

Correct Answer: d

Source: Page 427

Explanation: Neuropsychologists are specially trained clinicians who focus on the relationship between brain functioning and behavior. They use a very wide range of specialized tests to assess different aspects of brain functioning, such as spatial perception, motor performance, and speed of information processing.

9.

Correct Answer: a

Source: Page 430

Explanation: The Ages and Stages Questionnaire is used to screen for autism. The questionnaire assesses development and social-emotional functioning from early infancy through age five and a half based on parent responses to a questionnaire. If concerns about an autism spectrum disorder are identified through screening, the child is typically referred for a multidisciplinary comprehensive evaluation.

10.

Correct Answer: b

Source: Page 431

Explanation: In 2010, the CDC found that about 9% of adults in the United States met diagnostic criteria for a depressive disorder. Depression is common throughout the world and afflicts people of all ages.

11.

Correct Answer: b

Source: Page 433

Explanation: Individuals with Alzheimer's disease suffer a gradual loss of memory, thinking, and speaking skills, and often have behavioral and emotional symptoms such as anxiety, agitation, and depression. At this point, Alzheimer's disease cannot be definitively diagnosed until after a patient dies through pathology studies of the brain.

12.

Correct Answer: c

Source: Page 432

Explanation: Comorbidity is when one or more disorders co-occur with the primary disorder or disease. For example, alcoholism often co-occurs with depression. This can create challenges in psychological testing.

Short Answer

1. Clinical and counseling psychologists are similar to other mental health professionals in that they work with clients and treat illnesses that range from less serious (such as career indecision) to serious mental illness (such as schizophrenia). They also all work in a variety of settings and with a variety of people of all ages from young to old. The difference between clinical and counseling psychologists is that clinical psychologists tend to treat more serious problems and counseling psychologists tend to treat more everyday problems. There is, however, a great deal of overlap. Both clinical and counseling psychologists are usually licensed by the same state public health or education authorities and they work under the same license and regulations. In addition, clinical and counseling psychologists have either a PhD or a doctorate in psychology (PsyD). In contrast, other mental workers such as social workers, counselors, and psychiatric nurses normally have a master's degrees. Psychiatrists, on the other hand, are medical doctors who have a medical degree and complete a four-year residency, with a minimum of three years working with patients with mental disorders.

2. The American Psychological Association (APA) advocates that psychologists should use evidence-based practice, which is defined as "the integration of the best available research with clinical expertise in the context of patient characteristics, culture, and preferences" (APA, 2014, para. 2). Evidence-based assessment means that psychologists select tests and assessments based on clinical research findings showing that they accurately diagnose mental health conditions and are useful for planning treatment. The evidence-based approach minimizes theory, personal preferences, case studies, and qualitative evidence and instead focuses on high quality quantitative studies to guide assessment decisions.

3. Depression is common and present throughout the world and affects people of all ages. In fact, in 2010, the Centers for Disease Control found that approximately 9% of the population in the United States met the criteria for a depressive disorder. Depression can be diagnosed in several different ways. The Structured Clinical Interview for DSM Disorders along with self-report tests can be used to provide evidence of a depressive disorder, but many psychologists

believe it is too time consuming. The Beck Depression Inventory-II (BDI) is especially useful for screening large populations for depression and for monitoring the severity of depression during treatment. The BDI is a well-researched self-report test that is easily scored by the clinician. Tests with many scales such as the Minnesota Multiphasic Inventory-2 and the Personality Assessment Inventory both have depression scales and can be used as well. Assessing can be difficult if the client is non-cooperative or has low cognitive capabilities. In addition, the clinician must be aware of cultural differences and standards that can affect the diagnosis of depression. Finally comorbid disorders can complicate diagnosis. For example, alcohol and drug dependency can co-occur with depression.

4. Projective testing is the most controversial type of psychological testing. The controversy surrounds the lack of research evidence to support their reliability and validity and, thus, their use. Proponents of projective testing, however, contend that with proper standardized administration and scoring, the tests can still be useful for treatment planning and developing a broad understanding of the client's functioning and needs. The Rorschach inkblot test is perhaps the most well-known projective technique. This test involves showing 10 inkblots to the client, one at a time, and the client is asked what each one might be. In the more recent versions of the test, the client is also asked to elaborate on what made the inkblot look like the image they described. Although various scoring systems have been developed to improve the reliability and validity of the Rorschach, there still remains much controversy over its use, but there does seem to be consensus that it can be useful for assessing thought disorders, such as schizophrenia. The Thematic Apperception Test (TAT) is another commonly used projective test. The TAT was developed in the 1930s and still uses the same set of stimuli. It consists of 31 black-and-white drawings, each one on a different card. The clinician administers a subset of the 31 cards, asking the client to make up a story for each one and to include specific details in the story. Like the Rorschach, scoring rules have been developed, but reliability and validity still remain worrisome. A third type of projective test is the Draw-A-Person test, which is often used by clinicians who work with child victims of emotional and sexual violence. The child is given a blank piece of paper and asked to draw a person. After a person is drawn, the clinician asks the child to draw another person who is of the opposite sex. Again, there have been attempts to develop standardized scoring systems and there is some evidence that it is possible to distinguish between sexually abused and non-abused children.

5. Feedback and a written report are generally the two final parts of the psychological testing process. Providing feedback to the client is an ethical obligation under the APA Standards. In addition, receiving feedback can be a therapeutic experience for the client. The purpose of the feedback session is to provide the client with information about test findings and conclusions and make recommendations for treatment or intervention if it is needed. The second product testing is generally a written report. The report will commonly be sent to the individual who referred the patient for testing and the report also might become part of a legal, educational, or medical record. Because of this, the report needs to be carefully and accurately prepared. It is important to write reports that are easy to read, answer referral questions, include recommendations, and are appropriate for the audience of the report.

References

Archer, R. P., Buffington-Vollum, J. K., Stredny, R. V., & Handel, R. W. (2006). A survey of psychological test use patterns among forensic psychologists. *Journal of Personality Assessment, 87*(1), 84–94. doi: 10.1207/s15327752jpa8701_07

American Educational Research Association, American Psychological Association, & National Council on Measurement in Education. (2014). *Standards for educational and psychological testing*. Washington, DC: American Educational Research Association.

Pillay, S. (2010). The dangers of self diagnosis. *Psychology Today*. Retrieved from https://www.psychology-today.com/blog/debunking-myths-the-mind/201005/the-dangers-self-diagnosis

Psychology Today. (n.d.). *Tests*. Retrieved from https://cdn.psychologytoday.com/tests

Stanford. (n.d). *Test yourself*. Retrieved from http://wellmd.stanford.edu/test-yourself.html

Ward, J. T. (September, 2013). What is forensic psychology? *American Psychological Association*. Retrieved from http://www.apa.org/ed/precollege/psn/2013/09/forensic-psychology.aspx

15

How Are Tests Used in Organizational Settings?

Chapter Overview

In Chapter 15, we begin with a brief history of the role psychological assessment has played in organizations. We examine various types of tests that are used for hiring employees, such as interviews and tests of performance, personality, and integrity. We consider legal constraints on employment testing legislated by Congress and interpreted by the executive branch and the federal court system. Finally, we describe how organizations use psychological assessment to evaluate employee performance.

Learning Objectives

After completing your study of this chapter, you should be able to do the following:

- Discuss the history of employment testing in the United States during the 20th century.
- Report the strengths and weaknesses of the traditional interview and the structured interview for assessing job candidates.
- Describe the characteristics of a performance test, and discuss two types of performance tests used by organizations.
- Describe the five-factor model of personality, and name two tests that are based on this model.
- Discuss two types of integrity tests, and describe the criticism these tests have received.
- Describe the three ways in which validity evidence can be generalized to new situations.
- Discuss performance appraisal instruments, give examples of three types of rating scales, and describe four types of rating errors.

Chapter Outline

A Short History of Employment Testing
　　The Scientific Selection of Salesmen
　　The Legacy of World War I
　　Testing From World War II to the Present
Pre-Employment Testing
　　The Employment Interview
　　Performance Tests
　　Situational Judgment Tests
　　Personality Inventories
　　Integrity Testing
　　Cognitive Tests
　　Legal Constraints
　　Generalizing Validity Evidence
Performance Appraisal
　　Ranking Employees
　　Rating Employees
　　Rating Errors
　　Who Should Rate?
Chapter Summary

Key Concepts

anchors:	Numbers or words on a rating scale that the rater chooses to indicate the category that best represents the employee's performance on the specified dimension.
assessment center:	A large-scale replication of a job that requires test takers to solve typical job problems by role-playing or to demonstrate proficiency at job functions such as making presentations and fulfilling administrative duties; used for assessing job-related dimensions such as leadership, decision making, planning, and organizing.
behavioral checklist:	When a rater evaluates performance by rating the frequency of important behaviors required for the job.
behavioral interviews:	Interviews that focus on behaviors rather than on attitudes or opinions.
behaviorally anchored rating scale (bars):	A type of performance appraisal that uses behaviors as anchors; the rater rates by choosing the behavior that is most representative of the employee's performance.
central tendency errors:	Rating errors that result when raters use only the middle of the rating scale and ignore the highest and lowest scale categories.
cognitive tests:	Assessments that measure the test taker's mental capabilities, such as general mental ability tests, intelligence tests, and academic skills tests.

false positive:	When an innocent test taker mistakenly is classified as guilty.
five-factor model:	A widely accepted personality theory that proposes there are five central personality dimensions: surgency, emotional stability, agreeableness, conscientiousness, and intellect or openness to experience.
forced distribution:	A method of ranking employees that requires the supervisor to assign a certain number of employees to each performance category.
forced ranking:	A method of performance appraisal in which managers rank employees in terms of predetermined dimensions or criteria.
graphic rating scale:	A graph for rating employees' performance that represents a dimension, such as quality or quantity of work, divided into categories defined by numbers, words, or both.
halo effect:	A rating error that occurs when raters let their judgment on one-dimension influence judgments on other dimensions.
high-fidelity test:	A test that is designed to replicate the job tasks and settings as realistically as possible.
job analysis:	A systematic assessment method for identifying the knowledge, skills, abilities, and other characteristics required to perform a job.
leniency errors:	Systematic rating errors that occur when raters give all employees better ratings than they deserve.
low-fidelity tests:	Tests that simulate the job and its tasks using a written, verbal, or visual description.
meta-analysis:	A statistical technique that accumulates the results of multiple studies on comparable constructs into a single result in an attempt to get the best possible estimate of the relationship between a predictor and a criterion.
performance appraisal:	A formal evaluation of an employee's job performance.
personality traits:	Characteristics or qualities of a person (e.g., kind, optimistic); ongoing cognitive constructs.
polygraph:	A physiological measure associated with evaluating how truthfully an individual responds to questioning; also known as a *lie detector test.*
protected class:	Persons in a group, such as ethnic class or gender, who are protected from discrimination by federal law.
severity errors:	Systematic rating errors that occur when raters give all employees worse ratings than they deserve.
situational judgment test:	A type of low-fidelity simulation that presents test takers with short scenarios that pose dilemmas along with a number of possible courses of action that could be taken in response. The task is to choose the most (or sometimes least) effective course of action from the choices provided.
structured interview:	A predetermined set of questions that the assessor asks the respondent; the assessor then scores the answers based on their content to arrive at a diagnosis or a hiring decision.

synthetic validity:

A method used to generalize evidence of validity by combining validity coefficients on a group of tests that have each been shown to be valid predictors of a component of a job. By combining multiple tests, all the important job components can be represented, and an estimate of the overall validity of the group can be computed without having to conduct local validity studies on each test. Also referred to as *job component validity*.

360 feedback:

A method of performance appraisal in which employees receive ratings from their supervisors, peers, subordinates, and customers as well as from themselves.

traditional interview:

A pre-employment interview in which the interviewer pursues different areas of inquiry with each job.

transportability:

One strategy used for test validity generalization in which a case is made that a test that has been shown to be valid for one job is also valid for a different job based on evidence that the jobs are substantially similar in their requirements.

work sample:

A small-scale assessment in which test takers complete a job-related task such as building a sawhorse or designing a doghouse.

KEY CONCEPTS CROSSWORD

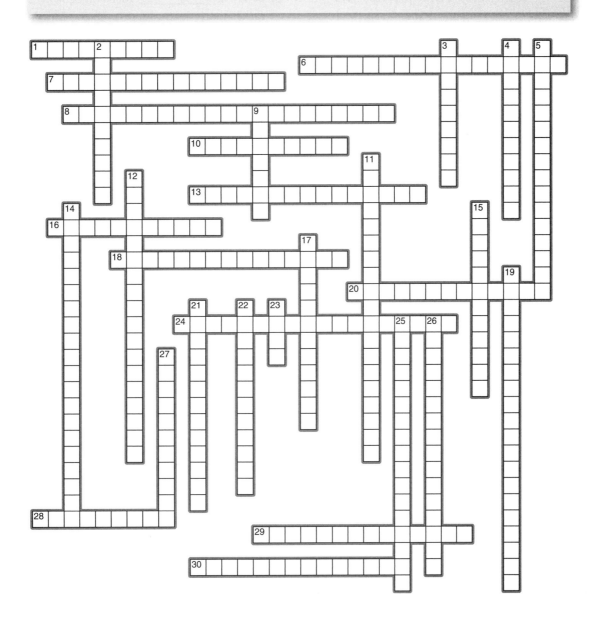

ACROSS

1. Type of test/assessment that measures the test taker's mental capabilities, such as general mental ability tests, intelligence tests, and academic skills tests.
6. A widely accepted personality theory that proposes there are five central personality dimensions: extraversion (surgency), emotional stability, agreeableness, conscientiousness, and intellect or openness to experience.
7. Persons in a group, such as ethnic class or gender, who are protected from discrimination by federal law.
8. A formal evaluation of an employee's job performance.
10. Type of interview with a predetermined set of questions that the assessor asks the respondent; the assessor then scores the answers based on their content to arrive at a diagnosis or a hiring decision.
13. Systematic rating errors that occur when raters give all employees worse ratings than they deserve.
16. Type of pre-employment interview in which the interviewer pursues different areas of inquiry with each job.
18. Systematic rating errors that occur when raters give all employees better ratings than they deserve.
20. Type of test that is designed to replicate the job tasks and settings as realistically as possible.
24. Characteristics or qualities of a person (e.g., kind, optimistic); ongoing cognitive constructs.
28. When using a behavioral _____ a rater evaluates performance by rating the frequency of important behaviors required for the job.
29. A method of performance appraisal in which managers rank employees in terms of predetermined dimensions or criteria.
30. When an innocent test taker mistakenly is classified as guilty.

DOWN

2. Behavioral _____ focus on behaviors rather than on attitudes or opinions.
3. A physiological measure associated with evaluating how truthfully an individual responds to questioning; also known as a *lie detector test*.
4. A small-scale assessment in which test takers complete a job-related task such as building a sawhorse or designing a doghouse.
5. Type of rating errors that result when raters use only the middle of the rating scale and ignore the highest and lowest scale categories.
9. Numbers or words on a rating scale that the rater chooses to indicate the category that best represents the employee's performance on the specified dimension.
11. A method of ranking employees that requires the supervisor to assign a certain number of employees to each performance category.
12. A method used to generalize evidence of validity by combining validity coefficients on a group of tests that have each been shown to be valid predictors of a component of a job.
14. A graph for rating employees' performance that represents a dimension, such as quality or quantity of work, divided into categories defined by numbers, words, or both.
15. A method of performance appraisal in which employees receive ratings from their supervisors, peers, subordinates, and customers as well as from themselves.
17. Type of test that simulates the job and its tasks using a written, verbal, or visual description.
19. Type of low-fidelity simulation that presents test takers with short scenarios that pose dilemmas along with a number of possible courses of action that could be taken in response. The task is to choose the most (or sometimes least) effective course of action from the choices provided.

21. A statistical technique that accumulates the results of multiple studies on comparable constructs into a single result in an attempt to get the best possible estimate of the relationship between a predictor and a criterion.

22. A systematic assessment method for identifying the knowledge, skills, abilities, and other characteristics required to perform a job.

23. Abbreviation for a type of performance appraisal that uses behaviors as anchors; the rater rates by choosing the behavior that is most representative of the employee's performance.

25. A large-scale replication of a job that requires test takers to solve typical job problems by role-playing or to demonstrate proficiency at job functions such as making presentations and fulfilling administrative duties.

26. One strategy used for test validity generalization in which a case is made that a test that has been shown to be valid for one job is also valid for a different job based on evidence that the jobs are substantially similar in their requirements.

27. A rating error that occurs when raters let their judgment on one-dimension influence judgments on other dimensions.

LEARNING ACTIVITIES BY LEARNING OBJECTIVE

The following are some study tips and learning activities you can engage in to support the learning objectives for this chapter.

Learning Objectives	*Study Tips and Learning Activities*
After completing your study of this chapter, you should be able to do the following:	The following study tips and learning activities will help you meet these learning objectives:
Discuss the history of employment testing in the United States during the 20th century.	• Make a timeline of the events described in your textbook. Now place other events, either personal (e.g., a relative's birth) or historical (e.g., women earn the right to vote), on the timeline. Share with your classmates.
Report the strengths and weaknesses of the traditional interview and the structured interview for assessing job candidates.	• Make a list of strengths and weaknesses of the interviews. Why do you think the structured interview is a better predictor of job performance? Check your answer with a classmate or your instructor.
Describe the characteristics of a performance test, and discuss two types of performance tests used by organizations.	• Think about high-fidelity and low-fidelity tests. What do you think are the advantages and weakness of each? Include expense of development and administration, accuracy of results, and ease of scoring. Compare your answers with those of a classmate, or discuss with your instructor.
Describe the five-factor model of personality, and name two tests that are based on this model.	• Go online and read more about the five-factor model of personality. You will find information in books and journal articles on personality.
Discuss two types of integrity tests, and describe the criticism these tests have received.	• Make a list of why employers use integrity tests, and then make a list of problems that could arise from making decisions based on inaccurate test results.
Describe the three ways in which validity evidence can be generalized to new situations.	• Go online and do a search for a test that might be used for employee selection, such as a sales aptitude test, a clerical skills test, or a personality test. Then go the publisher's website and see if you can determine what types of jobs the evidence for validity might generalize to. Can you think of some jobs that use of the test might be inappropriate for? Explore your ideas with your instructor.
Discuss performance appraisal instruments, give examples of three types of rating scales, and describe four types of rating errors.	• Get a copy of the form that students use to evaluate their instructors at your college or university. What type of appraisal is it? Do you have suggestions for improving the form based on information in this textbook? Share your ideas with a classmate or your instructor.

EXERCISES

1. In the table below, indicate the rating error (leniency, severity, central tendency, or halo) in each scenario.

Rating Scenario	Type of Error
1. A supervisor notices that an employee is very personable and, as a result, rates him high on all performance dimensions.	
2. A supervisor wants to avoid difficult performance conversations with employees so he rates them higher than they deserve.	
3. A supervisor does not differentiate among employees, rating them all as average so they will all receive the same rewards based on the evaluation.	
4. A new supervisor wants to be viewed as tough by her employees and, as a result, gives everyone low ratings.	

2. In the table below, indicate if the described testing scenario would be best classified as an assessment center, work sample, low-fidelity test, or a behavioral interview.

Testing Scenario	Type
1. A job candidate is asked to describe a time when he had to give a presentation to a group that was not receptive to the presentation's content or message.	
2. A job candidate must attend an all-day session where she must participate in a role-play exercise, give a presentation, take a personality test, and answer interview questions.	
3. A job candidate is asked to take a multiple-choice situational judgment test.	
4. A job candidate for a truck-driving job is asked to back a truck up to a loading dock.	

ADDITIONAL LEARNING ACTIVITIES

Activity 15-1 85 Years of Research Findings in Personnel Selection

Background

As described in the textbook, the scientific selection of employees has deep roots dating back to 1915 when Walter Dill Scott published *The Scientific Selection of Salesmen*. There is a lot of published research in this area. Schmidt and Hunter (1998), in their article titled "The Validity and Utility of Selection Methods in Personnel Psychology: Practical and Theoretical Implications of 85 Years of Research Findings," summarized the research by performing a meta analysis of the validity of testing methods used in organizations. Schmidt and Hunter analyzed many validity coefficients from prior research studies. Remember that a validity coefficient is a correlation coefficient used to infer the strength of the evidence of validity based on the relationship between a test and an external criterion. A coefficient of 0.00 indicates no evidence of validity, and a coefficient of 1.00 indicates a perfect relationship so the larger the coefficient, the more useful a test method is in predicting on the job performance. The Schmidt and Hunter study is very useful because it helps practitioners make informed judgments about the types of selection methods to use.

Questions

1. The table below contains 19 personnel selection methods that may be used as predictors of job performance. After reviewing each method, make an educated guess about the rank order of the 19 personnel selection methods as predictors of job performance (numbering from 1 to 19). For example, assign the number 1 to the method you believe has the best evidence of validity and the number 19 to the method you believe has the least evidence of validity. Enter your rankings in Column 1. Then, locate the Schmidt and Hunter (1998) article and write the actual validity coefficient (found in Table 1 of the article) in the second column.

Rank	Validity Coefficient	Selection Method
		General mental ability tests
		Work samples tests
		Integrity tests
		Conscientiousness tests
		Employment interviews—structured
		Employment interviews—unstructured
		Job knowledge tests

Rank	Validity Coefficient	Selection Method
		Job tryout procedure
		Peer ratings
		Training and education consistency method
		Reference checks
		Job experience (years)
		Biographical data measures
		Assessment center
		Training and education point method
		Years of education
		Interests
		Graphology
		Age

2. How well did your ranking match the actually validity coefficient? Where were you most accurate and where were you least accurate?

3. Can you explain why you thought some of you most inaccurate rankings were more predictive than they actually were? What were some of those reasons?

4. Compare your results with some classmates and discuss them.

Activity 15-2 Utility Analysis Speaking the Language of Business

Background

In Chapter 8, we learned about evidence of validity based on test–criterion relationships. As you have learned, the validity coefficient indicates the strength of that relationship. However, several researchers have proposed that the validity coefficient might not be the best way to understand the overall usefulness of a selection procedure in an organizational setting. They believed that it would be better to estimate the dollar value of the usefulness of the procedure, which would be more easily understood by managers. What they proposed is a technique called utility analysis.

It has long been known that the validity coefficient is just one piece of information concerning the usefulness of a test. There are other factors, such as the number of people selected, the cost of testing, the rate that employees would be successful if no test was given (often called the *base rate*), the proportion of applicants that are actually hired (called the *selection ratio*), and the typical variation in employees' performance in the specific setting. A complete description of every one of these factors is beyond the scope of space allotted here, but Brogden (1949) and Cronbach and Gleser (1965) developed a formula that uses several pieces of information to compute an easily understood dollar value (called *utility*) of the selection procedure. The formula, shown below, has come to be known as the Brodgen-Cronbach-Gleser model:

$$\Delta U = (N)(T)(SD_y)(r_{xy})(\bar{Z}_x) - (N)(C)$$

where,

ΔU is the increase in the average dollar payoff of using the selection procedure instead of random selection;

(N) is the number of employees selected by the procedure;

(T) is the expected tenure of the selected employees;

(SD_y) is the standard deviation in dollars of job performance without the selection procedure, which describes how much performance would be expected to vary among workers if the selection procedure was not used;

(r_{xy}) is the validity coefficient;

$(\bar{Z}_x)$ is the average standard predictor score of the selected group;

C is the cost of testing one applicant.

During the 1970s, 1980s, and into the 1990s, there was a concerted effort from researchers in different fields (accounting, economics, and industrial/organizational psychology) to place a dollar value on the human assets in organizations. For a variety of reasons, however, this proved to be difficult, and the research and use of utility analysis has greatly declined. Two well-known studies suggest at least one reason why.

Gary Latham and Glen Whyte conducted two studies that examined the impact of utility analysis on managerial decision making (Latham & Whyte, 1994; Whyte & Latham, 1997). Each of these studies showed that managers did not prefer to use the utility analysis information when deciding to implement a specific personnel selection procedure (a test). The researchers found that the utility analysis information either had no effect or a negative effect on managers' acceptance of a selection procedure. There have been several proposed explanations for this finding, but there are two that seem to be the most popular. First, utility analysis estimates tend to result in very large dollar values and it is possible that the managers simply did not believe the numbers. For example, one condition in Latham and Whyte's research showed the utility of a selection procedure to be worth $60,208,786. Second, managers are not rational decision makers. They are more likely to be swayed by soft interpersonal data than by hard quantitative data (Mintzberg, 1975), and the adoption of personnel practices is often determined by bandwagon effects and imitation (Subramony, 2006). In other words, managers often adopt a practice simply because others have adopted the practice.

Questions

1. Imagine you are a manager and a consultant tells you that a new selection tool would result in a net benefit to your organization of $60,208,786. What would your reaction be?

2. Some jobs are probably easier than others to put a dollar value on employee performance. Describe which types of jobs you believe a dollar value can be ascribed to performance and describe which types may be more difficult or impossible.

PRACTICE TEST QUESTIONS

The following are some practice questions to assess your understanding of the material presented in this chapter.

Multiple Choice

1. Who proposed a system that evaluated constructs such as "native intellectual ability" and that assessed "character" and "manner"?

   a. Walter Dill Scott

   b. Hugo Münsterberg

   c. Walter Bingham

   d. Millicent Pond

2. Which one of the following drew attention to issues of test validity and fairness during the latter half of the 20th century in the United States?

   a. The Psychological Corporation

   b. U.S. Army Alpha and Beta tests

   c. The civil rights movement

   d. Use of assessment centers during World War II

3. What is the MOST popular method for assessing job candidates?

   a. Assessment center

   b. Traditional employment interview

   c. Structured employment interview

   d. Performance appraisal

4. Which one of the following is the LEAST accurate method of predicting job performance?

   a. Traditional employment interview

   b. Structured interview

   c. Assessment center

   d. Work sample

5. The best prediction of job performance is obtained when interviews focus on an applicant's

   a. attitudes.

   b. opinions.

   c. beliefs.

   d. behaviors.

6. When designing a structured interview, developers use job analysis to establish evidence of validity based on

   a. relationships with other variables.

   b. reliability.

   c. constructs.

   d. content.

7. Which one of the following is an example of a high-fidelity test?

   a. Paper-and-pencil attitude survey

   b. Flight simulator

   c. Performance appraisal

   d. Traditional interview

8. Hunter and Hunter's (1984) meta-analysis suggests that personality tests are among the poorest predictors of job performance. Which one of the following has caused psychologists to look more favorably on personality tests?

   a. The traditional interview

   b. Integrity testing

   c. The five-factor model of personality

   d. Job analysis

9. The U.S. Congress has prohibited using which pre-employment test in most job settings?

   a. The polygraph

   b. Traditional interviews

   c. Assessment centers

   d. Personality tests

10. Which one of the following is most likely to make the "Othello error"—taking signs of distress as proof of unfaithfulness or dishonesty?

   a. Developers of integrity tests

   b. Employment interviewers

   c. Polygraph users

   d. Assessment center raters

11. Which one of the following is a concern of integrity test critics?

   a. Test publishers conducted many of the available studies.

   b. Integrity is too broad a concept to be useful in test development.

   c. Assessment centers are a better way of establishing honesty.

   d. The tests are based on the five-factor model of personality.

12. When Lilienfeld (1993) administered integrity tests to monks and nuns, college students, and incarcerated criminals, what did the test results show?

   a. Incarcerated criminals are the most dishonest.

   b. College students are the most dishonest.

   c. Monks and nuns are the most dishonest.

   d. All groups were equally dishonest.

13. Which one of the following is true about The *Uniform Guidelines on Employee Selection Procedures* the U.S. federal government published in 1978?

   a. They prohibit using polygraph tests for employment testing.

   b. They prohibit using integrity tests during the selection process.

   c. They consist of laws passed by Congress, which organizations must abide by.

   d. They include suggested procedures to follow when testing job candidates.

14. At the BKH Construction Company, supervisors are required to rank employees so that a certain number fall into each performance category. What is this method of performance appraisal is known as?

   a. Forced distribution

   b. Forced choice

   c. Graphic rating

   d. 360° feedback

15. Naomi supervises several employees. When she rates their performance, however, she often lets her judgment of their conscientiousness influence her ratings of their decision-making and leadership ability. Which one of the following rating errors is Naomi making?

   a. Leniency error

   b. Severity error

   c. Halo effect

   d. Central tendency error

16. What test shows high validity for job performance criteria and even higher validity for predicting training criteria?

   a. Personality tests

   b. Cognitive tests

   c. Integrity tests

   d. Performance tests

17. In 2012, Van Iddekinge, Roth, Raymark, and Olde-Dusseau conducted a meta-analysis investigating the relationship between integrity tests and external criteria. What was their finding about the size of the validity coefficients?

   a. They depended on the statistical method used for the meta-analysis.

   b. They depended on the criterion measure used.

   c. They were much larger than those found in previous research.

   d. They were much smaller than those found in previous research.

18. What type of relationship has been found between conscientiousness and job performance by recent researchers using item response theory?

   a. Positive linear

   b. Negative linear

   c. Curvilinear

   d. No relationship

19. What term is used to describe a situation where test takers do not reply in an honest fashion to personality tests?

   a. Misrepresentation

   b. Test cheating

   c. Dishonesty

   d. Faking

Short Answer

1. List the major events in the history of pre-employment testing described in your textbook.

2. Compare and contrast high- and low-fidelity tests. Give examples of each.

3. What are the differences between the traditional interview and the structured interview? Which do organizations use most often?

4. How might a small employer demonstrate evidence of validity for a test to select supervisors for his company that has only been validated for use in a different company?

5. Are personality tests valid predictors of job performance? What is the role of the five-factor model in personality tests?

6. Discuss various ways to assess employee honesty. What does the research reveal about the utility of employee honesty tests?

7. Describe how organizations evaluate employee performance.

8. What rating errors might individuals make when judging employee performance? What can be done to avoid the errors?

9. Compare and contrast the Hogan Personality Inventory (HPI) and the Wonderlic Basic Skills Test (WBST). What do the tests have in common? What are their differences?

ANSWER KEYS

Crossword

ACROSS

1. COGNITIVE—Type of test/assessment that measures the test taker's mental capabilities, such as general mental ability tests, intelligence tests, and academic skills tests.

6. FIVE-FACTOR MODEL—A widely accepted personality theory that proposes there are five central personality dimensions: extraversion (surgency), emotional stability, agreeableness, conscientiousness, and intellect or openness to experience.

7. PROTECTED CLASS—Persons in a group, such as ethnic class or gender, who are protected from discrimination by federal law.

8. PERFORMANCE APPRAISAL—A formal evaluation of an employee's job performance.

10. STRUCTURED—Type of interview with a predetermined set of questions that the assessor asks the respondent; the assessor then scores the answers based on their content to arrive at a diagnosis or a hiring decision.

13. SEVERITY ERRORS—Systematic rating errors that occur when raters give all employees worse ratings than they deserve.

16. TRADITIONAL—Type of pre-employment interview in which the interviewer pursues different areas of inquiry with each job.

18. LENIENCY ERRORS—Systematic rating errors that occur when raters give all employees better ratings than they deserve.

20. HIGH-FIDELITY—Type of test that is designed to replicate the job tasks and settings as realistically as possible.

DOWN

2. INTERVIEWS—Behavioral _____ focus on behaviors rather than on attitudes or opinions.

3. POLYGRAPH—A physiological measure associated with evaluating how truthfully an individual responds to questioning; also known as a *lie detector test*.

4. WORK SAMPLE—A small-scale assessment in which test takers complete a job-related task such as building a sawhorse or designing a doghouse.

5. CENTRAL TENDENCY—Type of rating errors that result when raters use only the middle of the rating scale and ignore the highest and lowest scale categories.

9. ANCHORS—Numbers or words on a rating scale that the rater chooses to indicate the category that best represents the employee's performance on the specified dimension.

11. FORCED DISTRIBUTION—A method of ranking employees that requires the supervisor to assign a certain number of employees to each performance category.

12. SYNTHETIC VALIDITY—A method used to generalize evidence of validity by combining validity coefficients on a group of tests that have each been shown to be valid predictors of a component of a job.

14. GRAPHIC RATING SCALE—A graph for rating employees' performance that represents a dimension, such as quality or quantity of work, divided into categories defined by numbers, words, or both.

15. 360 FEEDBACK—A method of performance appraisal in which employees receive ratings from their supervisors, peers, subordinates, and customers as well as from themselves.

24. PERSONALITY TRAITS—Characteristics or qualities of a person (e.g., kind, optimistic); ongoing cognitive constructs.
28. CHECKLIST—When using a behavioral _____ a rater evaluates performance by rating the frequency of important behaviors required for the job.
29. FORCED RANKING—A method of performance appraisal in which managers rank employees in terms of predetermined dimensions or criteria.
30. FALSE POSITIVE—When an innocent test taker mistakenly is classified as guilty.

17. LOW-FIDELITY—Type of test that simulates the job and its tasks using a written, verbal, or visual description.
19. SITUATIONAL JUDGMENT—Type of low-fidelity simulation that presents test takers with short scenarios that pose dilemmas along with a number of possible courses of action that could be taken in response. The task is to choose the most (or sometimes least) effective course of action from the choices provided.
21. META-ANALYSIS—A statistical technique that accumulates the results of multiple studies on comparable constructs into a single result in an attempt to get the best possible estimate of the relationship between a predictor and a criterion.
22. JOB ANALYSIS—A systematic assessment method for identifying the knowledge, skills, abilities, and other characteristics required to perform a job.
23. BARS—Abbreviation for a type of performance appraisal that uses behaviors as anchors; the rater rates by choosing the behavior that is most representative of the employee's performance.
25. ASSESSMENT CENTER—A large-scale replication of a job that requires test takers to solve typical job problems by role-playing or to demonstrate proficiency at job functions such as making presentations and fulfilling administrative duties.
26. TRANSPORTABILITY—One strategy used for test validity generalization in which a case is made that a test that has been shown to be valid for one job is also valid for a different job based on evidence that the jobs are substantially similar in their requirements.
27. HALO EFFECT—A rating error that occurs when raters let their judgment on one-dimension influence judgments on other dimensions.

Exercises

1.

Rating Scenario	Type of Error
1. A supervisor notices that an employee is very personable and, as a result, rates him high on all performance dimensions.	Halo
2. A supervisor wants to avoid difficult performance conversations with employees so he rates them higher than they deserve.	Leniency
3. A supervisor does not differentiate among employees, rating them all as average so they do not receive differential rewards based on the evaluation.	Central Tendency
4. A new supervisor wants to be viewed as tough by her employees and, as a result, gives everyone low ratings.	Severity

2.

Testing Scenario	Type
1. A job candidate is asked to describe a time when he had to give a presentation to a group that was not receptive to the presentation's content or message.	Behavioral Interview
2. A job candidate must attend an all-day session where she must participate in a role-play exercise, give a presentation, take a personality test, and answer interview questions.	Assessment Center
3. A job candidate is asked to take a multiple-choice situational judgment test.	Low Fidelity
4. A job candidate for a truck-driving job is asked to back a truck up to a loading dock.	Work Sample

Multiple-Choice

1.

Correct Answer: a

Source: Page 439

Explanation: Walter Dill Scott was one of the first psychologists to apply psychological and experimental techniques to business problems. In 1915, he wrote the influential and historically important book *The Scientific Selection of Salesmen*. In this book he asserted that companies should use group tests that evaluated constructs such as "native intellectual ability," "character," and "manner." His approach greatly influenced the applied psychology movement during World War I.

2.

Correct Answer: c

Source: Page 440

Explanation: The latter half of the 20th century saw a great increase in the use of psychological tests in the workplace. The civil rights movement drew attention to issues and fairness, reliability, and validity in the society in general and in the workplace. When Congress passed Title VII of the Civil Rights Act in 1964, it further stimulated governmental involvement in testing and led to the development of the *Uniform Guidelines on Employee Selection Procedures* (1978), which is an extremely important document for testing in the workplace.

3.

Correct Answer: b

Source: Page 443

Explanation: Although the other methods listed may demonstrate higher validity, the most used method for assessing job candidates is the traditional employment interview, which is unstructured.

4.

Correct Answer: a

Source: Page 443–444

Explanation: The traditional employment interview is the least accurate method of the answer options. For example, one meta-analysis discussed in the textbook found that it had a validity coefficient of .20. In comparison the structured interview was found to have a validity coefficient of .57. Traditional unstructured interviews can still serve a useful purpose, however. For example, they can provide interviewees an opportunity to ask questions and develop a realistic view of the job.

5.

Correct Answer: d

Source: Page 444

Explanation: Behavioral questions tend to have high evidence of validity based on content by drawing on real-life work situations that applicants are likely to face on the job. Also they focus on behaviors rather than more subjective attributes such as attitudes and personality traits that can easily be faked and are harder to accurately assess.

6.

Correct Answer: d

Source: Page 444–446

Explanation: Job analysis is a technique that identifies tasks, knowledge, skill, ability, and other characteristics (KSA&Os) that are required to successfully perform a job. From this information interview questions that are related to the job can be developed. By first identifying the KSA&Os and then developing related interview questions, content-related evidence of validity can be established.

7.

Correct Answer: b

Source: Page 449

Explanation: High-fidelity tests replicate job settings as realistically as possible. Often test takers use the same equipment that is used on the job and complete actual job tasks. However, this is not always safe or practical. For instance, it would be unwise to evaluate a person to determine if they could fly a plane by putting them in an actual plane. Of course the test would be highly valid, but it could lead to disastrous results for unqualified pilots. In such a case a flight simulator would be a much better choice.

8.

Correct Answer: c

Source: Page 456

Explanation: While there is still controversy over the use of personality tests for personnel selection, recent meta-analyses using the five-factor model of personality have shown that some factors can be good predictors of job performance. For example, conscientiousness has consistently been found to be a valid predictor of job performance for all jobs studied.

9.

Correct Answer: a

Source: Page 461

Explanation: The Employee Polygraph Protection Act of 1988 outlawed the use of the polygraph in employment testing for most private organizations. However, the law has an exemption for security firms (armored car, alarm, and guard) and government agencies allowing those organizations to continue to use the polygraph in employment settings.

10.

Correct Answer: c

Source: Page 461

Explanation: Lilienfeld (1993) concluded that there was no scientific evidence that a specific "lie response" exists. Instead physiological responses may occur for a variety of reasons and thus polygraph users are making the "Othello error" or taking signs of distress as proof of dishonesty.

11.

Correct Answer: a

Source: Page 463

Explanation: Ones, Viswesvaran, and Schmidt in 1993 published a meta-analysis of validation studies of integrity tests and found that the tests were valid across a variety of situations for thefts and counterproductive behaviors. However, others have criticized this meta-analysis because the studies they used were conducted by the test publishers and independent researchers. Such studies are likely to contain methodological flaws.

12.

Correct Answer: c

Source: Page 463

Explanation: Lilienfeld's (1993) study showed that a well-known honesty test actually found that monks and nuns were more dishonest than college students and incarcerated criminals.

13.

Correct Answer: d

Source: Page 464

Explanation: The *Uniform Guidelines* on *Employee Selection Procedures* was published by several government agencies and not passed by Congress so it is not law. However, the document has been given great deference by the courts as outlining the proper procedures that should be used when using tests in an employment setting. Interestingly, according to the Guidelines nearly all tools used to make employment decisions could be considered a test. As a result, all such tools need to adhere to the requirements set forth in the Guidelines.

14.

Correct Answer: a

Source: Page 469

Explanation: A forced distribution requires that a certain number of employees fall into each performance category, such as "poor," "average," and "outstanding." Many management consultants, however, advise against using forced distributions because the process may force supervisors to place an employee into a category that does not accurately describe his or her performance.

15.

Correct Answer: c

Source: Page 470

Explanation: The halo effect is a common and well-known rating error. It occurs when raters allow one performance dimension to influence the judgments on other dimensions. In contrast, leniency errors result when raters give all employees better ratings than they deserve, severity errors result when raters give all employees worse ratings than they deserve, and central tendency errors result when raters use only the middle of the rating scale and ignore the highest and lowest scale categories.

16.

Correct Answer: b

Source: Page 464

Explanation: A meta-analysis performed by Hunter and Hunter (1984) found that cognitive tests were among the most valid predictors of job performance. However, they are the most accurate for "thinking" jobs like manager and salesperson. In addition, while they are excellent predictors of job performance, they are even better predictors of training success.

17.

Correct Answer: b

Source: Page 463

Explanation: Van Iddekinge and his colleagues (2012) found that some of the validity coefficients were below .2, and many approached .1, even when corrected for unreliability in the criterion. However, the authors also found higher validity coefficients when the tests were used to predict self-reported counterproductive work behavior (.26 uncorrected, and .32 corrected for unreliability). Like previous researchers, they found that the validity coefficients from studies conducted by the test publishers were higher (.27) than the coefficients from studies that were not conducted by the test publishers (.12).

18.

Correct Answer: c

Source: Page 460

Explanation: Carter, Dalal, Boyce, O'Connell, Kung, & Delgado (2014) investigated the nature of the relationship between conscientiousness and job performance. Using item response theory (IRT), they found a curvilinear relationship, meaning that job performance improved as conscientiousness scores increased, but only to a certain point. Once that point was reached, job performance began to decrease.

19.

Correct Answer: d

Source: Page 457

Explanation: When a test taker does not respond to a test in an honest fashion, it is generically referred to as "faking." Usually, but not always, faking occurs when a person tries to respond to test questions in a way that he or she believes will present him- or herself in the most positive fashion. Presenting oneself in the most positive fashion is also called *socially desirable responding* (Edwards, 1957) and when this behavior is intentional, it is called *impression management* (Paulhaus, 1984).

Short Answer

1. The textbook provides a short history of employment testing. It begins in 1915 when Walter Dill Scott published *The Scientific Selection of Salesmen*, which proposes that employers

should use group tests for personnel selection. Scott was highly influential in the academic and military communities, but because of infighting among psychologists, he was not involved in the development of the U.S. Army's Alpha and Beta tests during World War I. The use of these tests set off concerns about the fairness of intelligence testing and the appropriate use of test scores that continues today. Following World War I, research continued on employment testing. Psychologists began studying methods for measuring job performance and placing workers in jobs based on their skills and qualifications. For example, the Strong-Campbell Interest Inventory, which is still in use today, originated from this work. Also during this time, two consulting firms that specialized in using tests in organizations were formed. One was founded by Walter Dill Scott, and the other, named the Psychological Corporation (now called Harcourt Assessment), was organized by J. McKeen Cattell. Psychologists and psychological testing became important again during World War II. Psychologist Walter Bingham oversaw the development of the Army General Classification Test used to place U.S. Army recruits. Also the Office of Strategic Services (the forerunner to the Central Intelligence Agency) began to use assessment centers in their selection of spies and undercover agents. During the latter half of the 20th century, the use of tests by organizations greatly expanded. The civil rights movement and the passage of Title VII of the Civil Rights Act of 1964 set important standards for fair employment practices. Later, the federal government developed the *Uniform Guidelines on Employee Selection Procedures* (1978) to help ensure consistency and fairness in employment decisions. Today pre-employment testing is commonly used by both large and small organizations. Companies employ many different types of psychological tests to meet their business needs.

2. Both high- and low-fidelity assessments are performance tests that mimic or inquire about work-related tasks and activities. Where they differ is in the degree of realism. High-fidelity tests replicate job settings and tasks as realistically as possible. Examples include a flight simulator for pilots and having instructors prepare and present a lecture. Using realistic simulations is often easier, safer, and cheaper than having test takers perform in a real-live situation. In contrast, a low-fidelity test is less realistic and simulates job-related tasks using written, verbal, or visual descriptions. Low-fidelity tests tend to be cheaper and easier to develop, safer to use, and simpler to administer than high-fidelity simulations. An example is a behavioral interview. For example, a pilot might be asked to describe landing procedures or discuss in detail how he or she responded to an emergency situation. Instructors could be asked about how they have or would go about developing and presenting a lecture or be asked to describe how they dealt with a situation when a student disrupted his or her lecture.

3. The employment interview is the most popular type of selection test used by organizations. There are two basic types of interviews: the traditional interview and the structured interview. Organizations tend to use the traditional interview more than structured interview even though research shows that structured interviews have greater reliability/precision and validity. Knowledge of the shortcomings of the traditional interview dates back to the initial development of employment testing when Scott in 1915 recognized and reported low agreement among hiring managers using traditional *unstructured* interviews. In contrast, structured interviews are standardized to ensure consistency. In a fully structured interview, all candidates are asked the same questions in the same order. The interviewer usually rates the candidates' answers using an anchored rating scale. Interviewers undergo training on question delivery, note taking, and rating.

This training standardizes the candidates' experience during the interview and the process used to evaluate them. The result of the standardization is increased interrater reliability, internal consistency, and validity.

4. It is often too time consuming and costly for a small employer to develop and validate a selection test. Also a small employer will not likely be able to obtain a large enough sample to be confident of any study results. Therefore, the company may try to generalize validity evidence found in a different setting to its own situation. There are three approaches that are endorsed by the Society for Industrial and Organizational Psychology. They are meta-analysis, synthetic validity, and transportability. Meta-analysis is a statistical technique that assembles and analyzes the results of many studies into a single result. Research has shown that much of the variation in validity coefficients obtained in different settings is the result of sampling error and statistical artifacts. Combining the results of multiple studies in a single larger analysis can remove these situational effects and provide the researcher with a better idea of the true relationship between the predictor and the criteria. Once this is done, if a relationship exists, then this provides evidence to "generalize" the relationship to other situations. The second approach, synthetic validity, also known as *job component validity*, is based on the idea that jobs are composed of various components. A validity coefficient can be "synthesized" by combining the known validities of a variety of different tests that have been validated on similar jobs so long as each test measures a necessary "component" of the job in question. This enables the employer to estimate the validity of tests for predicting performance in the employer's setting without having to conduct a new validity study. The third, and final, approach is transportability, which attempts to show that a valid test in one situation can be transported to another similar situation. For example, if a test has been shown to be a valid predictor of sales performance for car sales, clothing sales, insurance sales, and furniture sales, then it is likely to also be a valid predictor for other sales representative jobs such as flower sales or pharmaceutical sales as long as the sales skills required in each of the jobs are substantially the same.

5. There are many different personality assessments that can be used in an organizational setting, and their use goes back to the 1940s with the publication of Cattell's 16 Personality Factor Questionnaire. Research has shown that the 16PF has a predictive relationship with absenteeism, turnover, tenure, safety, and job performance. More recent work has focused on the "big-five" personality factors, a five-factor model of personality consisting of extroversion (sometimes referred to as *surgency*), emotional stability (sometimes called *neuroticism*), agreeableness, conscientiousness, and openness to experience (sometimes called *intellect*). Earlier work such as Hunter and Hunter's (1984) meta-analysis suggested that personality was a poor predictor of job performance. However, more recent work suggests otherwise. For example, Barrick and Mount (1991) found that conscientiousness is a valid predictor of job performance in all types of jobs and that extraversion and emotional stability are valid predictors of performance for some, but not all, jobs. Also, Ones, Dilchert, Viswesvaran, and Judge (2007) stated that the Big Five predict important organizational behaviors such as job performance, leadership, work attitudes, and motivation. With this said, however, there is still disagreement in the literature concerning the degree to which faking on personality measures can influence their validity. For example, Holden (2007) found that faking can substantially reduce the validity coefficient between test and criterion. However, Ones, Viswesvaran, and Reiss in a large-scale meta-analysis found that faking did not decrease the correlation between the Big Five personality dimensions and job performance.

6. Research shows that employee theft is quite costly for employers. For example, a survey by the University of Florida showed that employees are responsible for 48.5% of retail theft costing $15 billion annually (Horan, 2003). As a result, employers are very concerned with the integrity and honesty of the employees that they hire. One method that was previously used to test employee honesty is the polygraph. The idea behind the use of the polygraph is that when an individual gives an untruthful response, he or she exhibits increases in skin resistance, pulse or heart rate, and respiration, which the machine measures and records. The level of these physiological responses is compared to the level of physiological responses to "neutral" questions (such as "Is your name John?") to determine when the person is being deceptive. However, research suggests that there is no such "lie response," and that the test results in a high rate of false positives (identifying someone as dishonest when in fact they are honest). Because of these problems, the Employee Polygraph Protection Act of 1988 prohibited the use of the polygraph in most employment settings. There are some exemptions to the law allowed, such as for those companies that provide security services and government agencies. Paper-and-pencil integrity tests are another means used to test the honesty of employees or potential employees. There are two types: overt tests and personality-oriented tests. Overt tests ask test takers to provide information about their past behavior or to respond to how they would deal with hypothetical situations. Personality-oriented tests purport to measure characteristics that are predictive of honest behavior and positive organizational citizenship using items related to the Big Five personality factors. Research shows that both types of tests do have low-to-moderate predictive validities for predicting theft and counterproductive behaviors. Critics counter, however, that these research results come from the test publishers themselves and that the studies have methodological flaws. Interestingly, a study conducted by Lilienfeld (1993) found that the tests identified monks and nuns as more dishonest than college students and incarcerated criminals. In addition, Van Iddekinge et al. (2012) more recently conducted a meta-analysis of 104 studies that investigated the evidence of validity of integrity tests based on their relationship with external criteria. When the researchers looked specifically at the results of studies that met what they termed generally accepted professional standards for validity research, they found that the validity coefficients to be modest. Most of the estimates were below .2, and many approached .1.

7. Because performance appraisals are used to make employment decisions, they are considered a test under the *Uniform Guidelines on Employee Selection Procedures* (1978). There are two basic approaches that organizations use when appraising employees. The first is ranking. Forced ranking is a method that requires raters place employees in the order of their performance, such as best employee, second best, and so on. A forced distribution is another ranking method. Here raters are required to place a specific number or percentage of employees into each performance category, such as "poor," "average," and "outstanding." Often, the percentage of employees in each category is set to approximate a normal distribution. Ranking approaches do have drawbacks. For example, consider the case when an organization has a large number of poor performers. With a forced ranking approach, there will still be a best employee even though he or she may not be performing adequately. The second approach is rating. This is the traditional approach where supervisors rate employees using various scales, such as behavioral anchored rating scales (BARS), graphical rating scales, and behavioral checklists. Using a rating approach, employees are evaluated using the written anchors provided on the rating scale and not by directly comparing one employee to another.

8. Rating employees is a challenging task. Because it is a subjective process there are a number of common errors that raters routinely make. Leniency errors result when raters give all employees better ratings than they deserve, and severity errors result when raters give all employees worse ratings than they deserve. Central tendency is another common error. These errors result when raters use only the middle of the rating scale and ignore the highest and lowest scale categories. A halo effect occurs when raters let their judgment on one- dimension influence judgments on other dimensions. For example, if an employee is a good communicator, but does poorly on all other parts of the job yet still receives excellent scores across the board, this could be a halo error. Organizations can provide rater training to try to improve the accuracy of the raters. However, research shows that rater training only has limited short-term effects.

9. The Hogan Personality Inventory (HPI) and the Wonderlic Basic Skills Test (WBST) share several common features. They are both professionally developed tests that can be used in an employment setting when making employment decisions. Because they have been professionally developed and perfected over many years, they both have good reliability/precision and validity for their intended uses. However, they measure completely different constructs. The HPI is a personality inventory consisting of the following seven primary scales: adjustment, ambition, sociality, interpersonal sensitivity, prudence, inquisitiveness, and learning approach. In contrast, the WBST is a short measure of adult language and math skills designed to measure job readiness of teenagers and adults.

References

Barrick, M. R., & Mount, M. K. (1991). The Big Five personality dimensions and job performance: A meta-analysis. *Personnel Psychology*, 44, 1–26.

Brogden, H. E. (1949). A new coefficient: Application to biserial correlation and to estimation of selective efficiency. *Psychometrika*, 14(3), 169–182. Retrieved from http://link.springer.com/article/10.1007/BF02289151

Carter, N. T., Dalal, D. K., Boyce, A. S., O'Connell, M. S., Kung, M., & Delgado, K. M. (2104). Uncovering curvilinear relationships between conscientiousness and job performance: How theoretically appropriate measurement makes an empirical difference. *Journal of Applied Psychology*, 99, 564–586.

Cronbach, L. J., & Gleser, G. C. (1965). *Psychological tests and personnel decisions*. Urbana: University of Illinois Press.

Edwards, A. L. (1957). *The social desirability variable in personality assessment research*. New York: Dryden.

Holden, R. R. (2007). Socially desirable responding does moderate personality scale validity both in experimental and nonexperimental contexts. *Canadian Journal of Behavioral Science/Revue Candadienne des Sciences du Comportment*, 39, 184–201.

Horan, D. J. (2003, December). Controlling theft by key holders. *Chain Store Age*, p. 166.

Hunter, J. E., & Hunter, R. F. (1984). Validity and utility of alternative predictors of job performance. *Psychological Bulletin*, 96, 72–98.

Latham, G. P., & Whyte, G. (1994). The futility of utility analysis. *Personnel Psychology*, 47(1), 31–46. doi:10.1111/j.1744-6570.1994.tb02408.x

Lilienfeld, S. O. (1993, Fall). Do "honesty" tests really measure honesty? *Skeptical Inquirer*, pp. 32–41.

Mintzberg, H. (1975). The manager's job: Folkore and fact. *Harvard Business Review, July-August*, 49–61. Retrieved from https://hbr.org/1990/03/the-managers-job-folklore-and-fact/ar/1

Ones, D. S., Dilchert, S., Viswesvaran, C., & Judge, T. (2007). In support of personality assessment in organizational settings. *Personnel Psychology, 60,* 995–1027.

Ones, D. S., Viswesvaran, C., & Schmidt, F. L. (1993). Comprehensive meta-analysis of integrity test validities: Findings and implications for personnel selection and theories of job performance. *Journal of Applied Psychology, 78,* 679–703.

Paulhaus, D. L. (1984). Two component model of socially desirable responding. *Journal of Personality and Social Psychology, 88,* 348–355.

Schmidt, F. L., & Hunter, J. E. (1998). The validity and utility of selection methods in personnel psychology: Practical and theoretical implications of 85 years of research findings. *Personnel Psychology, 124,* 262–274. Retrieved from http://psycnet.apa.org/psycinfo/1998-10661-006

Subramony, M. (2006). Why organizations adopt some human resource management practices and reject others: An exploration of rationales. *Human resource management, 45*(2), 195–210. doi:10.1002/hrm.20104

Van Iddekinge, C., Roth, P., Raymark, P., & Olde-Dusseau, H. (2012). The criterion-related validity of integrity tests: An updated meta-analysis. *Journal of Applied Psychology, 97,* 499–530.

Whyte, G., & Latham, G. (1997). The futility of utility analysis revisited: When even an expert fails. *Personnel Psychology, 50*(3), 601–610. doi:10.1111/j.1744-6570.1997.tb00705.x